Betty Crocker's

COOKING BASICS

Betty Crocker's
COOKING
BASICS

Learning to Cook with Confidence

MACMILLAN • USA

MACMILLAN
A Simon & Schuster Macmillan Company
1633 Broadway
New York, NY 10019-6785

Library of Congress Cataloging-in-Publication Data
Crocker, Betty
   [Cooking basics]
   Betty Crocker's cooking basics. — 1st ed.
     p.   cm.
   Includes index.
   ISBN 0-02-862451-3 (alk. paper)
   1. Cookery. I. Title.
TX714.C7616   1998
641.5—dc21   98-20522
                               CIP

GENERAL MILLS, INC.
Betty Crocker Kitchens
Director: Marcia Copeland
Editors: Marcia Copeland, Joyce Gauck
Recipe Development: Betty Crocker Kitchens
Food Stylists: Kate Condon, Mary Johnson, Cindy Lund
Nutritionist: Elyse A. Cohen, M.S.L.N.
Photographer: Steven B. Olsen

Cover: George J. McKeon
Design: George J. McKeon

For consistent baking results, the Betty Crocker Kitchens recommend Gold Medal Flour.

Manufactured in the United States of America
10 9 8 7 6 5 4
First Edition

INTRODUCTION

Have you been wanting to cook something new, or just learn to cook with more fun and confidence? Then let BETTY CROCKER'S COOKING BASICS be your guide! We've heard from so many people that cooking a simple supper, bringing a dish to a friend's house, or cooking a treat for dessert is something they would like to do, but there doesn't seem to be a book that shows new cooks how to cook with confidence. Until now, that is!

We heard those requests, so we went out and asked you exactly what you'd like to make cooking clear, easy and stress-free. . . . You told us pictures were important, so every recipe has a photo, plus photos that show techniques used in the recipe—nothing is a mystery.

You told us to make the recipes simple to follow, and not to overload them with unnecessary information. No problem! These recipes are easy to read and a cinch to follow. We asked you to tell us exactly what you wanted to cook. The 100 recipes are just what you asked for, from how to cook a perfect hamburger to elegant Chicken Breasts with Orange Glaze.

We heard that many of you yearned to cook Thanksgiving dinner—or at least bring a dish to a friend's house or family gathering. Great idea! We included a complete Thanksgiving menu, plus an easy-to-use timetable, so you can sit down to your feast right when you want to. And everyone wants a simple way to entertain friends. The answer? A hearty do-ahead meal of Vegetable Lasagna that even the busiest person can make the night before and serve up the next day.

Then, you told us that setting up a kitchen seemed very expensive, not to mention confusing. What is a zester anyway? Betty Crocker guides you through kitchen equipment—what you really need, what's less critical, though nice to have. Every item is pictured, so there's no more wondering what that thing is you found in the back of the kitchen drawer.

And, we explain all the cooking terms you need to know, give you the scoop on herbs and spices, pass on advice for what foods to have on hand and how to store food safely. We added great information on grilling, as well as how to set your table, even have a buffet. What's left? Common cooking techniques, such as dicing, slicing and peeling. We gave you a photo of each, so you can do it confidently in your own kitchen.

Want to cook something? Go right ahead. With Betty Crocker, you can be confident that it's easy, it's delicious and it's just what you want.

Betty Crocker

CONTENTS

CHAPTER 1

THE BASICS OF GETTING STARTED

UNDERSTANDING THE RECIPE

You will feel confident, organized and well prepared when trying a recipe for the first time if you read through the entire recipe before starting to cook. This will give you an opportunity to ask an experienced cook for help if there is a direction that isn't clear. Also, you will have time to make sure you have all the ingredients, utensils and pans needed to prepare the recipe. And you'll know if the recipe makes as many servings as you need and how much time the food needs to cook or bake. After reviewing the recipe, you'll be ready to cook with confidence.

Some ingredients need to be prepared before they can be added to a recipe. This might involve slicing a carrot or draining the liquid from a can of black beans. The recipe is easier to assemble if you prepare each ingredient first, so it is ready to use when you need it. If you will be using the oven or broiler, check the shelves or racks in the oven to be sure they are in the right place before turning on the heat. For most baked recipes, the oven shelf should be near the middle. For broiling, you will need to place the shelf closer to the heating element, which is usually at the top of the oven. A recipe requiring broiling usually will tell you how far from the heat to broil the food.

In this book, equipment that is absolutely necessary for preparation is identified at the top of each recipe. For example, the equipment could be a baking pan, electric mixer or a blender. You may need to use additional equipment or utensils other than those listed to complete the recipe, but their exact size is not always critical. We also tell you at the top of each recipe how long the food needs to cook, bake, chill or stand, so you can plan your time more easily. The time needed to prepare the ingredients is not included because this will vary, depending on your cooking experience.

The first time you make a recipe, it's a good idea to follow the directions exactly and use the ingredients called for. Often the results will be just what you wanted, but sometimes a certain flavor may seem too strong or be one you don't like. If that happens, the next time you make the recipe, try adjusting the flavorings, herbs and spices slightly. Put a reminder near the recipe of changes you'd like to try. As you gain cooking experience, you'll learn more about ingredients and how to make changes to suit your taste.

Finally, cleanup will be easy if you wash utensils or rinse and put them in the dishwasher, as you use them. This way, cooking and baking will be enjoyable and rewarding.

Cooking or
Baking Time

Easy
Step-by-Step
Directions

Suggestions
for Serving

Tips and
Useful
Information

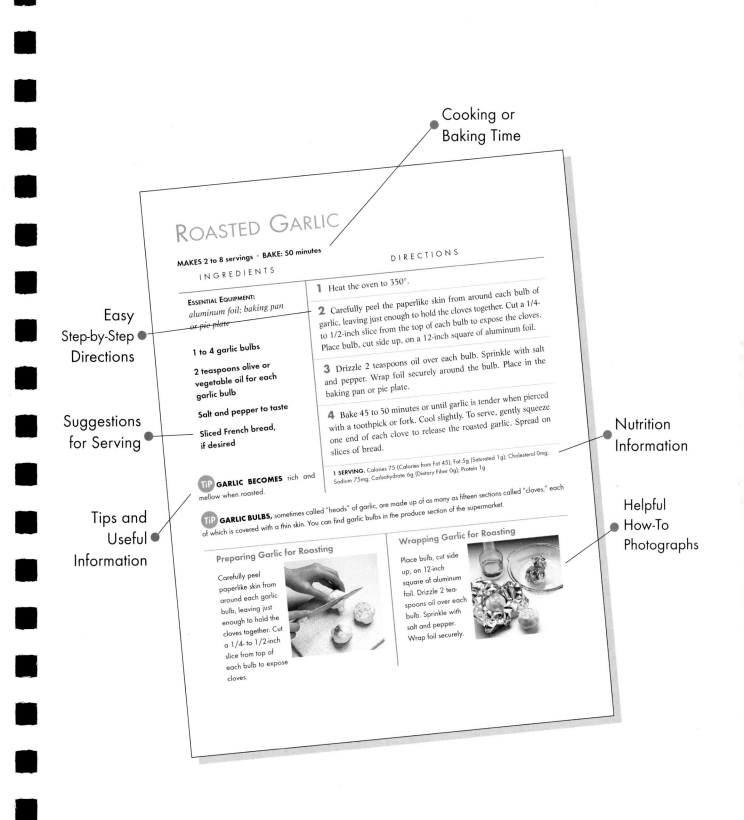

ROASTED GARLIC

MAKES 2 to 8 servings • BAKE: 50 minutes

INGREDIENTS

ESSENTIAL EQUIPMENT:
*aluminum foil; baking pan
or pie plate*

1 to 4 garlic bulbs

2 teaspoons olive or
vegetable oil for each
garlic bulb

Salt and pepper to taste

Sliced French bread,
if desired

DIRECTIONS

1 Heat the oven to 350°.

2 Carefully peel the paperlike skin from around each bulb of garlic, leaving just enough to hold the cloves together. Cut a 1/4- to 1/2-inch slice from the top of each bulb to expose the cloves. Place bulb, cut side up, on a 12-inch square of aluminum foil.

3 Drizzle 2 teaspoons oil over each bulb. Sprinkle with salt and pepper. Wrap foil securely around the bulb. Place in the baking pan or pie plate.

4 Bake 45 to 50 minutes or until garlic is tender when pierced with a toothpick or fork. Cool slightly. To serve, gently squeeze one end of each clove to release the roasted garlic. Spread on slices of bread.

1 SERVING. Calories 75 (Calories from Fat 45); Fat 5g (Saturated 1g); Cholesterol 0mg; Sodium 75mg; Carbohydrate 6g (Dietary Fiber 0g); Protein 1g

TiP GARLIC BECOMES rich and mellow when roasted.

TiP GARLIC BULBS, sometimes called "heads" of garlic, are made up of as many as fifteen sections called "cloves," each of which is covered with a thin skin. You can find garlic bulbs in the produce section of the supermarket.

Nutrition
Information

Helpful
How-To
Photographs

Preparing Garlic for Roasting

Carefully peel paperlike skin from around each garlic bulb, leaving just enough to hold the cloves together. Cut a 1/4- to 1/2-inch slice from top of each bulb to expose cloves.

Wrapping Garlic for Roasting

Place bulb, cut side up, on 12-inch square of aluminum foil. Drizzle 2 teaspoons oil over each bulb. Sprinkle with salt and pepper. Wrap foil securely.

COMMON ABBREVIATIONS

Be prepared. In our recipes we don't use abbreviations, but other recipes do, so we've rounded up some common abbreviations to help you out.

t	=	teaspoon
tsp	=	teaspoon
T	=	tablespoon
Tbsp	=	tablespoon
c	=	cup
oz	=	ounce
pt	=	pint
qt	=	quart
gal	=	gallon
lb	=	pound
#	=	pound

MEASURING GUIDE

What's different, yet exactly the same? All these measurements! In our recipes, we have used the larger measurement—1/4 cup, not 4 tablespoons—but this equivalency chart will help you out for the other measuring you do in the kitchen.

3 teaspoons	=	1 tablespoon
4 tablespoons	=	1/4 cup
5 tablespoons + 1 teaspoon	=	1/3 cup
8 tablespoons	=	1/2 cup
1 cup	=	1/2 pint
2 cups	=	1 pint
4 cups (2 pints)	=	1 quart
4 quarts	=	1 gallon
16 ounces	=	1 pound
Dash or pinch	=	less than 1/8 teaspoon

HOW TO MEASURE INGREDIENTS

Successful cooking starts with measuring correctly. Not all ingredients are measured the same way or with the same type of cups or spoons. Here are some tips to help you measure successfully.

MEASURING CUPS: For liquids usually are glass. They have a spout for pouring and space above the top measuring line. They can be purchased in 1-, 2-, 4- and 8-cup sizes.

Dry ingredients and solid ingredients such as shortening are measured using a set of cups that stack or "nest" inside one another. These cups are made to hold an exact amount when filled to the top. They are purchased as a set that contains 1/4-, 1/3-, 1/2- and 1-cup sizes. Some sets also may have a 1/8-cup (2 tablespoons) and/or a 2-cup size.

MEASURING SPOONS: Are sold as a set that includes 1/4-, 1/2- and 1-teaspoon sizes plus a 1-tablespoon size. Some sets may have a 1/8-teaspoon size. These special spoons are designed for measuring and should be used instead of spoons intended for eating. They are used for both liquid and dry ingredients.

LIQUIDS: When measuring liquids, use the smallest measuring cup size you have that is large enough to hold the amount needed. For example, to measure 1/2 cup milk, you'd use a 1-cup measuring cup instead of a 2-cup measuring cup. Place the cup on a level surface, then bend down to check the amount at eye level. To measure sticky liquids such as honey, molasses and corn syrup, lightly spread the cup with oil first, or spray with cooking spray, so the liquid will be easier to remove.

DRY: For dry ingredients, gently fill the measuring cup to heaping, using a large spoon. Do not shake the cup or pack down the ingredients. While holding the cup over the canister or storage container to catch the excess of the ingredient, level the cup off, using something with a straight edge, such as a knife or the handle of a wooden spoon.

SOLID FATS AND BROWN SUGAR: Fill the measuring cup, using a spoon or rubber spatula. Pack down the ingredient, and level off if necessary.

SHREDDED CHEESE, CEREAL, CHOPPED NUTS: Fill the measuring cup lightly without packing down the ingredient, and level off.

MARGARINE AND BUTTER IN STICKS: Cut off the amount needed, following guideline marks on the wrapper, using a sharp knife. An entire 1/4-pound stick equals 1/2 cup, half a stick is 1/4 cup, an eighth of a stick is 1 tablespoon.

SALT, PEPPER, HERBS AND SPICES: Fill measuring spoon with salt, pepper or a ground spice such as cinnamon; level off. For dried herbs, lightly fill the spoon to the top.

ESSENTIAL EQUIPMENT AND TOOLS

Having the right equipment makes cooking easier and fun. The following are the basic tools you should consider having for your kitchen. You may already have many of these things, and sometimes you can improvise by using another tool.

CAN OPENER: Purchase one that's easy to wash after each use.

COLANDER: For draining pasta and other foods after cooking and for draining fresh produce after washing. If you are purchasing a new colander, choose one that will be easy to clean.

CUTTING BOARD: Plastic boards can be easily and thoroughly washed. Wash them immediately after cutting raw meat, poultry or fish.

GRATER: A box grater has different size openings on each side for shredding cheeses or vegetables and for grating fruit peels. Other types are available, but all should have several sizes of openings for a variety of shredding and grating.

KITCHEN SCISSORS OR SHEARS: Good for snipping fresh herbs and for all-purpose cutting and trimming of ingredients.

KNIVES: With three good knives—paring, chef's and all-purpose—cutting, slicing, dicing and chopping are easy. (See page 9.)

MEASURING CUPS AND SPOONS: Measuring accurately ensures recipe success. (See page 5.)

MIXING BOWLS: Choose two or three deep bowls in different sizes. A large mixing bowl can double as a salad bowl.

POTATO MASHER: You'll need this for making mashed potatoes or twice-baked potatoes.

SPATULA, WIDE METAL OR PLASTIC, OR PANCAKE TURNER: Not just for pancakes, it's great for turning chicken breasts and fish fillets as well as serving lasagna and desserts.

SPATULA, RUBBER: For scraping the last bit of food out of mixing bowls or measuring cups.

SPOON, LARGE METAL: Use to stir mixtures and to spoon juices over meats or poultry as they roast. Use also to lift large pieces of meat from the cooking pan to the serving plate.

SPOON, SLOTTED: Use to lift solid foods out of cooking liquids.

SPOON, WOODEN OR PLAS-TIC: For all-purpose mixing. It is especially good for stirring hot foods because the handle will stay cool.

STRAINER: For draining cans of fruit or vegetables and for draining the liquid off cooked foods.

THERMOMETER, MEAT: An easy way to be sure meats, poultry and fish are cooked properly.

TIMER: To ensure that your foods are cooked to perfection. If the recipe gives a range of time, set the timer for the minimum time to check for doneness.

TONGS FOR COOKING: Especially good to use when grilling foods, but can also can be used to lift or turn food without piercing it. Cooking tongs should be made of metal, in contrast to salad tongs, which might be wooden or plastic and usually have a larger end for tossing a salad.

VEGETABLE BRUSH: Use to clean celery and potatoes.

VEGETABLE PEELER: Much easier to use than a knife to remove a thin peel from apples, potatoes and carrots.

WIRE WHISK: Great for beating eggs and preparing sauces and dressings as well as for all-purpose mixing.

BLENDER: Can be used for certain types of chopping as well as to whirl smoothies and puree vegetables for creamy soups.

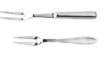

FORK, LONG-HANDLED: Great for holding meat and poultry in place while it is being sliced or carved.

JUICER: To squeeze fresh juice from oranges, lemons, limes and other citrus fruits.

LADLE: A large ladle is best to dish up soups, stews and chili.

ELECTRIC MIXER: An easy way to whip cream and beat cakes and other desserts. It also can be used to mash potatoes.

HAND BEATER: Also called an egg beater or a rotary beater.

PASTRY BLENDER: Used to mix shortening, butter or margarine with dry ingredients such as flour and sugar to produce a crumbly mixture.

SPATULA, NARROW METAL: When measuring dry ingredients, this spatula is handy to use to level off the measuring cup. It's also helpful when frosting a cake.

SPATULA, WOODEN, OR SPECIALLY COATED UTENSILS: Use to stir when cooking or frying in a nonstick pan to protect the surface of the pan.

STEAMER BASKET: Use to suspend vegetables above boiling water. It adapts to many pan sizes and folds for easy storage.

ALL ABOUT KNIVES

Invest in good knives to make food preparation easy, fast and efficient. Before purchasing a knife, pick it up. It should fit your hand and feel comfortable to use. The blade of a good knife extends through the full length of the knife handle. If this extension, called the tang, is not visible, make sure the knife has three rivets, which indicate that the blade is inside the handle.

Good knives are expensive but will last for a very long time if they are cared for properly. Storing them in a block of wood designed for knife storage is perfect, but the cardboard sleeve the knife was packaged in works well, too. The idea is to keep knives from getting dull edges by bumping into other utensils in a drawer. Preserve knife handles by washing and drying knives by hand instead of in the dishwasher. If knives become too soaked with water, wooden handles will dry and warp and the blades may loosen. Sharp knives are the easiest and safest to use. Refer to manufacturers' recommendations for keeping your knives sharp.

Slicing, dicing, cutting and chopping can be done easily, quickly and correctly if you have three good knives. You'll need a paring knife, a chef's knife and a multipurpose knife with a serrated edge.

THREE ESSENTIAL KNIVES

PARING KNIFE: Has a small blade, about 2 1/2 to 3 inches long, and a rounded or pointed tip. If you plan to have only one paring knife, choose one with a pointed tip. You'll need it to cut up fruits and vegetables, cut fat from a steak or a pork chop, cut into meats and poultry to check for doneness and for many other uses.

CHEF'S KNIFE: Has a heavy, triangular blade, anywhere from 6 to 12 inches long. A medium-size blade, about 8 to 10 inches, is the most versatile size. It is used for chopping, slicing and dicing as well as for crushing a clove of garlic. This knife also is called a cook's knife.

MULTIPURPOSE KNIFE: Has a scalloped or serrated edge and comes in several sizes, but the most helpful one has a blade that is at least 7 to 8 inches long. It may be called a bread knife, a slicer, or a carver and its uses include slicing bread, tomatoes, cooked meats and carving a turkey.

POTS AND PANS FOR COOKING

You'll be able to make most recipes if you have a small collection of pans with lids, in sizes ranging from 1 to 4 quarts, and a large skillet. Pans can be purchased in large sets, but if you don't need everything in the set, you can collect some unmatched pots and pans that will work just as well.

THREE ESSENTIAL SAUCEPANS

SAUCEPANS (1-, 2-, 3-QUART): Essential for cooking or reheating foods on a range top. Although one or two saucepans may be adequate, a collection of saucepans will make cooking more efficient. Each pan should have a tight-fitting lid, which is important when cooking dishes that require the retention of moisture. Pans with a non-stick finish require plastic or coated utensils to prevent scratching the surface of the pan.

MORE ESSENTIAL SAUCEPANS

SKILLET: Used for sautéing vegetables, panfrying meats and stir-frying almost any food. Available in an assortment of materials and sizes. When purchasing a skillet, look for a solid, thick-bottomed pan that will transmit heat evenly and that has a tight-fitting lid. Although a 10-inch skillet is used most often, some recipes work better in a skillet that is slightly larger. A smaller skillet, about 8 inches in diameter, is nice to have when cooking smaller quantities.

DUTCH OVEN (4 QUARTS OR LARGER): A large pot that is used most often on top of the range to prepare a large batch of soup or chili or to cook pasta. It should have a tight-fitting lid. Many Dutch ovens are ovenproof and can be used when cooking pot roast or stew in the oven.

# PANS FOR BAKING

You will need a few baking pans for meats, vegetables and main dishes as well as for cakes, cookies and other desserts. The dimensions of a pan are often given on its bottom. If the dimensions are not there, measure across the bottom to determine the size. Some baking pans have a nonstick finish or lining. This surface will scratch easily, so use care when cutting main dishes or desserts that are served from the pan, and wash the pans with a nonabrasive or plastic scrubber.

SQUARE BAKING PAN: An 8- or 9-inch square pan that can be used for main dishes, such as lasagna, as well as for cakes, bar cookies and other desserts.

13×9-INCH RECTANGULAR PAN: A popular pan size for baking brownies, bars and cakes. Some main dishes, vegetables and casseroles also can be prepared in this pan.

9-INCH ROUND PAN: One of the most popular sizes for baking layer cakes. Most layer cakes require two of these pans.

COOKIE SHEET: Available in an assortment of sizes. To ensure proper heat circulation, select one that is at least 2 inches narrower on each side than your oven. Although a cookie sheet may have a small lip edge, it should not have straight sides that are 1 inch or more in height. (A large rectangular pan with 1-inch sides is usually called a jelly roll pan rather than a cookie sheet and will not bake or brown cookies in the same way that a cookie sheet does.)

9-INCH PIE PAN: Not only is a pie pan essential for making pies, it also can be used to bake a meat loaf or small cuts of meat and poultry. If you are uncertain about the size of your pie pan, measure across the top of the pan, excluding the lip edge.

BEEF AND PORK
MAIN DISHES

# JUICY HAMBURGERS—THREE WAYS

BROILING, GRILLING AND PANFRYING

MAKES 4 servings

INGREDIENTS

DIRECTIONS

---

1 pound regular or lean ground beef

3 tablespoons water

1/2 teaspoon salt

1/4 teaspoon pepper

4 hamburger buns

BROILING HAMBURGERS

1 You may need to move the oven rack so it is 5 to 6 inches below the broiler. Set the oven control to broil.

2 Mix the beef, water, salt and pepper in a bowl. Shape the mixture into 4 uniform, flat patties, each about 3/4 inch thick. Handle the patties as little as possible. The more the beef is handled, the less juicy the burgers will be.

3 Place the patties on the rack in a broiler pan. (For easy cleanup, line the bottom of the broiler pan with aluminum foil before placing patties on rack.)

4 Broil patties with tops about 3 inches from heat 5 to 7 minutes on each side for doneness, turning once, until no longer pink in center and juice is clear. Serve on buns.

CHEESEBURGERS: About 1 minute before the hamburgers are done, top each burger with 1 slice (1 ounce) American, Cheddar, Swiss or Monterey Jack cheese. Broil until cheese is melted and bubbling.

GRILLING HAMBURGERS

1 Prepare the coals or a gas grill for direct heat (pages 236–237). Heat to medium heat, which will take about 40 minutes for charcoal or about 10 minutes for a gas grill.

2 Shape the hamburger patties as described in step 2 of Broiling Hamburgers.

3 Place the patties on the grill about 4 inches from medium heat. Grill uncovered 7 to 8 inches on each side for doneness, turning once, until no longer pink in center and juice is clear. Loosen patties gently with a turner to prevent crumbling. Serve on buns.

PANFRYING HAMBURGERS

1 Shape the hamburger patties as described in step 2 of Broiling Hamburgers.

2 Cook the patties in a skillet over medium heat about 10 minutes for doneness, turning occasionally, until no longer pink in center and juice is clear. Serve on buns.

Shaping Patties

Shaping the patties to have smooth edges will keep them together during cooking and result in uniform doneness. Gently pinch to close any cracks in the patty.

TiP **DON'T PRESS THE BEEF PATTIES** with a spatula while cooking. Pressing squeezes natural juices out and makes the burgers dry and less tender.

TiP **FOR MORE FLAVOR** and better burgers, use lean or regular ground beef; hamburgers made with extra-lean ground beef may crumble when broiled. For a moister hamburger, use coarsely ground instead of finely ground beef.

✔ **STORE THE UNCOOKED MEAT** immediately in the coldest part of your refrigerator, or freeze as soon as possible. Ground meat deteriorates more quickly than other cuts, so it should be used promptly.

MEAT LOAF

MAKES 4 servings • BAKE: 1 hour • LET STAND: 5 minutes

INGREDIENTS

ESSENTIAL EQUIPMENT: *baking pan, such as 8-inch square pan or 9-inch pie pan*

1 pound lean ground beef

1 clove garlic or 1/8 teaspoon garlic powder

1 small onion

2 slices bread with crust

1/4 cup milk

2 teaspoons Worcestershire sauce

1 teaspoon chopped fresh or 1/4 teaspoon dried sage leaves

1/4 teaspoon salt

1/4 teaspoon ground mustard (dry)

1/8 teaspoon pepper

1 egg

1/3 cup ketchup, chili sauce or barbecue sauce

DIRECTIONS

1 Heat oven to 350°. Break up the beef into small pieces in a large bowl, using a fork or spoon.

2 Peel and finely chop the garlic. Peel the onion, and chop enough of the onion into small pieces to measure 3 tablespoons. Wrap remaining piece of onion, and refrigerate for another use. Add the garlic and onion to the beef.

3 Tear the bread into small pieces and add to beef mixture.

4 Add the milk, Worcestershire sauce, sage, salt, mustard, pepper and egg to the beef mixture. Mix with a fork, large spoon or your hands until the ingredients are well mixed.

5 Place the beef mixture in the ungreased baking pan. Almost any size pan will work; just be sure the pan has sides on it to catch the juices that will accumulate while the meat loaf bakes. Shape the mixture into an 8×4-inch loaf in the pan, and spread ketchup over the top.

6 Bake uncovered 50 to 60 minutes or until beef in center of loaf is no longer pink. A meat thermometer inserted in the center of the loaf should read 160°. Let the loaf stand 5 minutes, so it will be easier to remove from the pan. Cut the loaf into slices.

1 SERVING: Calories 320 (Calories from Fat 160); Fat 18g (Saturated 7g); Cholesterol 120mg; Sodium 550mg; Carbohydrate 15g (Dietary Fiber 0g); Protein 25g

Lighter **MEAT LOAF** For 12 grams of fat and 270 calories per serving, substitute ground turkey for the ground beef, substitute 1/4 cup fat-free cholesterol-free egg product for the egg and use skim milk. Bake until 180°.

TiP FOR MORE FLAVOR, purchase a meat loaf mixture of ground beef, lamb and pork, already prepared in your supermarket meat case.

TiP TO SAVE TIME, purchase fresh garlic already chopped or crushed. You'll find it in the produce section of the supermarket. Store it in the refrigerator after opening the jar.

Checking for Doneness

Cut a small slit near center of loaf; meat and juices should no longer be pink.

Mea Loaf, Dilled Carrots with Pea Pods (page 182)

MEXICAN BEEF AND BEAN CASSEROLE

MAKES 4 servings • BAKE: 50 minutes

INGREDIENTS

ESSENTIAL EQUIPMENT: *10-inch skillet; 2-quart baking pan or casserole*

1 pound ground beef

2 cans (15 to 16 ounces each) pinto beans

1 can (8 ounces) tomato sauce

1/2 cup mild chunky-style salsa

1 teaspoon chili powder

1 cup shredded Monterey Jack cheese (4 ounces)

DIRECTIONS

1 Heat the oven to 375°.

2 Cook the beef in the skillet over medium heat 8 to 10 minutes, stirring occasionally, until brown; drain.

3 Rinse and drain the beans in a strainer. Mix the beef, beans, tomato sauce, salsa and chili powder in the ungreased baking pan.

4 Cover with lid or aluminum foil and bake 40 to 45 minutes, stirring once or twice, until hot and bubbly. Carefully remove the lid, and sprinkle cheese over the top. Continue baking uncovered about 5 minutes or until the cheese is melted.

1 SERVING: Calories 520 (Calories from Fat 235); Fat 26g (Saturated 12g); Cholesterol 90mg; Sodium 1020mg; Carbohydrate 45g (Dietary Fiber 14g); Protein 41g

Lighter **MEXICAN BEEF AND BEAN CASSEROLE:** For 18 grams of fat and 465 calories per serving, substitute ground turkey for the beef and reduced-fat Cheddar cheese for the Monterey Jack cheese.

TiP FOR A FLAVOR WITH MORE ZIP, use Monterey Jack cheese with jalapeño peppers or, as it's also known, pepper Jack cheese.

TiP TO SPICE UP THE FLAVOR, next time try a higher spice level of salsa. If it is too hot, cool it with sour cream. Salsa comes in mild, hot and extra-hot.

Rinsing Pinto Beans

Rinse and drain the beans in a strainer. Rinsing canned beans results in a cleaner taste and can reduce digestive problems.

Mexican Beef and Bean Casserole

CHILI

MAKES 4 servings • **COOK: 1 hour 20 minutes**

INGREDIENTS

DIRECTIONS

ESSENTIAL EQUIPMENT: *3-quart saucepan or 12-inch skillet with high side*

1 large onion

2 cloves garlic

1 pound ground beef

1 tablespoon chili powder

2 teaspoons fresh chopped or 1 teaspoon dried oregano leaves

1 teaspoon ground cumin

1/2 teaspoon salt

1/2 teaspoon red pepper sauce

1 can (16 ounces) whole tomatoes, undrained

1 can (15 to 16 ounces) red kidney beans, undrained

1 Peel and chop the onion. Peel and crush the garlic.

2 Cook the beef, onion and garlic in the saucepan over medium heat 8 to 10 minutes, stirring occasionally, until beef is brown; drain.

3 Stir in the chili powder, oregano, cumin, salt, pepper sauce and tomatoes with their liquid, breaking up the tomatoes with a spoon or fork.

4 Heat the mixture to boiling over high heat. Once mixture is boiling, reduce heat just enough so mixture bubbles gently. Cover and cook 1 hour, stirring occasionally.

5 Stir in the beans with their liquid. Heat to boiling over high heat. Once mixture is boiling, reduce heat just enough so mixture bubbles gently. Cook uncovered about 20 minutes, stirring occasionally, until desired thickness.

1 SERVING: Calories 350 (Calories from Fat 155); Fat 17g (Saturated 7g); Cholesterol 65mg; Sodium 920mg; Carbohydrate 27g (Dietary Fiber 7g); Protein 29g

CINCINNATI-STYLE CHILI: For each serving, spoon about 3/4 cup beef mixture over 1 cup hot cooked spaghetti. Sprinkle each serving with 1/4 cup shredded Cheddar cheese and 2 tablespoons chopped onion. Top with sour cream if desired.

TiP **TO SAVE TIME,** increase chili powder to 2 table-spoons, and omit the cumin, oregano and pepper sauce.

TiP **IF YOU REALLY LIKE IT HOT,** top chili with sliced fresh jalapeño chilies.

Breaking up Tomatoes

Break up tomatoes with a spoon or fork. This distributes the tomatoes evenly throughout the chili and makes serving the chili easier.

Chili

QUICK LASAGNA

MAKES 4 servings • **BAKE: 40 minutes** • **LET STAND: 10 minutes**

INGREDIENTS

ESSENTIAL EQUIPMENT: *10-inch skillet; 8- or 9-inch square pan*

1 clove garlic

1/2 pound ground beef

1 teaspoon Italian seasoning

1 cup spaghetti sauce

6 purchased precooked or oven-ready lasagna noodles (each about 7 × 3 inches)

1 container (12 ounces) reduced-fat cottage cheese (1 1/2 cups)

1 cup shredded mozzarella cheese (4 ounces)

2 tablespoons grated Parmesan cheese

DIRECTIONS

1 Heat the oven to 400°. Peel and finely chop the garlic. Cook the beef and garlic in the skillet over medium heat about 5 minutes, stirring occasionally, until the beef is brown; drain.

2 Stir the Italian seasoning and spaghetti sauce into the beef. Spread 1/4 cup of the beef mixture in the ungreased square pan.

3 Top with 2 noodles, placing them so they do not overlap or touch the sides of the pan because they will expand as they bake. Spread about 1/2 cup of the remaining beef mixture over the noodles.

4 Spread about 1/2 cup of the cottage cheese over the beef mixture. Sprinkle with about 1/3 cup of the mozzarella cheese.

5 Repeat layering twice more, beginning with 2 more noodles and following directions in steps 3 and 4 Sprinkle with the Parmesan cheese.

6 Cover with aluminum foil and bake 30 minutes. Carefully remove the foil, and continue baking about 10 minutes longer or until lasagna is bubbly around the edges and looks very hot. Let stand 10 minutes, so the lasagna will become easier to cut and serve.

1 SERVING: Calories 430 (Calories from Fat 160); Fat 18g (Saturated 8g); Cholesterol 55mg; Sodium 980mg; Carbohydrate 33g (Dietary Fiber 2g); Protein 36g

TiP **TO MAKE AHEAD,** assemble the lasagna, but do not bake it. Cover with aluminum foil and refrigerate no longer than 24 hours. Bake as directed in step 6, increasing the first bake time to 40 minutes.

TiP **YOU CAN SUBSTITUTE** ricotta cheese for the cottage cheese. Ricotta is drier in texture than cottage cheese. Look for it in the dairy case near the cottage cheese.

Layering Beef and Noodles

Spread 1/4 cup beef mixture in pan; top with noodles. Spread 1/2 cup beef mixture over noodles.

Layering Cheese

After beef mixture and noodles are layered, spread 1/2 cup cottage cheese over beef mixture. Sprinkle with 1/3 cup mozzarella cheese.

Quick Lasagna

GREAT STEAK—THREE WAYS

BROILING, GRILLING AND PAN FRYING

TYPES OF STEAK

Porterhouse   *Rib Eye*   *Sirloin*   *T-Bone*   *Tenderloin*

Select a steak that is bright red in color. Vacuum-packed beef will have a darker, purplish red color because the meat is not exposed to air. These cuts of steak, porterhouse, rib eye, sirloin, T-bone and tenderloin, are the most tender and are best for broiling, grilling and panfrying.

BROILING A STEAK

1 Select a 3/4- to 1-inch-thick steak from those shown in the photos.

2 You may need to move the oven rack so it is 5 to 6 inches below the broiler. Set the oven control to broil.

3 To prevent the steak from curling during broiling, cut outer edge of fat on steak diagonally at 1-inch intervals with a sharp knife. Do not cut into the meat or it will dry out during broiling.

4 Place steak on the rack in a broiler pan. (For easy cleanup, line the bottom of the broiler pan with aluminum foil before placing steak on rack.) Place in oven with the top of the steak the number of inches from heat listed in the chart.

5 Broil uncovered for about half the time listed in the chart or until the steak is brown on one side.

6 Turn the steak and continue cooking until desired doneness. To check doneness, cut a small slit in the center of boneless cuts or in the center near the bone of bone-in cuts. Medium-rare is very pink in the center and slightly brown toward the edges. Medium is light pink in center and brown toward the edges. Or insert a meat thermometer in the center of the steak to check for desired doneness. Sprinkle salt and pepper over both sides of steak after cooking if desired. Serve immediately.

Cutting Fat

Cut fat diagonally at 1-inch intervals with sharp knife.

GRILLING A STEAK

1 Select a 3/4- to 1-inch-thick steak from those shown in the photos.

2 Prepare the coals or a gas grill for direct heat (pages 236–237). Heat to medium heat, which will take about 40 minutes for charcoal or about 10 minutes for a gas grill.

3 Cut edges of fat on steak as described in step 3 of Broiling a Steak.

4 Place steak on the grill the number of inches from heat listed in the chart.

5 Turn the steak and continue cooking until desired doneness. Check for doneness as described in step 6 of Broiling a Steak.

TiP **MARBLING IN MEATS,** refers to the small flecks of fat throughout the lean meat. The flavor and juiciness of the meat is improved with marbling.

TiP **SOME STEAKS ARE AGED;** aging is a process done by a butcher and results in meat with firmer texture and a more concentrated beef flavor. Aged steaks are usually more expensive.

 TIMETABLE FOR BROILING OR GRILLING STEAKS

Type of Steak	Inches from Heat	Approximate Total Broiling Time in Minutes		Approximate Total Grilling Time in Minutes	
		145° (medium-rare)	*160° (medium)*	*145° (medium-rare)*	*160° (medium)*
Porterhouse and T-Bone	3 to 4	10	15	19	14
Rib Eye	2 to 4	8	15	7	12
Sirloin (boneless)	2 to 4	10	21	12	16
Tenderloin	2 to 3	10	15	11	13

PANFRYING A STEAK

1 Select a 1/2- to 1-inch-thick steak from those shown in the photos.

2 If the steak is very lean and has little fat, coat a heavy skillet or frying pan with a small amount of vegetable oil, or spray it with cooking spray. Or use a nonstick skillet.

3 If the steak is more than 1/2 inch thick, heat the skillet over medium-low to medium heat 1 to 2 minutes. If the steak is 1/2 inch, use medium to medium-high heat.

4 Place the steak in the hot skillet. You do not need to add oil or water or cover the skillet; covering will cause the steak to be steamed rather than panfried.

5 Cook for the time listed in the chart. If the steak has extra fat on it, fat may accumulate in the skillet; remove this fat with a spoon as it accumulates. Turn steaks thicker than 1/2 inch occasionally, turn steaks that are 1/2 inch thick once, until brown on both sides and desired doneness. To check doneness, cut a small slit in the center of boneless cuts or in the center near the bone of bone-in cuts. Medium-rare is very pink in center and slightly brown toward the edges. Medium is light pink in center and brown toward the edges. Or insert a meat thermometer in the center of the steak to check for desired doneness. Sprinkle salt and pepper over both sides of steak after cooking if desired. Serve immediately.

 TIMETABLE FOR PANFRYING STEAKS

Type of Steak	Thickness in Inches	Range-top Temperature	Approximate Total Cooking Time in Minutes 145° to 160° (medium-rare to medium)
Porterhouse and T-Bone	1/2	Medium	8 to 10
Rib Eye	1/2	Medium-high	3 to 5
Sirloin (boneless)	3/4 to 1	Medium-low to Medium	10 to 12
Tenderloin	3/4 to 1	Medium	6 to 9

*T-Bone Steak, Corn (page 163),
Baked Potato Wedges (page 172)*

BEEF WITH PEA PODS

MAKES 4 servings • COOK: 8 minutes

INGREDIENTS

ESSENTIAL EQUIPMENT: *2-quart saucepan; 10-inch skillet or wok*

1 pound beef boneless sirloin steak

1 clove garlic

Hot Cooked Rice (below)

1 tablespoon vegetable oil

1/4 teaspoon salt

Dash of pepper

2/3 cup beef broth

1 tablespoon cornstarch

2 tablespoons water

1 tablespoon soy sauce

1 teaspoon finely chopped gingerroot or 1/4 teaspoon ground ginger

1 package (6 ounces) frozen snow (Chinese) pea pods, thawed

HOT COOKED RICE

1 cup uncooked regular long-grain white rice

2 cups water

DIRECTIONS

1 Cut and discard most of the fat from the beef. Cut the beef with the grain into 2-inch strips, then cut the strips across the grain into 1/4-inch slices. Peel and finely chop the garlic.

2 Prepare Hot Cooked Rice. While the rice is cooking, continue with the recipe.

3 Heat the skillet over high heat 1 to 2 minutes. Add the oil to the hot skillet. If using a wok, rotate it to coat the side with oil. Add the beef and garlic to the skillet. Stir-fry with a turner or large spoon about 3 minutes, lifting and stirring constantly, until beef is brown.

4 Sprinkle salt and pepper over beef, and stir in the broth. Heat to boiling over high heat.

5 Mix the cornstarch, water and soy sauce, and stir into the beef mixture. Cook, stirring constantly, until the mixture thickens and boils. Continue boiling 1 minute, stirring constantly. The sauce will be thin.

6 Stir in the gingerroot and pea pods. Cook uncovered about 2 minutes, stirring occasionally, until pea pods are crisp-tender when pierced with a fork. Serve over rice.

HOT COOKED RICE Heat the rice and water to boiling in the saucepan over high heat, stirring occasionally to prevent sticking. Once mixture is boiling, reduce heat just enough so mixture bubbles gently. Cover and cook about 15 minutes or until rice is fluffy and tender.

1 SERVING: Calories 345 (Calories from Fat 65); Fat 7g (Saturated 2g); Cholesterol 55mg; Sodium 620mg; Carbohydrate 46g (Dietary Fiber 1g); Protein 26g

BEEF WITH PEA PODS: For 4 grams of fat and 320 calories per serving, omit the oil and use a non-stick skillet or wok. Spray the room-temperature skillet or wok with cooking spray before heating in step 3.

TiP FOR EASY PREPARATION, place beef in the freezer for 1 hour before slicing; it will be easier to slice when partially frozen.

TiP FOR MORE FLAVOR, use any leftover beef broth to replace part of the water used for cooking the rice.

Slicing Beef

Cut beef with grain into 2-inch strips; cut strips across grain into 1/4-inch slices.

Thawing Frozen Pea Pods

Place frozen pea pods in a strainer, then run cold water over them until the pea pods can be separated easily.

Beef with Pea Pods

BEEF STROGANOFF

MAKES 6 servings • COOK: 20 minutes

INGREDIENTS

ESSENTIAL EQUIPMENT: *10-inch skillet; 3-quart saucepan*

1 1/2 pounds beef boneless top loin steak, about 1 inch thick

2 tablespoons margarine or butter

Hot Cooked Noodles (below)

1 clove garlic

1 1/2 cups beef broth

2 tablespoons ketchup

1 teaspoon salt

1 medium onion

1/2 pound mushrooms

3 tablespoons all-purpose flour

1 cup sour cream or plain yogurt

HOT COOKED NOODLES

6 cups water

3 cups uncooked egg noodles (6 ounces)

DIRECTIONS

1 Cut the beef across the grain into about 1/8-inch strips. Cut longer strips crosswise in half.

2 Melt the margarine in the skillet over medium-high heat. Cook the beef in the margarine 8 to 10 minutes, stirring occasionally, until brown. While the beef is cooking, heat the water for Hot Cooked Noodles and continue with step 3.

3 Peel and finely chop the garlic. Reserve 1/3 cup of the beef broth. Stir the remaining broth, the ketchup, salt and garlic into beef. Heat to boiling over high heat. Once mixture is boiling, reduce heat just enough so mixture bubbles gently. Cover and cook about 10 minutes or until beef is tender.

4 While the beef is cooking, peel and chop the onion and cut the mushrooms into slices. Finish preparing the noodles.

5 Stir the onion and mushrooms into the beef mixture. Cover and cook about 5 minutes or until onion is tender.

6 Shake the reserved 1/3 cup beef broth and the flour in a tightly covered jar or container. Gradually stir this mixture into beef mixture. Heat to boiling over high heat, stirring constantly. Continue boiling 1 minute, stirring constantly, until thickened. Reduce heat just enough so mixture bubbles gently.

7 Stir in the sour cream. Cook until hot, but do not heat to boiling or the mixture will curdle. Serve over noodles.

HOT COOKED NOODLES Heat water to boiling in the saucepan over high heat. Stir in the noodles. Boil vigorously 8 to 10 minutes, stirring occasionally to prevent sticking, until noodles are tender. Boiling vigorously allows pasta to move freely so it cooks evenly, but watch carefully so the water doesn't boil over. Drain noodles in a strainer or colander.

1 SERVING: Calories 390 (Calories from Fat 170); Fat 19g (Saturated 8g); Cholesterol 105mg; Sodium 820mg; Carbohydrate 28g (Dietary Fiber 1g); Protein 28g

TiP **FOR A BIT OF COLOR** and fresh flavor, sprinkle freshly chopped parsley over the noodles.

TiP **FOR A MORE FLAVORFUL** and exotic version, use chanterelle, morel or shiitake mushrooms instead of regular white mushrooms.

Cleaning and Slicing Mushrooms

Rinse mushrooms, and cut off the stem ends. Cut mushrooms into 1/4-inch slices.

Thickening the Stroganoff

Stir broth-and-flour mixture gradually into beef mixture. For the right consistency, it is important to boil and stir 1 minute.

Beef Stroganoff

SPICY BEEF SALAD

MAKES 6 servings • COOK: 5 minutes • REFRIGERATE: 30 minutes plus 1 hour

INGREDIENTS

DIRECTIONS

ESSENTIAL EQUIPMENT: *10-inch nonstick skillet or wok*

1 pound beef boneless sirloin steak

2 tablespoons dry sherry or apple juice

1 tablespoon soy sauce

2 teaspoons sugar

1 small head lettuce

8 medium green onions with tops

2 medium tomatoes

3/4 pound mushrooms

Spicy Dressing (below)

SPICY DRESSING
1 clove garlic

1/4 cup rice vinegar or white wine vinegar

2 tablespoons soy sauce

1 teaspoon finely chopped gingerroot

1 teaspoon sesame oil

1/8 teaspoon ground red pepper (cayenne)

1 Cut and discard most of the fat from the beef. Cut the beef with the grain into 2-inch strips, then cut the strips across the grain into 1/8-inch slices. (For easier cutting, partially freeze beef about 1 hour.)

2 To marinate the beef, toss the beef, sherry, soy sauce and sugar in a glass or plastic bowl. Cover and refrigerate 30 minutes.

3 Wash the lettuce, and let drain. Peel and cut the green onions into 1/8-inch slices. Coarsely chop the tomatoes. Cut the mushrooms into slices. Tear or shred the lettuce into bite-size pieces.

4 Heat the skillet over medium-high heat 1 to 2 minutes. Add half of the beef to the hot skillet. Stir-fry with a turner or large spoon about 3 minutes, lifting and stirring constantly, until beef is brown. Remove beef from the skillet; drain. Repeat with remaining beef.

5 Toss the beef and green onions in a large salad or serving bowl. Layer the tomatoes, mushrooms and lettuce on the beef. Cover and refrigerate at least 1 hour but no longer than 10 hours.

6 Prepare Spicy Dressing. Pour the dressing over the salad, then toss until well coated.

SPICY DRESSING Peel and finely chop the garlic. Shake garlic and remaining ingredients in a tightly covered jar or container.

1 SERVING: Calories 120 (Calories from Fat 25); Fat 3g (Saturated 1g); Cholesterol 35mg; Sodium 430mg; Carbohydrate 9g (Dietary Fiber 2g); Protein 16g

TiP **TO SAVE TIME,** purchase fresh mushrooms that are already sliced.

TiP **SESAME OIL** is an Asian oil with a strong flavor and fragrance. It's usually with the Asian foods, but if you can't find it, you can substitute vegetable oil. Also, if you don't have rice or white wine vinegar, regular white vinegar will do.

Cutting Grain of Meat

The "grain" of meat refers to the muscle fibers that run the length of a cut of meat. Cut with the grain into 2-inch strips, then cut across the grain into 1/8-inch slices.

Preparing Gingerroot

Peel gingerroot with a paring knife, cut into thin slices and chop finely.

Spicy Beef Salad

ITALIAN BEEF KABOBS

MAKES 2 servings • **REFRIGERATE: 1 hour** • **BROIL: 8 minutes**

INGREDIENTS

ESSENTIAL EQUIPMENT: *four 10-inch metal or bamboo skewers; broiler pan with rack*

3/4 pound beef bone-in sirloin or round steak, 1 inch thick

2 cloves garlic

1/4 cup balsamic vinegar

1/4 cup water

1 tablespoon chopped fresh or 1 teaspoon dried oregano leaves

2 tablespoons olive or vegetable oil

1 1/2 teaspoons chopped fresh or 1/2 teaspoon dried marjoram leaves

1 teaspoon sugar

DIRECTIONS

1 Cut and discard most of the fat and the bone from the beef. Cut beef into 1-inch pieces.

2 Peel and finely chop the garlic. Make a marinade by mixing the vinegar, water, oregano, oil, marjoram, sugar and garlic in a medium glass or plastic bowl. Stir in the beef until coated. Cover and refrigerate, stirring occasionally, at least 1 hour but no longer than 12 hours. If you are using bamboo skewers, soak them in water 30 minutes before using to prevent burning.

3 You may need to move the oven rack so it is near the broiler. Set the oven control to broil.

4 Remove the beef from the marinade, reserving the marinade. Thread the beef on the skewers, leaving a 1/2-inch space between each piece. Brush the kabobs with the marinade.

5 Place the kabobs on the rack in the broiler pan. Broil kabobs with tops about 3 inches from heat 6 to 8 minutes for medium-rare to medium doneness, turning and brushing with marinade after 3 minutes. Discard any remaining marinade.

1 SERVING: Calories 195 (Calories from Fat 70); Fat 8g (Saturated 2g); Cholesterol 80mg; Sodium 60mg; Carbohydrate 1g (Dietary Fiber 0g); Protein 30g

TiP **TO SAVE TIME,** omit the garlic, vinegar, water, oregano, oil, marjoram and sugar, and instead, marinate the beef in 2/3 cup purchased Italian dressing in step 2.

✔ **ALTHOUGH YOU MIGHT BE TEMPTED** to serve the extra marinade with the cooked kabobs, you should discard any marinade that has been in contact with raw meat. Bacteria from the raw meat could transfer to the marinade.

Broiling

The distance from the heat to the food is important. If the food is too close to the heat, it will burn.

Italian Beef Kabobs

BEEF STEW

MAKES 4 servings • COOK: 3 hours 20 minutes

INGREDIENTS

DIRECTIONS

ESSENTIAL EQUIPMENT: *12-inch skillet or Dutch oven (about 4-quart size)*

1 pound beef boneless chuck, tip or round roast

1 tablespoon vegetable oil or shortening

3 cups water

1/2 teaspoon salt

1/8 teaspoon pepper

2 medium carrots

1 large potato

1 medium green bell pepper

1 medium stalk celery

1 small onion

1 teaspoon salt

1 dried bay leaf

1/2 cup cold water

2 tablespoons all-purpose flour

1 Cut and discard most of the fat from the beef. Cut the beef into 1-inch cubes.

2 Heat the oil in the skillet over medium heat 1 to 2 minutes. Cook the beef in the oil about 15 minutes, stirring occasionally, until brown on all sides.

3 Remove the skillet from the heat, then add the water, 1/2 teaspoon salt and the pepper. Heat to boiling over high heat. Once mixture is boiling, reduce heat just enough so mixture bubbles gently. Cover and cook 2 to 2 1/2 hours or until beef is almost tender.

4 Peel the carrots, and cut into 1-inch pieces. Scrub the potato thoroughly with a vegetable brush, but do not peel. Cut the potato into 1 1/2-inch pieces. Cut the bell pepper lengthwise in half, and cut out seeds and membrane. Cut the bell pepper into 1-inch pieces. Cut the celery into 1-inch pieces. Peel and chop the onion; cut in half.

5 Stir the vegetables, 1 teaspoon salt and bay leaf into the beef mixture. Cover and cook about 30 minutes or until vegetables are tender when pierced with a fork. Remove and discard bay leaf.

6 Shake the cold water and flour in a tightly covered jar or container. Gradually stir this mixture into beef mixture. Heat to boiling over high heat, stirring constantly. Continue boiling 1 minute, stirring constantly, until thickened.

1 SERVING: Calories 310 (Calories from Fat 145); Fat 16g (Saturated 5g); Cholesterol 65mg; Sodium 950mg; Carbohydrate 21g (Dietary Fiber 3g); Protein 24g

TiP **TO SAVE TIME,** use a 16-ounce bag of frozen mixed vegetables instead of the carrots, potato, bell pepper, celery and onion. There's no need to thaw the vegetables; just stir them into the beef mixture in step 5.

TiP **TO SAVE TIME,** cut up the vegetables about 1 hour in advance, putting the potato pieces in cold water to keep them from turning brown.

Browning the Beef

Cook the beef in the oil about 15 minutes, stirring occasionally, until brown on all sides. Browning helps develop the flavor of the stew.

Beef Stew

NEW ENGLAND POT ROAST

MAKES 4 servings • COOK: 3 hours

INGREDIENTS

ESSENTIAL EQUIPMENT: *Dutch oven (about 4-quart size) or 12-inch skillet*

2- to 2 1/2-pound beef arm, blade or cross rib pot roast

3/4 teaspoon salt

1/2 teaspoon pepper

1/2 cup prepared horseradish

1/2 cup water

8 small potatoes

6 medium carrots

4 small onions

Pot Roast Gravy (below)

POT ROAST GRAVY

Water

1/4 cup cold water

2 tablespoons all-purpose flour

DIRECTIONS

1 Place the pot roast in the room-temperature Dutch oven. Cook over medium heat, turning about every 6 minutes, until all sides are brown. Browning is important because it helps develop the rich flavor of the roast. If the roast sticks to the Dutch oven, loosen it carefully with a fork or turner. Remove the Dutch oven from the heat.

2 Sprinkle the salt and pepper over the roast. Spread the horseradish on top of the roast. Pour the water into the Dutch oven along the side of the roast, leaving the horseradish on top. Heat to boiling over high heat. Once water is boiling, reduce heat just enough so water bubbles gently. Cover and cook 2 hours. If more water is needed to keep the Dutch oven from becoming dry, add it 2 tablespoons at a time.

3 After the roast has been cooking for 1 1/2 hours, scrub the potatoes thoroughly with a vegetable brush, but do not peel. Cut each potato in half. Peel the carrots, and cut each into 4 equal lengths. Peel the onions and cut each in half. Add the potatoes, carrots and onions to the Dutch oven. Cover and cook about 1 hour or until the roast and vegetables are tender when pierced with a fork. Vegetables that are in the cooking liquid will cook more quickly, so you may want to move some of the vegetables from the top of the roast into the liquid to cook all uniformly.

4 Remove the roast and vegetables to a warm ovenproof platter or pan; keep warm by covering with aluminum foil or placing in oven with the temperature set at 200° or lower for no longer than 10 minutes. Prepare Pot Roast Gravy.

5 While keeping the gravy warm over low heat, cut the roast into 1/4-inch slices. Serve with the gravy and vegetables.

POT ROAST GRAVY Gravy is easy if you measure the water and flour accurately. Remove all but about 1 tablespoon of fat from the Dutch oven by skimming off the liquid with a large spoon and discarding the fat. Add enough water to the liquid to measure 1 cup. Shake 1/4 cup water and the flour in a tightly covered jar. Gradually stir this mixture into the liquid. Heat to boiling over high heat, stirring constantly. Continue boiling 1 minute, stirring constantly, until thickened.

1 SERVING: Calories 555 (Calories from Fat 190); Fat 21g (Saturated 8g); Cholesterol 90mg; Sodium 590mg; Carbohydrate 66g (Dietary Fiber 9g); Protein 35g

TiP **CUT LEFTOVER COLD POT ROAST** into slices, for a hearty sandwich.

TiP **LOOK FOR PREPARED HORSERADISH** in glass jars in the condiment section of your supermarket.

Browning the Pot Roast

Start the pot roast in a room-temperature Dutch oven. If it sticks during browning, loosen carefully with a fork or turner.

Making Pot Roast Gravy

Remove excess fat from the liquid; keep 1 tablespoon. Heat the liquid and flour-water mixture to boiling, then boil and stir 1 minute.

New England Pot Roast

SUCCULENT PORK CHOPS—THREE WAYS

BROILING, GRILLING AND PANFRYING

Loin or Rib Chop

Loin Chop, boneless

Blade Chop

Fresh, lean pork should be grayish pink in color and fine grained in texture.

BROILING OR GRILLING PORK CHOPS

1 Select pork chop from those shown in the photos.

2 To Broil: You may need to move the oven rack so it is 5 to 6 inches below the broiler. Set the oven control to broil.

To Grill: Prepare the coals or a gas grill for direct heat (pages 236–237). Heat to medium heat, which will take about 40 minutes for charcoal or about 10 minutes for a gas grill.

3 To Broil: Place pork chop on the rack in a broiler pan. (For easy cleanup, line the bottom of the broiler pan with aluminum foil before placing pork on rack.) Place in oven with the top of the pork chop the number of inches from heat listed in the chart.

To Grill: Place pork chop on the grill the number of inches from heat listed in the chart.

4 Broil or **Grill** uncovered for about half the time listed in the chart or until pork chop is brown on one side.

5 Turn the pork chop and continue cooking until the doneness listed in the chart.* To check doneness, cut a small slit in the center of boneless cuts or in the center near the bone of bone-in cuts. Medium pork is slightly pink in center. Well-done pork is no longer pink in center. Or insert a meat thermometer in the center of the pork chop to check for desired doneness. Sprinkle salt and pepper over both sides of pork chop after cooking if desired. Serve immediately.

Well-done pork, although a little less juicy, is recommended for some cuts because the pork will be more flavorful.

 TIMETABLE FOR BROILING OR GRILLING PORK CHOPS

Pork Cut	Approximate Thickness	Inches from Heat	Approximate Doneness	Approximate Total Broiling Time in Minutes	Total Grilling Time in Minutes
Loin or Rib Chops (bone-in)	3/4 inch	3 to 4	160° (medium)	8 to 11	6 to 8
	1 1/2 inches	3 to 4	160° (medium)	19 to 22	12 to 16

Pork Cut	Approximate Thickness	Inches from Heat	Approximate Doneness	Approximate Total Broiling Time in Minutes	Total Grilling Time in Minutes
Loin Chop (boneless)	1 inch	3 to 4	160° (medium)	11 to 13	8 to 10
Blade Chop (bone-in)	3/4 inch	3 to 4	170° (well)	13 to 15	11 to 13
	1 1/2 inches	3 to 4	170°(well)	26 to 29	19 to 22

PANFRYING PORK CHOPS

1 Select pork chop from those shown in the photos.

2 If the pork is very lean and has little fat, coat a heavy skillet or frying pan with a small amount of vegetable oil, or spray it with cooking spray. Or use a nonstick skillet.

3 Heat the skillet over medium heat 1 to 2 minutes.

4 Place the pork chop in the hot skillet. You do not need to add oil or water or cover the skillet; covering will cause the pork chop to be steamed rather than panfried.

5 Cook for the time listed in the chart, turning pork chop occasionally. If the pork chop has extra fat on it, fat may accumulate in the skillet; remove this fat with a spoon as it accumulates. Cook until brown on both sides and the doneness listed in chart.* To check doneness, cut a small slit in the center of boneless cuts or in the center near the bone of bone-in cuts. Medium pork is slightly pink in center. Well-done pork is no longer pink in center. Or insert a meat thermometer in the center of the pork chop to check for desired doneness. Sprinkle salt and pepper over both sides of pork chop after cooking if desired. Serve immediately.

Well-done pork, although a little less juicy, is recommended for some cuts because the pork will be more flavorful.

 TIMETABLE FOR PANFRYING PORK CHOPS

Pork Cut	Thickness in Inches	Pork Doneness	Approximate Total Cooking Time in Minutes
Loin or Rib Chops (bone-in)	1/2	160° (medium)	7 to 8
	1	160° (medium)	12 to 14
Loin Chops (boneless)	1/2	160° (medium)	7 to 8
	1	160° (medium)	10 to 12

PORK CHOPS AND APPLES

MAKES 2 servings • BAKE: 45 minutes

INGREDIENTS

ESSENTIAL EQUIPMENT: *1 1/2-quart casserole; small non-stick skillet (8- or 10-inch size)*

1 medium apple, such as Granny Smith, Wealthy or Rome Beauty

2 tablespoons packed brown sugar

1/4 teaspoon ground cinnamon

2 pork rib chops, 1/2 to 3/4 inch thick (about 1/4 pound each)

Cooking spray

DIRECTIONS

1 Heat the oven to 350°.

2 Cut the apple into fourths, and remove the seeds. Cut each fourth into 3 or 4 wedges. Place apple wedges in the casserole. Sprinkle the brown sugar and cinnamon over the apples.

3 Cut and discard most of the fat from the pork chops. Spray the skillet with cooking spray, and heat over medium heat 1 to 2 minutes. Cook pork chops in hot skillet about 5 minutes, turning once, until light brown.

4 Place the pork chops in a single layer on the apple wedges. Cover with lid or aluminum foil and bake about 45 minutes or until pork is slightly pink when you cut into the center and apples are tender when pierced with a fork.

1 SERVING: Calories 200 (Calories from Fat 55); Fat 6g (Saturated 2g); Cholesterol 45mg; Sodium 30mg; Carbohydrate 24g (Dietary Fiber 2g); Protein 15g

TiP SERVE WITH baked Acorn Squash (page 165) and a green salad with Honey-Dijon Dressing (page 148).

TiP FOLLOW COOK TIMES for pork carefully. Today's pork is lean and requires shorter cooking times. Overcooking pork will make it tough.

Cutting Fat from Pork Chop

Use a sharp knife to cut most of the fat from pork chop, being careful not to cut into the meat.

Slicing Apple

Cut apple into fourths, and remove seeds. Cut each fourth into wedges.

Pork Chops and Apples

ORANGE-GLAZED PORK CHOPS

MAKES 4 servings • COOK: 15 minutes

INGREDIENTS

ESSENTIAL EQUIPMENT: *10-inch skillet*

4 pork loin or rib chops, about 1/2 inch thick (about 1 1/4 pounds total)

Cooking spray

1/4 teaspoon salt

1/8 teaspoon pepper

1/2 cup orange juice

1/4 cup dry white wine or chicken broth

1 tablespoon chopped fresh or 1/2 teaspoon dried tarragon leaves

1 tablespoon cornstarch

2 tablespoons water

DIRECTIONS

1 Cut and discard most of the fat from the pork chops. Spray the room-temperature skillet with cooking spray, and heat over medium heat 1 to 2 minutes. Sprinkle salt and pepper over both sides of pork chops. Cook pork chops in hot skillet about 5 minutes, turning once, until light brown. Remove the skillet from the heat.

2 Add the orange juice, wine and tarragon to the skillet. Heat to boiling over high heat. Once mixture is boiling, reduce heat just enough so mixture bubbles gently. Cover and cook 10 to 15 minutes, stirring occasionally, until pork is slightly pink when you cut a small slit near the bone.

3 While the pork chops are cooking, mix the cornstarch and water.

4 When the pork chops are done, remove from the skillet to a serving platter. Cover with aluminum foil or lid to keep warm. Stir cornstarch mixture into orange juice mixture in skillet. Cook over medium heat, stirring constantly, until mixture thickens and boils. Continue boiling 1 minute, stirring constantly. Pour over pork chops.

1 SERVING: Calories 180 (Calories from Fat 70); Fat 8g (Saturated 3g); Cholesterol 65mg; Sodium 190mg; Carbohydrate 5g (Dietary Fiber 0g); Protein 22g

TiP **SERVE WITH** roasted sweet potatoes: Scrub fresh medium sweet potato with a vegetable brush, and pierce with fork or knife. Bake at 350° about 1 hour or until tender when pierced with a fork. Serve with butter.

TiP **FOR RECIPE SUCCESS,** stir the cornstarch mixture constantly while you are heating it; otherwise, the consistency will be lumpy and uneven.

Thickening the Glaze

Stir cornstarch mixture into skillet. Cook over medium heat, stirring constantly, until mixture thickens and boils.

Checking Pork for Doneness

Cut a small slit in the center near the bone of the pork chop. The meat should be just slightly pink.

Orange-Glazed Pork Chops

STIR-FRIED BROCCOLI AND PORK

MAKES 4 servings • **REFRIGERATE: 20 minutes** • **COOK: 10 minutes**

INGREDIENTS

ESSENTIAL EQUIPMENT: *2-quart saucepan; 12-inch skillet or wok*

1 pound pork boneless loin or leg

1 clove garlic

2 small onions

1 can (8 ounces) whole water chestnuts

1 tablespoon soy sauce

2 teaspoons cornstarch

1/2 teaspoon ground red pepper (cayenne)

Hot Cooked Rice (below)

2 tablespoons vegetable oil

3 cups broccoli flowerets or 1 bag (16 ounces) frozen broccoli cuts, thawed

1/4 cup chicken broth

1/2 cup peanuts

HOT COOKED RICE

1 cup uncooked regular long-grain white rice

2 cups water

DIRECTIONS

1 Cut and discard most of the fat from the pork. Cut pork into 2×1×1/8-inch slices. Peel and finely chop the garlic. Peel the onions, and cut each into 8 pieces; set aside. Drain the water chestnuts in a strainer.

2 To make a marinade, mix the garlic, soy sauce, cornstarch and red pepper in a glass or plastic bowl. Stir in pork. Cover and refrigerate 20 minutes.

3 While the pork is marinating, prepare Hot Cooked Rice.

4 About 10 minutes before rice is done, heat the skillet over high heat 1 to 2 minutes. Add the oil to the hot skillet, then the pork. Stir-fry with a turner or large spoon 5 to 6 minutes, lifting and stirring constantly, until pork is no longer pink.

5 Add the onions, broccoli and water chestnuts to pork mixture. Stir-fry 2 minutes.

6 Stir in the broth, and heat to boiling over high heat. Stir in the peanuts. Serve pork mixture with rice.

HOT COOKED RICE Heat the rice and water to boiling in the saucepan over high heat, stirring occasionally to prevent sticking. Once mixture is boiling, reduce heat just enough so mixture bubbles gently. Cover and cook about 15 minutes or until rice is fluffy and tender.

1 SERVING: Calories 570 (Calories from Fat 225); Fat 25g (Saturated 5g); Cholesterol 70mg; Sodium 200mg; Carbohydrate 56g (Dietary Fiber 5g); Protein 35g

TiP **SAVE A FEW MINUTES** by buying broccoli at the salad bar. It's already cut up, and you can buy only what you need.

TiP **FOR MORE FLAVOR AND VARIETY,** substitute fried rice from the deli or frozen food case for the Hot Cooked Rice.

Marinating Pork

For easier marinating, use a resealable plastic bag. The bag makes it much easier to turn the pork to coat all sides.

Stir-Frying Pork

Because stir-frying is done over high heat, you must constantly lift and turn the pork to prevent scorching and to cook evenly.

Stir-Fried Broccoli and Pork

TERIYAKI PORK TENDERLOIN

MAKES 3 servings • **REFRIGERATE: 1 hour** • **BAKE: 30 minutes**

INGREDIENTS

ESSENTIAL EQUIPMENT: *baking pan, such as 8-inch square or 11×7-inch rectangle*

1 clove garlic

2 tablespoons soy sauce

1 tablespoon water

1 teaspoon packed brown sugar

2 teaspoons lemon juice

2 teaspoons vegetable oil

1/8 teaspoon coarsely ground pepper

1 pork tenderloin (about 3/4 pound)

Cooking spray

DIRECTIONS

1 Peel and finely chop the garlic. To make a teriyaki marinade, mix the garlic, soy sauce, water, brown sugar, lemon juice, oil and pepper in a shallow glass or plastic dish. Add pork, and turn to coat with marinade. Cover and refrigerate, turning occasionally, at least 1 hour but no longer than 24 hours.

2 Heat the oven to 425°. Spray the baking pan with cooking spray. Remove the pork from the marinade, and discard marinade. Place pork in the sprayed pan.

3 Bake uncovered 27 to 30 minutes or until meat thermometer inserted in thickest part of pork reads 160° or pork is slightly pink when you cut into the center. Cut pork crosswise into thin slices.

1 SERVING: Calories 155 (Calories from Fat 45); Fat 5g (Saturated 2g); Cholesterol 70mg; Sodium 220mg; Carbohydrate 1g (Dietary Fiber 0g); Protein 26g

✔**FOR FOOD SAFETY,** be sure to use a glass or plastic dish to marinate the pork. Acidic ingredients such as lemon juice can react with a metal pan, causing discoloration of the pan and an off flavor. You also can use a tightly sealed plastic bag for marinating.

TiP SERVE WITH Garlic Mashed Potatoes (page 167) and Brown Sugar-Glazed Carrots (page 85) for an impressive and quick dinner.

Slicing Pork

Use a sharp knife to cut pork crosswise into thin slices.

Teriyaki Pork Tenderloin, Garlic Mashed Potatoes, Brown Sugar-Glazed Carrots

PORK TENDERLOIN WITH ROSEMARY

MAKES 3 servings • BAKE: 30 minutes

INGREDIENTS

DIRECTIONS

ESSENTIAL EQUIPMENT: *baking pan, such as 8-inch square or 11×7-inch rectangle*

Cooking spray

1 clove garlic

1/4 teaspoon salt

1/8 teaspoon pepper

1 pork tenderloin (about 3/4 pound)

1 1/2 teaspoon finely chopped rosemary or 1/2 teaspoon dried rosemary leaves, crumbled

1 Heat the oven to 425°. Spray the baking pan with cooking spray.

2 Peel and crush the garlic. Sprinkle salt and pepper over all sides of the pork tenderloin. Rub rosemary and garlic on all sides of pork. Place pork in the sprayed pan.

3 Bake uncovered 27 to 30 minutes or until meat thermometer inserted in thickest part of pork reads 160° or pork is slightly pink when you cut into the center. Cut pork crosswise into thin slices.

1 SERVING: Calories 140 (Calories from Fat 35); Fat 4g (Saturated 2g); Cholesterol 70mg; Sodium 100mg; Carbohydrate 0g (Dietary Fiber 0g); Protein 26g

TiP **SERVE WITH** Stir-Fried Green Beans and Pepper (page 180), which you can easily prepare while the pork is baking.

Crushing Garlic

Garlic can be crushed in a special tool, called a garlic press, or by pressing with the side of a knife or mallet to break into small pieces.

Crumbling Rosemary Leaves

When using dried rosemary, crumble the herbs in the palm of your hand to release more flavor before rubbing them onto the pork.

Pork Tenderloin with Rosemary, Stir-Fried Green Beans and Pepper

BARBECUED RIBS

MAKES 6 servings • BAKE: 1 hour 45 minutes

INGREDIENTS

ESSENTIAL EQUIPMENT: *shallow roasting pan (about 13×9-inch rectangle); 1-quart saucepan or 1 cup microwavable measuring cup*

4 1/2 pounds pork spareribs

Spicy Barbecue Sauce (below)

SPICY BARBECUE SAUCE

1/3 cup margarine or butter

2 tablespoons white vinegar

2 tablespoons water

1 teaspoon sugar

1/2 teaspoon garlic powder

1/2 teaspoon onion powder

1/2 teaspoon pepper

Dash of ground red pepper (cayenne)

DIRECTIONS

1 Heat the oven to 325°.

2 Cut the ribs into 6 serving pieces. Place the ribs, meaty sides up, in the roasting pan.

3 Bake uncovered 1 hour. While the ribs are baking, prepare Spicy Barbecue Sauce.

4 Brush the sauce over the ribs. Bake uncovered about 45 minutes longer, brushing frequently with sauce, until tender.

SPICY BARBECUE SAUCE Heat all ingredients in the saucepan over medium heat, stirring frequently, until margarine is melted. Or microwave all ingredients in a 1-cup microwavable measuring cup on high about 30 seconds or until margarine is melted.

1 SERVING: Calories 615 (Calories from Fat 450); Fat 50g (Saturated 17g); Cholesterol 160mg; Sodium 240mg; Carbohydrate 2g (Dietary Fiber 0g); Protein 39g

COUNTRY-STYLE SAUCY RIBS: Use 3 pounds pork country-style ribs. Cut the ribs into 6 serving pieces. Place in 13×9-inch rectangular pan. Cover with aluminum foil and bake at 325° for 2 hours; drain. Pour Spicy Barbecue Sauce over the ribs. Bake uncovered about 30 minutes longer or until tender.

TiP **SERVE WITH** Creamy Coleslaw (page 150) and crusty rolls from your favorite bakery.

TiP **TO SERVE SAUCE WITH RIBS,** heat any remaining sauce to boiling, stirring constantly. Continue boiling 1 minute, stirring constantly.

Cutting Ribs

Using a sharp knife or kitchen scissors, cut pork ribs into serving-size pieces.

Brushing on Sauce

Coat the ribs liberally with sauce, using a pastry brush. Turn ribs with tongs, and brush the other side.

Barbecued Ribs

Glazed Baked Ham

INGREDIENTS

ESSENTIAL EQUIPMENT: *shallow roasting pan (about 13×9-inch rectangle), and rack*

BROWN-SUGAR GLAZE

1/2 cup packed brown sugar

2 tablespoons orange or pineapple juice

1/2 teaspoon ground mustard (dry)

TiP FOR EASY CLEANUP, line bottom of roasting pan with aluminum foil before placing ham on rack.

TiP FOR MORE FLAVOR, use dark brown sugar instead of light.

DIRECTIONS

1 Select a fully cooked ham from those listed in Timetable for Roasting Ham (right). Allow about 1/3 pound ham per person, slightly less for a boneless ham and slightly more for ham with a bone.

2 Place the ham, fat side up, on a rack in the roasting pan. The rack keeps the ham out of the drippings and prevents scorching. It is not necessary to brush the ham with pan drippings while it bakes.

3 Insert a meat thermometer so the tip is in the thickest part of the ham and does not touch bone or rest in fat.

4 Bake uncovered in 325° oven for the time listed in the chart. It is not necessary to preheat the oven. While the ham is baking, prepare Brown Sugar Glaze (below).

5 Remove the ham from the oven 30 minutes before it is done. Remove any skin from the ham. Make cuts about 1/2 inch apart in a diamond pattern in the fat surface of the ham, not into the meat. Insert a whole clove in the corner of each diamond if desired. Pat or spoon glaze over the ham.

6 Bake uncovered about 30 minutes longer or until thermometer reads 135°. Cover the ham with a tent of aluminum foil and let stand 15 to 20 minutes or until thermometer reads 140°. (Temperature will continue to rise about 5° and roast will be easier to carve as juices set up.)

BROWN-SUGAR GLAZE Mix all ingredients. Makes enough for a 4- to 8-pound ham.

1 SERVING. Calories 240 (Calories from Fat 110); Fat 12g (Saturated 4g); Cholesterol 75mg; Sodium 1930mg; Carbohydrate 4g (Dietary Fiber 0g); Protein 29g

Cutting Diamond Pattern in Ham

Make cuts about 1/2 inch apart and 1/4 inch deep in diamond pattern in fat surface of ham, not into the meat.

Carving Ham

Place ham, fat side up and bone to your right, on carving board. Cut a few slices from thin side. Turn ham cut side down, so it rests firmly. Make vertical slices down to the leg bone, then cut horizontally along bone to release slices.

TIMETABLE FOR ROASTING HAM

Fully Cooked Smoked Ham	Oven Temperature	Approximate Weight in Pounds	Approximate Cooking Time in Minutes per Pound
Boneless Ham	325°	1 1/2 to 2	29 to 33
		3 to 4	19 to 23
		6 to 8	16 to 20
		9 to 11	12 to 16
Bone-in Ham	325°	6 to 8	13 to 17
		14 to 16	11 to 14

Glazed Baked Ham

CHAPTER 3

POULTRY AND SEAFOOD MAIN DISHES

FAST AND FLAVORFUL CHICKEN BREASTS— THREE WAYS

BROILING, GRILLING AND PANFRYING

BROILING OR GRILLING CHICKEN BREASTS

1 Select skinless, boneless chicken breast halves (about 1/4 pound each) or skinless bone-in chicken breast halves (about 1/2 pound each). If the chicken is frozen, place it in the refrigerator the night before you plan to use it or for at least 12 hours. Cut and discard fat from chicken with kitchen scissors or knife. Rinse chicken under cold water, and pat dry with paper towels.

2 To Broil: You may need to move the oven rack so it is 5 to 7 inches below the broiler. Brush the rack of broiler pan with vegetable oil, or spray it with cooking spray. Set the oven control to broil.

To Grill: Brush the grill rack with vegetable oil, or spray it with cooking spray. Prepare the coals or a gas grill for direct heat (pages 236–237). Heat to medium heat, which will take about 40 minutes for charcoal or about 10 minutes for a gas grill.

3 To Broil: Place the chicken breast on the rack in a broiler pan.

To Grill: Place the chicken breast on the grill 4 to 6 inches from heat.

4 Broil or **Grill** uncovered for the time listed in the chart, turning frequently with tongs. If desired, brush the chicken breasts with prepared barbecue or teriyaki sauce from your supermarket during the last 15 to 20 minutes for bone-in chicken or the last 10 minutes for boneless chicken.

Cutting Fat from Chicken

Cut fat from chicken with kitchen scissors or knife.

Rinsing Chicken

Rinse chicken under cold water; pat dry with paper towels.

TIMETABLE FOR BROILING AND GRILLING CHICKEN BREASTS

Cut of Chicken	Approximate Broiling Time	Approximate Grilling Time	Doneness
Breast halves (bone in)	25 to 35 minutes, turning once (7 to 9 inches from heat)	20 to 25 minutes	Cook until juice of chicken is no longer pink when centers of thickest pieces are cut.
Breast halves (boneless)	15 to 20 minutes, turning once (4 to 6 inches from heat)	15 to 20 minutes	Cook until juice of chicken is no longer pink when centers of thickest pieces are cut.

PANFRYING CHICKEN BREASTS

1 Select skinless, boneless chicken breast halves (about 1/4 pound each) or skinless, bone-in chicken breast halves (about 1/2 pound each). If the chicken is frozen, place it in the refrigerator the night before you plan to use it or for at least 12 hours. Cut and discard fat from chicken with kitchen scissors or knife. Rinse chicken under cold water, and pat dry with paper towels.

2 Heat 1 teaspoon vegetable oil in a 8-inch nonstick skillet over medium heat 1 to 2 minutes. If you are preparing 3 to 4 chicken breast halves, use a 10- or 12-inch skillet. Add the chicken.

3 Cook 8 to 10 minutes, turning chicken over once with tongs, until outside of chicken is golden brown and the juice is no longer pink when you cut into the center of the thickest piece. Larger chicken breast halves may take 2 to 3 minutes longer. If desired, sprinkle with salt, pepper and paprika.

TiP **FOR MORE FLAVOR,** chicken breasts can be marinated before broiling, grilling or panfrying. A wide array of marinades are available in your supermarket, or you may wish to make your own. Allow about 1/4 to 1/2 cup marinade for each 1 to 2 pounds of chicken. Marinate chicken covered in the refrigerator for 15 minutes to 2 hours.

CHICKEN BREASTS WITH ORANGE GLAZE

MAKES 2 servings • **COOK: 25 minutes**

INGREDIENTS

ESSENTIAL EQUIPMENT: *8-inch skillet or 3-quart saucepan*

2 skinless, boneless chicken breast halves (about 1/4 pound each)

1 tablespoon margarine or butter

1/2 teaspoon cornstarch

1/4 teaspoon ground mustard (dry)

1/4 cup orange juice

2 tablespoons orange marmalade

1 tablespoon soy sauce

DIRECTIONS

1 If the chicken is frozen, place it in the refrigerator the night before you plan to use it or for at least 12 hours. Cut and discard fat from chicken with kitchen scissors or knife. Rinse chicken under cold water, and pat dry with paper towels.

2 Melt the margarine in the skillet over medium heat. Cook chicken in margarine about 15 minutes, turning chicken over once with tongs, until juice of chicken is no longer pink when you cut into the center of the thickest piece.

3 While the chicken is cooking, mix the cornstarch and mustard in a small bowl. Stir in the orange juice, orange marmalade and soy sauce, mixing well.

4 Place the chicken on a serving plate, and cover with aluminum foil or a pan lid to keep it warm. Discard any juices left in the skillet.

5 To make the glaze, pour the orange mixture into the same skillet. Heat to boiling over medium heat, stirring constantly. Continue boiling about 1 minute, stirring constantly, until the sauce is thickened. Pour the glaze over chicken on serving plate.

1 SERVING: Calories 255 (Calories from Fat 80); Fat 9g (Saturated 2g); Cholesterol 65mg; Sodium 650mg; Carbohydrate 17g (Dietary Fiber 0g); Protein 27g

TiP **YOU CAN SUBSTITUTE** apricot, peach or pineapple preserves for the orange marmalade in the glaze.

✔**PREVENT POULTRY FROM** contaminating any foods in your grocery cart by putting it in plastic bags and placing it in the cart so that juices do not drip on other foods.

Making Orange Glaze

For smooth orange glaze, heat to boiling, stirring constantly. Boil and stir 1 minute.

Chicken Breasts with Orange Glaze

PARMESAN-DIJON CHICKEN

MAKES 6 servings • BAKE: 30 minutes

INGREDIENTS

ESSENTIAL EQUIPMENT: *shallow microwavable dish or pie pan; rectangular pan (about 13×9 inches)*

6 skinless, boneless chicken breast halves (about 1/4 pound each)

1/4 cup (1/2 stick) margarine or butter

3/4 cup dry bread crumbs

1/4 cup grated Parmesan cheese

2 tablespoons Dijon mustard

DIRECTIONS

1 If the chicken is frozen, place it in the refrigerator the night before you plan to use it or for at least 12 hours. Cut and discard fat from chicken with kitchen scissors or knife. Rinse chicken under cold water, and pat dry with paper towels.

2 Heat the oven to 375°. Either place the margarine in the shallow microwavable dish and microwave uncovered on High about 15 seconds until melted, or place the margarine in a pie pan and place in the oven about 1 minute until melted.

3 Mix the bread crumbs and cheese in a large plastic bag. Stir the mustard into the melted margarine until well mixed.

4 Dip the chicken, one piece at a time, into the margarine mixture, coating all sides. Then place in the bag of crumbs, seal the bag and shake to coat with crumb mixture. Place the chicken in a single layer in the ungreased rectangular pan.

5 Bake uncovered 20 to 30 minutes, turning chicken over once with tongs, until juice of chicken is no longer pink when you cut into the center of the thickest pieces. If chicken sticks to the pan during baking, loosen it gently with a turner or fork.

1 SERVING: Calories 275 (Calories from Fat 115); Fat 13g (Saturated 3g); Cholesterol 70mg; Sodium 390mg; Carbohydrate 10g (Dietary Fiber 0g); Protein 30g

TiP **FOR RECIPE SUCCESS,** pat rinsed chicken until it's very dry before dipping it into the margarine mixture, or the coating will not adhere.

TiP **SERVE WITH** Twice-Baked Potatoes (page 170), which can bake at the same time as the chicken. Put the potatoes in the oven before you begin preparing the chicken.

Making Dry Bread Crumbs

Place 4 pieces of bread on a cookie sheet and heat in a 200° oven about 20 minutes or until dry; cool. Crush into crumbs with a rolling pin or clean bottle.

Coating Chicken

Dip chicken into margarine mixture, then shake in bag of crumb coating.

Parmesan-Dijon Chicken, Twice-Baked Potatoes

RANCH CHICKEN

MAKES 4 servings • **COOK: 15 minutes**

INGREDIENTS

ESSENTIAL EQUIPMENT: *shallow bowl or pie pan; 10- or 12-inch nonstick skillet*

4 skinless, boneless chicken breast halves (about 1/4 pound each)

1/4 cup ranch dressing

1/3 cup seasoned dry bread crumbs

2 tablespoons olive or vegetable oil

TiP YOU CAN USE reduced-fat ranch dressing in this recipe.

DIRECTIONS

1 If the chicken is frozen, place it in the refrigerator the night before you plan to use it or for at least 12 hours. Cut and discard fat from chicken with kitchen scissors or knife. Rinse chicken under cold water, and pat dry with paper towels.

2 Pour the dressing into the shallow bowl or pie pan. Place the bread crumbs on waxed paper or a plate.

3 Dip the chicken, one piece at a time, into the dressing, coating all sides. Then coat all sides with bread crumbs.

4 Heat the oil in the skillet over medium-high heat 1 to 2 minutes. Cook chicken in oil 12 to 15 minutes, turning chicken over once with tongs, until outside is golden brown and the juice is no longer pink when you cut into the center of the thickest pieces. If the chicken sticks to the pan, loosen it gently with a turner or fork.

1 SERVING: Calories 290 (Calories from Fat 145); Fat 16g (Saturated 3g); Cholesterol 70mg; Sodium 260mg; Carbohydrate 8g (Dietary Fiber 0g); Protein 28g

TiP SERVE WITH a big bowl of cooked pasta sprinkled with olive oil, grated Parmesan cheese and chopped fresh oregano. Round out the meal with a marinated-vegetable salad from the deli.

Selecting Chicken

When you select packaged chicken, buy trays or bags that have very little or no liquid in the bottom. Avoid torn and leaking packages.

Thawing Chicken in the Microwave

Uncooked frozen chicken can be thawed in the microwave oven, following the microwave manufacturer's directions.

Ranch Chicken

CREAMY CHICKEN AND DUMPLINGS

MAKES 4 servings • COOK: 30 minutes

INGREDIENTS

ESSENTIAL EQUIPMENT: *Dutch oven (about 4-quart size) or 3-quart saucepan*

1 pound skinless, boneless chicken breast halves

1 tablespoon vegetable oil

1 3/4 cups water

1 cup milk

1 envelope (about 1 ounce) chicken gravy mix

2 teaspoons chopped fresh or 3/4 teaspoon dried marjoram leaves

1/2 teaspoon salt

1 bag (16 ounces) frozen broccoli, cauliflower and carrots

Dumplings (below)

DUMPLINGS

1 2/3 cups Bisquick® Original baking mix

1/2 cup milk

DIRECTIONS

1 If the chicken is frozen, place it in the refrigerator the night before you plan to use it or for at least 12 hours. Cut and discard fat from chicken with kitchen scissors or knife. Rinse chicken under cold water, and pat dry with paper towels. Cut chicken into 1-inch pieces.

2 Heat the oil in the Dutch oven over medium heat. Cook chicken in oil 5 to 7 minutes, stirring frequently, until golden brown. Remove the Dutch oven from the heat.

3 Stir in the water, milk, gravy mix (dry), marjoram, salt and frozen vegetables. Although thawing the vegetables is not necessary, stir them into the chicken mixture to allow them to cook uniformly.

4 Heat chicken mixture to boiling over high heat. Once mixture is boiling, reduce heat just enough so mixture bubbles gently.

5 Prepare Dumplings. With the chicken mixture boiling gently with bubbles breaking the surface continually, drop the dumpling dough by 12 spoonfuls onto hot chicken mixture. The dumplings will cook completely through when they are dropped onto the chicken mixture rather than into the liquid. If they are dropped directly into the liquid, the dumplings will be doughy and will not cook through.

6 Cook uncovered 10 minutes. Cover and cook 10 minutes longer.

DUMPLINGS Mix baking mix and milk in small or medium bowl with a fork until baking mix is completely moistened and a soft dough forms.

1 SERVING: Calories 435 (Calories from Fat 135); Fat 15g (Saturated 4g); Cholesterol 70mg; Sodium 1460mg; Carbohydrate 45g (Dietary Fiber 3g); Protein 33g

TiP **YOU CAN SUBSTITUTE** 1 pound skinless, bone-less chicken thighs for the chicken breast halves.

TiP **FOR RECIPE SUCCESS,** mix the dumpling dough only until the baking mix and milk form a soft dough; overmixing will cause tough dumplings.

Mixing Dumpling Dough

Mix baking mix and milk with fork until a soft dough forms.

Dropping Dumplings onto Chicken Mixture

Drop dumpling dough by spoon-fuls onto hot chicken mixture.

Creamy Chicken and Dumplings

TERIYAKI CHICKEN STIR-FRY

MAKES 4 servings • COOK: 10 minutes

INGREDIENTS

ESSENTIAL EQUIPMENT: *12-inch skillet or wok; 2-quart saucepan*

1 pound skinless, boneless chicken breast halves

1 tablespoon vegetable oil

1/2 cup teriyaki baste and glaze

3 tablespoons lemon juice

1 bag (16 ounces) frozen broccoli, carrots and water chestnuts

Hot Cooked Couscous (below)

HOT COOKED COUSCOUS

2 cups water

1/2 teaspoon salt

1 tablespoon olive or vegetable oil

1 1/2 cups uncooked couscous

DIRECTIONS

1 If the chicken is frozen, place it in the refrigerator the night before you plan to use it or for at least 12 hours. Cut and discard fat from chicken with kitchen scissors or knife. Rinse chicken under cold water, and pat dry with paper towels. Cut into 1-inch pieces.

2 Heat the skillet over high heat 1 to 2 minutes. Add the oil to the hot skillet. If using a wok, rotate it to coat the side with oil.

3 Add the chicken. Stir-fry with a turner or large spoon 3 to 4 minutes, lifting and stirring constantly, until chicken is no longer pink in center.

4 Stir in the teriyaki glaze, lemon juice and frozen vegetables. Although thawing the vegetables is not necessary, stir them into the chicken mixture to allow them to cook uniformly.

5 Heat the mixture to boiling over high heat, stirring constantly. Reduce heat just enough so mixture bubbles gently. Cover and cook about 6 minutes or until vegetables are crisp-tender when pierced with a fork.

6 While chicken mixture is cooking, prepare Hot Cooked Couscous. Serve chicken mixture with couscous.

HOT COOKED COUSCOUS Heat the water, salt and oil just to boiling in the saucepan over high heat. Stir in the couscous. Cover and remove from heat. Let stand 5 minutes. Fluff couscous lightly with a fork before serving.

1 SERVING: Calories 490 (Calories from Fat 100); Fat 11g (Saturated 2g); Cholesterol 60mg; Sodium 1770mg; Carbohydrate 66g (Dietary Fiber 6g); Protein 38g

TiP **TRY A FLAVORED COUSCOUS,** such as roasted garlic and olive, herbed chicken or wild mushroom.

✔ **WHEN CUTTING RAW POULTRY,** use hard-plastic cutting boards. They are less porous than wooden cutting boards and are easily cleaned or washed in a dishwasher.

Stir-Frying Chicken

Stir-fry chicken over high heat with a turner or large spoon, lifting and stirring constantly.

Fluffing Couscous

Use a fork to fluff and lift the couscous after it cooks, which prevents the couscous from clumping and sticking.

Teriyaki Chicken Stir-Fry

QUICK CHICKEN SOUP

MAKES 6 servings • COOK: 15 minutes

INGREDIENTS

DIRECTIONS

ESSENTIAL EQUIPMENT: *Dutch oven (about 4-quart size)*

3/4 pound cooked chicken (about 2 cups cut up)

2 medium stalks celery

2 medium carrots

1 medium onion

2 cloves garlic

4 cans (14 1/2 ounces each) ready-to-serve 1/3-less-sodium chicken broth

1 cup frozen green peas

1 tablespoon chopped fresh parsley or 1 teaspoon parsley flakes

1 tablespoon chopped fresh or 1 teaspoon dried thyme leaves

1/4 teaspoon pepper

1 dried bay leaf

1 cup uncooked gemelli or rotini pasta (4 ounces)

1 Cut the chicken into 1/2-inch pieces. Slice the celery. Peel and slice the carrots. Peel and chop the onion. Peel and finely chop the garlic.

2 Heat the chicken, celery, carrots, onion, garlic, broth, frozen peas, parsley, thyme, pepper and bay leaf to boiling in the Dutch oven over high heat. Stir in the pasta. Heat to boiling over high heat, stirring occasionally to prevent sticking. Once mixture is boiling, reduce heat just enough so mixture bubbles gently.

3 Cook uncovered 10 to 15 minutes, stirring occasionally, until pasta is tender and vegetables are tender when pierced with a fork. Remove and discard bay leaf.

1 SERVING: Calories 255 (Calories from Fat 55); Fat 6g (Saturated 2g); Cholesterol 45mg; Sodium 650mg; Carbohydrate 26g (Dietary Fiber 3g); Protein 27g

TIP LEFTOVER CHICKEN SOUP freezes well. Place it in a moistureproof and vaporproof container such as a plastic container with tight-fitting lid; label and date before freezing.

✔ **FOR FOOD SAFETY**—and the best flavor—cooked poultry should be wrapped tightly and refrigerated no longer than 2 days.

Chopping Fresh Parsley and Thyme

Remove stems from parsley leaves. Place leaves in small bowl or measuring cup. Cut into very small pieces with kitchen scissors. Repeat with thyme.

Chopping Garlic

Hit garlic clove with flat side of heavy knife to crack the skin, which will then slip off easily. Finely chop garlic with knife.

Quick Chicken Soup

OVEN-FRIED CHICKEN

MAKES 6 servings • **BAKE: 1 hour**

INGREDIENTS

ESSENTIAL EQUIPMENT: *13×9-inch rectangular pan*

3- to 3 1/2-pound cut-up broiler-fryer chicken

1/4 cup (1/2 stick) margarine or butter

1/2 cup all-purpose flour

1 teaspoon paprika

1/2 teaspoon salt

1/4 teaspoon pepper

DIRECTIONS

1 If the chicken is frozen, place it in the refrigerator the night before you plan to use it or for at least 12 hours. Cut and discard fat from chicken with kitchen scissors or knife. Rinse chicken under cold water, and pat dry with paper towels.

2 Heat the oven to 425°. Place the margarine in the rectangular pan, and melt in the oven, which will take about 3 minutes.

3 Mix the flour, paprika, salt and pepper in a large plastic bag. Place the chicken, a few pieces at a time, in the bag, seal the bag and shake to coat with flour mixture. Place the chicken, skin sides down, in a single layer in margarine in pan.

4 Bake uncovered 30 minutes. Remove chicken from oven, and turn pieces over with tongs. Continue baking uncovered about 30 minutes longer or until juice of chicken is no longer pink when you cut into the center of the thickest pieces. If chicken sticks to the pan, loosen it gently with a turner or fork.

1 SERVING: Calories 245 (Calories from Fat 125); Fat 14g (Saturated 4g); Cholesterol 85mg; Sodium 120mg; Carbohydrate 2g (Dietary Fiber 0g); Protein 28g

Lighter **OVEN-FRIED CHICKEN:** For 6 grams of fat and 160 calories per serving, remove the skin from chicken before cooking. Do not melt margarine in pan; instead, spray pan with cooking spray. Decrease margarine to 2 tablespoons; melt the margarine, and drizzle over chicken after turning in step 4.

TiP **SERVE WITH** Garlic Mashed Potatoes (page 167). Peel potatoes after chicken goes into the oven to bake. Start to cook the potatoes and garlic just before turning the chicken.

Removing Chicken Skin

Remove chicken skin by lifting and pulling skin away from chicken. Loosen and cut away connective membrane with kitchen scissors or knife.

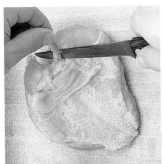

Turning Chicken Pieces

Chicken is baked skin sides down for the first 30 minutes; turn chicken with tongs or a turner. If chicken sticks to the pan, gently loosen it.

Oven-Fried Chicken

OVEN-BARBECUED CHICKEN

MAKES 6 servings • BAKE: 1 hour

INGREDIENTS

DIRECTIONS

ESSENTIAL EQUIPMENT: *13 × 9-inch rectangular pan*

3- to 3 1/2-pound cut-up broiler-fryer chicken

3/4 cup chili sauce

2 tablespoons honey

2 tablespoons soy sauce

1 teaspoon ground mustard (dry)

1/2 teaspoon prepared horseradish

1/2 teaspoon red pepper sauce

1 If the chicken is frozen, place it in the refrigerator the night before you plan to use it or for at least 12 hours. Cut and discard fat from chicken with kitchen scissors or knife. Rinse chicken under cold water, and pat dry with paper towels.

2 Heat the oven to 375°.

3 Place the chicken, skin sides down, in a single layer in the ungreased pan. Cover with aluminum foil and bake 30 minutes.

4 While the chicken is baking, mix the chili sauce, honey, soy sauce, mustard, horseradish and pepper sauce in a small bowl. Remove chicken from oven, and turn pieces over with tongs. Pour sauce over chicken, spooning sauce over chicken pieces if necessary to coat them completely.

5 Continue baking uncovered about 30 minutes longer or until juice of chicken is no longer pink when you cut into the center of the thickest pieces. Spoon remaining sauce over chicken before serving.

1 SERVING: Calories 280 (Calories from Fat 110); Fat 12g (Saturated 3g); Cholesterol 85mg; Sodium 790mg; Carbohydrate 15g (Dietary Fiber 0g); Protein 28g

TiP **TO SAVE TIME,** omit sauce ingredients and use 1 cup purchased barbecue sauce.

✔ **WHEN HANDLING** uncooked poultry, be sure to keep your hands, utensils and countertops soap-and-hot-water clean. When cleaning up after working with raw poultry, be sure to use disposable paper towels.

Turning Chicken

To retain juices and keep chicken from becoming dry, turn pieces with tongs instead of a fork.

Adding Sauce

The sauce is added the last 30 minutes. For uniform flavor and juiciness, be certain all pieces of chicken are coated with sauce.

Oven-Barbecued Chicken

Thyme-Baked Chicken with Vegetables

MAKES 6 servings • **BAKE: 1 1/2 to 2 hours**

INGREDIENTS

ESSENTIAL EQUIPMENT: *shallow roasting pan (about 13×9-inch rectangle)*

3- to 3 1/2-pound whole broiler-fryer chicken

6 medium carrots

4 medium stalks celery

3 medium baking potatoes (russet or Idaho), 8 to 10 ounces each

3 medium onions

2 tablespoons margarine or butter

1 tablespoon chopped fresh or 1 teaspoon dried thyme leaves

TiP FOR EASY CLEANUP, use a disposable aluminum pan. For easier handling of the heavy chicken and vegetables, buy a heavy-duty pan or use two lighter-weight pans.

TiP TO KEEP VEGETABLES HOT while you are carving the chicken, place them on an ovenproof serving platter or baking pan. Cover with aluminum foil and return to the still-warm oven, which has been turned off.

DIRECTIONS

1 Heat the oven to 375°. Rinse the chicken under cold water, and pat dry with paper towels. Pat the inside of the chicken with paper towels. Fold the wings of chicken across the back so tips are touching. There may be a little resistance, but once they are in this position, they will stay. Tie the drumsticks to the tail with string, but if the tail is missing, tie the drumsticks together.

2 Place the chicken, breast side up, in the roasting pan. Insert a meat thermometer so the tip is in the thickest part of inside thigh muscle and does not touch bone. Roast chicken uncovered 45 minutes.

3 While the chicken is roasting, prepare the vegetables. Peel the carrots, and cut into 1-inch pieces. Cut the celery into 1-inch pieces. Scrub the potatoes thoroughly with a vegetable brush or peel the potatoes, and cut into 1 1/2-inch pieces. Peel the onions, and cut into wedges.

4 Remove the chicken from the oven. Arrange the carrots, celery, potatoes and onions around the chicken. Melt the margarine. Stir the thyme into the margarine. Drizzle this mixture over the chicken and vegetables.

5 Cover the chicken and vegetables with aluminum foil and bake 45 to 60 minutes longer or until the thermometer reads 180°, the juice of chicken is no longer pink when you cut into the center of the thigh and the vegetables are tender when pierced with a fork. Another way to test for doneness is to wiggle the drumstick; if it moves easily, the chicken is done.

6 Remove the vegetables from the pan, and cover with aluminum foil to keep warm while carving the chicken. If you have an ovenproof platter, place the vegetables on the platter, cover with aluminum foil and place in the oven, which has been turned off.

7 Place chicken on a stable cutting surface, such as a plastic cutting board or platter. Place chicken, breast up and with its legs to your right if you're right-handed or to the left if left-handed. Remove ties from drumsticks. To carve chicken, see Carving the Turkey (page 87).

1 SERVING: Calories 350 (Calories from Fat 145); Fat 16g (Saturated 4g); Cholesterol 85mg; Sodium 170mg; Carbohydrate 25g (Dietary Fiber 4g); Protein 30g

Folding Wings of Chicken

Fold wings of the chicken across its back so that tips are touching.

Tying Drumsticks

Cross the drumsticks, and tie them to the tail with clean string.

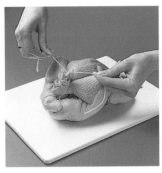

Thyme-Baked Chicken with Vegetables

TURKEY SALAD WITH FRUIT

MAKES 4 servings • **REFRIGERATE: 2 hours**

INGREDIENTS

DIRECTIONS

ESSENTIAL EQUIPMENT: *large serving bowl*

Mixed salad greens to line salad plates

10 ounces cooked turkey (about 2 cups cut up)

2 medium stalks celery

1 medium green onion with top

1 can (11 ounces) mandarin orange segments

1 can (8 ounces) sliced water chestnuts

1 container (6 ounces) peach, orange or lemon yogurt (2/3 cup)

1/4 teaspoon ground ginger

1 cup seedless green grapes

1 Wash the salad greens, let drain and refrigerate.

2 Cut the turkey into 1/2-inch pieces. Thinly slice the celery. Peel and cut the green onion into 1/8-inch slices. Drain the orange segments and water chestnuts in a strainer.

3 Mix the yogurt and ginger in the bowl. Stir in the turkey, celery, onion, orange segments, water chestnuts and grapes. Cover and refrigerate at least 2 hours. Arrange salad greens on 4 plates. Top greens with turkey salad.

1 SERVING: Calories 265 (Calories from Fat 45); Fat 5g (Saturated 2g); Cholesterol 60mg; Sodium 110mg; Carbohydrate 33g (Dietary Fiber 2g); Protein 24g

TiP **TO SAVE TIME,** purchase cooked turkey or chicken at the deli counter of your favorite supermarket.

TiP **SERVE WITH** Garlic Bread (page 142) or toasted pita breads, cut into wedges.

Cutting up Turkey

Cut turkey into 1/2-inch pieces. Some pieces will be irregular in shape.

Turkey Salad with Fruit

THANKSGIVING DINNER

You've always wanted to prepare and serve a traditional and delicious Thanksgiving dinner just like Grandma's—and now you can, with the help of this timetable and some planning. We provide dishes you can prepare in advance of the big day as well as help in dovetailing the preparations for this family-and-friends feast. If you receive offers of help, take them! Everyone likes to pitch in with this special dinner. So go ahead and send those dinner invitations with confidence.

This timetable was created for an 8- to 12-pound turkey, so you'll need to adjust the schedule slightly if your turkey is larger or smaller. To start off, we suggest a light and easy appetizer that doubles as the salad, to leave room for turkey and stuffing. Any apple and pear combination works for the appetizer. Purchase the dinner rolls from your favorite bakery. If time is really crunched, purchase the cranberry sauce and pumpkin pie, too. Or let a guest bring the pie.

There's no need to worry about matching linens. Select from the array of bright, colorful paper napkins and place mats available. Short on serving bowls? Try inexpensive sturdy plastic bowls available in the housewares or party supply section of your favorite store. For a stunning and colorful centerpiece, fill a large bowl or vegetable dish with chrysanthemums. Avoid last-minute frenzy by asking others to help you in carving the turkey and mashing the potatoes. Then sit down and enjoy a Thanksgiving dinner certain to bring well-deserved rave reviews.

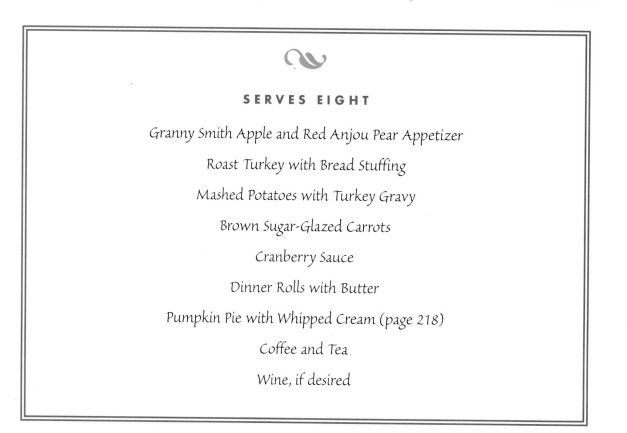

SERVES EIGHT

Granny Smith Apple and Red Anjou Pear Appetizer

Roast Turkey with Bread Stuffing

Mashed Potatoes with Turkey Gravy

Brown Sugar-Glazed Carrots

Cranberry Sauce

Dinner Rolls with Butter

Pumpkin Pie with Whipped Cream (page 218)

Coffee and Tea

Wine, if desired

READY, SET, GO

3 days before dinner

- Purchase groceries.
- Wrap rolls in aluminum foil and freeze to keep them fresh.

2 days before dinner

- **Thaw turkey,** if frozen, in refrigerator.
- Make Cranberry Sauce (page 85); cover and refrigerate.
- Whip cream for Pumpkin Pie (page 218); freeze as directed in recipe.
- Purchase flowers for centerpiece, order a floral centerpiece or purchase a low, pretty pot of mums for the table.

1 day before dinner

- Make Bread Stuffing (page 83); cover and refrigerate immediately.
- Peel, slice and cook carrots; cover and refrigerate.
- Chill wine.
- Set the table, and select serving dishes.
- Make Pumpkin Pie (page 218), or purchase from your favorite bakery.

Morning of the dinner

- Remove rolls from freezer.
- Wash apples and pears; core and slice. Dip into lemon juice to keep them from turning brown. Arrange apple and pear slices on a serving plate with lemon yogurt as the dip. Cover with plastic wrap and refrigerate.
- Prepare glaze ingredients for Brown Sugar-Glazed Carrots (page 85); place in skillet and leave at room temperature until ready to finish.

5 hours before dinner

- Wash turkey; pat dry with paper towels. Stuff with Bread Stuffing (page 83).
- Place turkey in oven for roasting immediately after stuffing.

- Peel potatoes for Mashed Potatoes (page 84); cover with cold water in saucepan to keep them from turning brown.

1 hour before dinner

- Place butter and Cranberry Sauce on the table.

45 minutes before dinner

- Begin cooking potatoes.
- Prepare coffee.
- Serve appetizer.
- Fill water glasses.

30 minutes before dinner

- Remove turkey from oven; place on carving board or platter and cover with aluminum foil to keep warm.
- Place rolls in aluminum foil in oven to heat.
- Remove stuffing from turkey; place in serving bowl and cover with aluminum foil to keep warm.
- Make Turkey Gravy (page 86).
- Mash the potatoes. The potatoes can stand for about 5 minutes but no longer than 10 minutes after they are mashed; keep them in a covered saucepan so they stay warm.
- Carve the turkey and arrange on a platter. If you aren't serving immediately, cover with aluminum foil to keep warm, and serve within 10 minutes.

10 minutes before dinner

- Heat the glaze for the carrots; add carrots.
- Remove whipped cream from freezer, and place in refrigerator.
- Make tea.
- Remove rolls from oven, and place in serving basket.
- Place carrots and gravy in serving bowls. Place the food on the table.
- Serve wine.

ROAST TURKEY

1 Select a turkey that is plump and meaty with smooth, moist-looking skin. The skin should be creamy colored. The cut ends of the bones should be pink to red in color.

2 If the turkey is frozen, thaw it slowly in the refrigerator, in cold water or quickly in the microwave, following the manufacturer's directions. A turkey weighing 8 to 12 pounds will thaw in about 2 days in the refrigerator. A turkey weighing 20 to 24 pounds will thaw in about 5 days in the refrigerator. A whole frozen turkey can be safely thawed in cold water. Leave the turkey in its original wrap, free from tears or holes. Place in cold water, allowing 30 minutes per pound for thawing, and change the water often.

3 Remove the package of giblets (gizzard, heart and neck), if present, from the neck cavity of the turkey, and discard. Rinse the cavity, or inside of the turkey, with cool water; pat dry with paper towels. Rub the cavity of turkey lightly with salt if desired. Do not salt the cavity if you will be stuffing the turkey.

4 Stuff the turkey just before roasting—not ahead of time. See Bread Stuffing (page 83). Fill the wishbone area (the neck) with stuffing first. Fasten the neck skin to the back of the turkey with a skewer. Fold the wings across the back so the tips are touching. Fill the body cavity lightly with stuffing. It is not necessary to pack the stuffing because it will expand during roasting. Tuck the drumsticks under the band of skin at the tail, or tie or skewer the drumsticks to the tail.

5 Place the turkey, breast side up, on a rack in a shallow roasting pan. Brush with melted margarine or butter. It is not necessary to add water or to cover the turkey. Place a meat thermometer in the thickest part of thigh muscle, so thermometer does not touch bone. Follow Timetable (below) for approximate roasting time. Place a tent of aluminum foil loosely over the turkey when it begins to turn golden. When two thirds done, cut the band or remove the skewer holding the drumsticks; this will allow the interior part of the thighs to cook through.

6 Roast until the thermometer reads 180° (for a whole turkey) and the juice is no longer pink when you cut into the center of the thigh. The drumstick should move easily when lifted or twisted. When the turkey is done, remove it from the oven and let it stand about 15 minutes for easiest carving. Keep turkey covered with aluminum foil so it will stay warm.

 TIMETABLE FOR ROASTING TURKEY

	Ready-to-Cook Weight	Oven Temperature	Roasting Time*
Whole Turkey	8 to 12 pounds	325°	3 to 3 1/2 hours
(stuffed)	12 to 14 pounds	325°	3 1/2 to 4 hours
	14 to 18 pounds	325°	4 to 4 1/4 hours
	18 to 20 pounds	325°	4 1/4 to 4 3/4 hours
	20 to 24 pounds	325°	4 3/4 to 5 1/4 hours

Begin checking turkey for doneness about one hour before end of recommended roasting time. For prestuffed turkeys, follow package directions very carefully—do not use this timetable.

BREAD STUFFING

MAKES 10 servings, about 1/2 cup each • **PREPARE: 30 minutes**

INGREDIENTS

ESSENTIAL EQUIPMENT: *Dutch oven (about 4-quart size) or 12-inch skillet*

2 large celery stalks with leaves

1 medium onion

3/4 cup (1 1/2 sticks) margarine or butter

9 cups soft bread cubes

1 1/2 teaspoons chopped fresh or 1/2 teaspoon dried thyme leaves

1 teaspoon salt

1/2 teaspoon ground sage

1/4 teaspoon pepper

DIRECTIONS

1 Chop the celery, including the leaves. Peel and chop the onion.

2 Melt the margarine in the Dutch oven over medium-high heat. Cook the celery and onion in margarine 6 to 8 minutes, stirring occasionally, until tender when pierced with a fork. Remove the Dutch oven from the heat.

3 Gently toss the celery mixture with the bread cubes, thyme, salt, sage and pepper, using a spoon, until bread cubes are evenly coated.

Lighter **BREAD STUFFING** For 6 grams of fat and 130 calories per serving, decrease margarine to 1/4 cup. Heat margarine and 1/2 cup chicken broth to boiling in Dutch oven over medium-high heat. Cook celery and onion in broth mixture.

Filling Wishbone Area

Fill wishbone area with stuffing. Fasten neck skin to back with skewer. Fold wings across back with tips touching.

Filling Body Cavity

Fill body cavity lightly with stuffing. Do not pack; stuffing will expand. Tuck drumsticks under band of skin at tail, or skewer to tail.

MASHED POTATOES

MAKES 4 to 6 servings • COOK: 25 minutes

INGREDIENTS

ESSENTIAL EQUIPMENT: *large saucepan (about 3-quart size); potato masher or electric mixer*

6 medium potatoes (about 2 pounds)

1/4 cup (1/2 stick) margarine or butter at room temperature

1/4 teaspoon salt, if desired

1/2 cup milk

1/2 teaspoon salt

Dash of pepper

DIRECTIONS

1 Wash and peel the potatoes, and cut into large pieces. Remove the margarine from the refrigerator so it can soften while the potatoes cook.

2 Add 1 inch of water (and the 1/4 teaspoon salt if desired) to the saucepan. Cover and heat to boiling over high heat. Add potato pieces. Cover and heat to boiling again. Once water is boiling, reduce heat just enough so water bubbles gently.

3 Cook covered 20 to 25 minutes or until tender when pierced with a fork. The cooking time will vary, depending on the size of the potato pieces and the type of potato used. Drain potatoes in a strainer.

4 Return the drained potatoes to the saucepan, and cook over low heat about 1 minute to dry them. While cooking, shake the pan often to keep the potatoes from burning, which can happen very easily once the water has been drained off.

5 Place the potatoes in a medium bowl to be mashed. You can mash them in the same saucepan they were cooked in if the saucepan will not be damaged by the potato masher or electric mixer.

6 Mash the potatoes with a potato masher or electric mixer until no lumps remain. Add the milk in small amounts, beating after each addition. You may not use all the milk because the amount needed to make potatoes smooth and fluffy depends on the type of potato used. Add the margarine, 1/2 teaspoon salt and the pepper. Beat vigorously until potatoes are light and fluffy.

BROWN SUGAR-GLAZED CARROTS

MAKES 8 servings • COOK: 15 minutes

INGREDIENTS

ESSENTIAL EQUIPMENT: *3-quart saucepan; 10- or 12-inch skillet*

2 pounds carrots (6 to 7 medium)

1/2 teaspoon salt, if desired

2/3 cup packed brown sugar

1/4 cup margarine or butter

1 teaspoon grated orange peel

1/2 teaspoon salt

DIRECTIONS

1 Peel the carrots, and cut into 1/4-inch slices. Heat 1 inch water to boiling in the saucepan over high heat. Add the 1/4 teaspoon salt if desired. Add the carrot slices. Cover and heat to boiling again. Reduce heat just enough so water bubbles gently. Cook covered 12 to 15 minutes or until carrots are tender when pierced with a fork.

2 While carrots are cooking, heat the brown sugar, margarine, orange peel and 1/2 teaspoon salt in the skillet over medium heat, stirring constantly, until sugar is dissolved and mixture is bubbly. Be careful not to overcook or the mixture will taste scorched. Remove the skillet from the heat.

3 Drain carrots in a strainer, then stir them into the brown sugar mixture. Cook over low heat about 5 minutes, stirring occasionally and gently, until carrots are glazed and hot.

CRANBERRY SAUCE

MAKES 16 servings • COOK: 20 minutes • REFRIGERATE: 3 hours

INGREDIENTS

ESSENTIAL EQUIPMENT: *3-quart saucepan*

4 cups 1 pound fresh or frozen cranberries (4 cups)

2 cups water

2 cups sugar

DIRECTIONS

1 Rinse the cranberries in a strainer with cool water, and remove any stems or blemished berries.

2 Heat the water and sugar to boiling in the saucepan over medium heat, stirring occasionally. Continue boiling 5 minutes longer, stirring occasionally.

3 Stir in the cranberries. Heat to boiling over medium heat, stirring occasionally. Continue boiling about 5 minutes longer, stirring occasionally, until cranberries begin to pop. Remove the saucepan from the heat, and pour the sauce into a bowl or container. Refrigerate about 3 hours or until chilled.

TURKEY GRAVY

MAKES 1 cup gravy • COOK: 5 minutes

INGREDIENTS

ESSENTIAL EQUIPMENT: *the pan the turkey was roasted in*

2 tablespoons turkey drippings (fat and juices)

2 tablespoons all-purpose flour

1 cup liquid (turkey juices, broth or water)

Browning sauce, if desired

Salt and pepper to taste

TiP **THIS RECIPE CAN EASILY** be doubled or tripled if there are enough drippings. Sprinkle carefully with salt and pepper, though; they do not need to be doubled or tripled.

DIRECTIONS

1 Place the turkey on a carving board or warm platter, and cover with aluminum foil while preparing gravy. Pan and drippings will be hot, so be careful when handling. Pour drippings from roasting pan into a bowl, leaving the brown particles in the pan. Return 2 tablespoons of the drippings to the roasting pan. Measuring accurately is important because too little fat makes the gravy lumpy and too much fat makes the gravy greasy.

2 Stir the flour into the drippings in the pan, using a long-handled fork or spoon. Cooking with the roasting pan on top of the burner may be unwieldy, so keep a pot holder handy to steady the pan. Cook over low heat, stirring constantly, until the mixture is smooth and bubbly. As you stir, the brown particles will be loosened from the bottom of the pan; they add more flavor to the gravy. Remove the pan from the heat.

3 Stir in the 1 cup liquid (turkey juices, broth or water). Heat to boiling over high heat, stirring constantly. Continue boiling 1 minute, stirring constantly. Stir in a few drops of browning sauce if you want the gravy to have a richer, deeper color. Taste the gravy, and add a desired amount of salt and pepper.

Returning Drippings to the Pan

Return 2 tablespoons drippings to the roasting pan.

Thickening Gravy

Stir in the 1 cup turkey juices. Heat to boiling, stirring constantly. Continue boiling 1 minute, stirring constantly.

CARVING THE TURKEY

Use a sharp carving knife for best results when carving a whole turkey. While carving, keep the turkey from moving by holding it in place with a meat fork. Carve on a stable cutting surface, such as a plastic cutting board or platter. Carving is easier if the turkey is allowed to stand for about 15 minutes after roasting.

1 Place the turkey, breast up and with its legs to your right if you're right-handed or to the left if left-handed. Remove the ties or skewers.

2 While gently pulling the leg and thigh away from the body, cut through the joint between leg and body. Separate the drumstick and thigh by cutting down through the connecting joint. Serve the drumstick and thighs whole, or carve them.

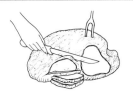

3 Make a deep horizontal cut into the breast just above the wing. Insert a fork in the top of the breast as shown, and starting halfway up the breast, carve thin slices down to the horizontal cut, working upward. Repeat steps 1 through 3 on the other side of the turkey.

Thanksgiving Dinner

FABULOUS FISH—FOUR WAYS

BROILED, GRILLED, PANFRIED AND BAKED

Fish is easy to fix and so good for you. Here are four simple and delicious ways to prepare it. Fish is available whole, drawn and pan-dressed, but you'll find it most often in steaks or fillets. You can purchase fish fresh or frozen. When you select fresh fish, the scales should be bright with a sheen, the flesh should be firm and elastic and there should be no odor. Frozen fish should be tightly wrapped and frozen solid; there should be no discoloration and no odor.

CUTS OF FISH

Fish Steaks

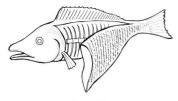

Fish Fillets

FISH STEAKS are the cross section of a large pan-dressed fish. Steaks are 1/2 to 3/4 inch thick. Allow 1/4 to 1/3 pound per serving.

FISH FILLETS are the sides of the fish, cut lengthwise from the fish. They can be purchased with or without skin. Fillets usually are boneless; however, small bones, called *pins,* may be present. Allow 1/4 to 1/3 pound per serving.

BROILED FISH STEAK

MAKES 1 serving   **BROIL: 10 minutes**

ESSENTIAL EQUIPMENT: *broiler pan with rack*

Fish steak, about 3/4 inch thick (1/4 to 1/3 pound)
Salt and pepper to taste
2 teaspoons margarine or butter, melted

1 You may need to move the oven rack so it is 5 to 6 inches below the broiler. Set the oven control to broil.

2 Sprinkle both sides of the fish steak with salt and pepper. Brush both sides with half of the margarine.

3 Place fish steak on the rack in the broiler pan. Broil with top of fish steak about 4 inches from heat 5 minutes. Brush with margarine.

4 Carefully turn fish over with a turner. If fish sticks to the rack, loosen it gently with a turner or fork. Brush other side with margarine.

5 Broil 4 to 6 minutes longer or until the fish flakes easily with a fork.

BROILED FISH FILLETS: Substitute 1/4 to 1/3 pound fish fillets for the fish steak. Sprinkle with salt and pepper and brush with margarine as directed for fish steaks. Broil with tops about 4 inches from heat 5 to 6 minutes or until fish flakes easily with a fork. Turning the fillets is not necessary.

GRILLED FISH STEAK

MAKES 1 serving   **GRILL: 20 minutes**

ESSENTIAL EQUIPMENT: *grill*

Fish steak, about 3/4 inch thick (1/4 to 1/3 pound)
Salt and pepper to taste
1 tablespoon margarine or butter, melted
1 teaspoon lemon juice

1 Prepare the coals or a gas grill for direct heat (pages 236–237). Heat to medium heat, which will take about 40 minutes for charcoal or about 10 minutes for a gas grill.

2 Sprinkle both sides of the fish steak with salt and pepper. Mix the margarine and lemon juice.

3 Grill the fish steak uncovered about 4 inches from medium heat 7 to 10 minutes, brushing 2 or 3 times with the margarine mixture.

4 Carefully turn the fish steak with a turner. If fish sticks to the grill, loosen it gently with a turner. Brush other side with margarine mixture.

5 Grill uncovered 7 to 10 minutes longer or until the fish flakes easily with a fork. Brush with margarine mixture.

PANFRIED FISH FILLETS

MAKES 6 servings   **COOK: 10 minutes**

ESSENTIAL EQUIPMENT: *shallow bowl or pie pan; 10-inch skillet*

1 1/2 pounds lean fish fillets, about 3/4 inch thick
1/2 teaspoon salt
1/8 teaspoon pepper
1 egg
1 tablespoon water
1/2 cup all-purpose flour, cornmeal or grated Parmesan cheese
Vegetable oil or shortening

1 Cut the fish fillets into 6 serving pieces. Sprinkle both sides of fish with salt and pepper.

2 Beat egg and water in the shallow bowl or pie pan until well mixed. Sprinkle the flour on waxed paper or a plate. Dip both sides of fish pieces into egg, then coat completely with flour.

3 Heat the oil (1/8 inch) in the skillet over medium heat about 2 minutes. Fry the fish in the oil 6 to 10 minutes, turning fish over once, until the fish flakes easily with a fork and is brown on both sides. Drain on paper towels.

BAKED FISH FILLETS

MAKES 4 servings   **BAKE: 15 to 20 minutes**

ESSENTIAL EQUIPMENT: *shallow baking pan, such as 11×7-inch rectangle or 8-inch square*

Shortening to grease pan
1 pound lean fish fillets, about 3/4 inch thick
3 tablespoons margarine or butter, melted
1 tablespoon lemon juice
1/4 teaspoon salt
1/4 teaspoon paprika

1 Heat the oven to 375°. Grease the bottom of the baking pan with the shortening.

2 Cut the fish fillets into 4 serving pieces if needed. Place the pieces, skin sides down, in the greased pan.

3 Mix the margarine, lemon juice, salt and paprika. Drizzle this mixture over the fish.

4 Bake uncovered 15 to 20 minutes or until the fish flakes easily with a fork.

SOLE WITH ALMONDS

MAKES 4 servings • **BAKE: 15 minutes**

INGREDIENTS

ESSENTIAL EQUIPMENT: *shallow baking pan, such as 11×7-inch rectangle or 9-inch square*

Vegetable oil for greasing pan

1 pound sole or other lean fish fillets, about 3/4 inch thick

1/3 cup sliced almonds or chopped walnuts

3 tablespoons margarine or butter at room temperature

1 1/2 tablespoons grated lemon peel

1 1/2 tablespoons lemon juice

1/2 teaspoon salt

1/2 teaspoon paprika

DIRECTIONS

1 Heat the oven to 375°. Grease the bottom of the baking pan with the oil.

2 Cut the fish fillets into 4 serving pieces if needed. Place the pieces, skin sides down, in the greased pan.

3 Mix the almonds, margarine, lemon peel, lemon juice, salt and paprika. Spoon this mixture over the fish.

4 Bake uncovered 15 to 20 minutes or until the fish flakes easily with a fork.

1 SERVING: Calories 220 (Calories from Fat 125); Fat 14g (Saturated 2g); Cholesterol 55mg; Sodium 480mg; Carbohydrate 3g (Dietary Fiber 1g); Protein 21g

Lighter **SOLE WITH ALMONDS:** For 9 grams of fat and 170 calories per serving, decrease almonds to 2 tablespoons and margarine to 2 tablespoons.

TiP **GRATE ONLY THE YELLOW PORTION,** or the "zest," of the lemon peel. The bright yellow peel provides the best flavor without bitterness. Also, grate the lemon peel before you squeeze the lemon for juice.

TiP **SERVE WITH** Green Beans (page 159) and packaged rice pilaf for an easy and impressive dinner ready in one hour.

Grating Lemon Peel

Grate the lemon peel by rubbing the lemon across the small rough holes of a grater.

Checking Fish for Doneness

You can test fish for doneness by placing a fork in the thickest part of the fish, then gently twisting the fork. The fish will flake easily when it's done.

Sole with Almonds, Green Beans

BAKED FLOUNDER TERIYAKI

MAKES 6 servings • **REFRIGERATE: 1 hour** • **BAKE: 20 minutes**

INGREDIENTS

ESSENTIAL EQUIPMENT: *13×9-inch rectangular pan*

Cooking spray

1 1/2 pounds flounder (about 6 small fillets) or other lean fish fillets

1 medium green onion with top

2 cloves garlic

1/3 cup dry sherry or apple juice

3 tablespoons lemon juice

2 teaspoons finely chopped gingerroot

1 teaspoon vegetable oil

2 teaspoons honey

1/4 teaspoon pepper

DIRECTIONS

1 Spray the rectangular pan with cooking spray. Cut the fish fillets into 6 serving pieces if needed. Place the pieces in the sprayed pan. If the pieces have skin, place with skin sides down.

2 Peel and cut the green onion into 1/8-inch slices. Peel and finely chop the garlic.

3 Mix the onion, garlic, sherry, lemon juice, gingerroot, oil, honey and pepper. Spoon this mixture over the fish. Cover with aluminum foil and refrigerate 1 hour.

4 Heat the oven to 375°. Bake covered 15 to 20 minutes or until the fish flakes easily with a fork.

1 SERVING: Calories 120 (Calories from Fat 20); Fat 2g (Saturated 0g); Cholesterol 55mg; Sodium 90mg; Carbohydrate 5g (Dietary Fiber 0g); Protein 20g

---

TiP YOU CAN SUBSTITUTE other lean fish, such as halibut, orange roughy, ocean perch, red snapper or scrod, for the flounder.

TiP SERVE WITH Sautéed Mushrooms (page 164) and Asparagus (page 158) for a light and healthful supper.

Folding Fish Fillets

Fish fillets are naturally uneven in thickness, so for even cooking, fold the thin end under before you spoon onion mixture over fish.

Baked Flounder Teriyaki, Asparagus

STIR-FRIED SCALLOPS WITH BROCCOLI AND MUSHROOMS

MAKES 4 servings • **COOK: 10 minutes**

INGREDIENTS

ESSENTIAL EQUIPMENT: *2-quart saucepan; 3-quart saucepan or 12-inch skillet*

1/2 pound broccoli

1/4 pound mushrooms

1 pound scallops

1 jar (2 ounces) sliced pimientos

Hot Cooked Rice (below)

2 tablespoons margarine or butter

1 can (10 1/2 ounces) condensed chicken broth

3 tablespoons cornstarch

2 teaspoons soy sauce

HOT COOKED RICE

1 cup uncooked regular long-grain white rice

2 cups water

DIRECTIONS

1 Trim the large leaves from the broccoli, and cut off any tough ends of lower stems. Rinse broccoli with cool water. Cut stems and flowerets into bite-sized pieces. Cut stem ends from the mushrooms, and cut the mushrooms into 1/4-inch slices.

2 If the scallops are larger than 1 inch in diameter, cut each in half. Rinse with cool water, and pat dry with paper towels. Drain the pimientos in a strainer.

3 Prepare Hot Cooked Rice. While the rice is cooking, continue with the recipe.

4 Melt the margarine in the 3-quart saucepan over medium heat. Cook the mushrooms in the margarine about 5 minutes, stirring frequently, until tender when pierced with a fork.

5 Stir in the scallops, broccoli and pimientos. Cook 3 to 4 minutes, stirring frequently, until scallops are white. Remove the saucepan from the heat.

6 Gradually stir the chicken broth into the cornstarch until the mixture is smooth. Stir the broth mixture and soy sauce into the scallop mixture. Heat to boiling over high heat, stirring constantly. Continue boiling 1 minute, stirring constantly. Serve over rice.

HOT COOKED RICE Heat the rice and water to boiling in the 2-quart saucepan over high heat, stirring occasionally to prevent sticking. Once mixture is boiling, reduce heat just enough so mixture bubbles gently. Cover and cook about 15 minutes or until rice is fluffy and tender.

1 SERVING: Calories 425 (Calories from Fat 80); Fat 9g (Saturated 2g); Cholesterol 35mg; Sodium 1030mg; Carbohydrate 54g (Dietary Fiber 2g); Protein 34g

TiP **TO SAVE TIME,** buy broccoli and mushrooms that are already cleaned and sliced at the salad bar.

TiP **SERVE WITH** a fruit salad of sliced bananas and halved strawberries drizzled with a tablespoon of orange or pineapple juice.

Thickening with Cornstarch

Gradually stir the broth into the cornstarch until smooth. Heat to boiling, stirring constantly. Boil and stir 1 minute.

Testing Scallops for Doneness

Scallops are very tender and cook quickly, turning white and opaque when they are done. Longer cooking results in tough scallops.

Stir-Fried Scallops with Broccoli and Mushrooms

SHRIMP SCAMPI

MAKES 2 or 3 servings • COOK: 12 minutes

INGREDIENTS

ESSENTIAL EQUIPMENT: *3-quart saucepan; 10-inch skillet*

3/4 pound uncooked peeled and cleaned medium shrimp

1 medium green onion with top

1 clove garlic

4 ounces uncooked fettuccine

1 tablespoon olive or vegetable oil

2 teaspoons chopped fresh or 1/2 teaspoon dried basil leaves

2 teaspoons chopped fresh parsley or 3/4 teaspoon parsley flakes

1 tablespoon lemon juice

1/8 teaspoon salt

Grated Parmesan cheese, if desired

DIRECTIONS

1 Fill the saucepan about half full of water. Add 1/4 teaspoon salt if desired. Cover and heat over high heat until the water is boiling rapidly. While water is heating, continue with the recipe.

2 Rinse the shrimp with cool water, and pat dry with paper towels. If the shrimp have tails, remove tails with knife. Peel the green onion, and cut into 1/4-inch slices. Peel and finely chop the garlic.

3 Once the water is boiling, add the fettuccine and stir to prevent sticking. Heat to boiling again. Boil uncovered 10 to 13 minutes, stirring frequently, until tender.

4 When fettuccine has been cooking for 5 minutes, heat the oil in the skillet over medium heat 1 to 2 minutes. Cook the shrimp, onion, garlic, basil, parsley, lemon juice and salt in the oil 2 to 3 minutes, stirring frequently, until shrimp are pink and firm. Do not overcook the shrimp or they will become tough. Remove the skillet from the heat.

5 Drain the fettuccine in a strainer or colander. Toss fettuccine and shrimp mixture in skillet. Sprinkle with cheese.

1 SERVING: Calories 365 (Calories from Fat 90); Fat 10g (Saturated 2g); Cholesterol 290mg; Sodium 440mg; Carbohydrate 38g (Dietary Fiber 2g); Protein 33g

TiP **IF YOU USE FRESH FETTUCCINE** instead of dried, it will cook much faster. You will need to start the shrimp as soon as the fettuccine begins to cook.

✔**SHRIMP IS VERY PERISHABLE.** Store it uncooked in refrigerator no longer than 1 to 2 days.

Cooking Shrimp
Cook the shrimp only 2 to 3 minutes, stirring frequently. Shrimp will turn pink and become firm when done.

Shrimp Scampi

PASTA AND MEATLESS MAIN DISHES

Italian Tomato Sauce with Pasta

MAKES 4 servings • COOK: 35 minutes

INGREDIENTS

ESSENTIAL EQUIPMENT: *medium saucepan (about 2-quart size); Dutch oven (about 4-quart size)*

1 medium onion

1 large clove garlic

1 small green bell pepper

1 tablespoon olive or vegetable oil

1 can (14.5 ounces) whole tomatoes, undrained

1 can (8 ounces) tomato sauce

1 tablespoon chopped fresh or 1 teaspoon dried basil leaves

1 1/2 teaspoons chopped fresh or 1/2 teaspoon dried oregano leaves

1/4 teaspoon salt

1/4 teaspoon fennel seed

1/8 teaspoon pepper

7 or 8 ounces uncooked spaghetti, fettuccine or linguine

DIRECTIONS

1 Peel and chop the onion. Peel and finely chop the garlic. Cut the bell pepper lengthwise in half, and cut out seeds and membrane. Chop enough bell pepper to measure 1/4 cup. Wrap and refrigerate any remaining bell pepper.

2 Heat the oil in the saucepan over medium heat 1 to 2 minutes. Cook the onion, garlic and bell pepper in the oil 2 minutes, stirring occasionally.

3 Stir in the tomatoes with their liquid, and break them up with a fork. Stir in the tomato sauce, basil, oregano, salt, fennel seed and pepper. Heat to boiling over high heat. Once mixture is boiling, reduce heat just enough so mixture bubbles gently and does not spatter.

4 Cover and cook 35 minutes, stirring about every 10 minutes to make sure mixture is just bubbling gently and to prevent sticking. Lower the heat if the sauce is bubbling too fast.

5 After the tomato sauce has been cooking about 20 minutes, fill the Dutch oven about half full of water. Add 1/2 teaspoon salt if desired. Cover and heat over high heat until the water is boiling rapidly. Add the spaghetti. Heat to boiling again. Boil uncovered 8 to 10 minutes, stirring frequently, until tender. If using fettuccine or linguine, boil 9 to 13 minutes.

6 Drain the spaghetti in a strainer or colander. Serve with the tomato sauce.

1 SERVING: Calories 275 (Calories from Fat 45); Fat 5g (Saturated 1g); Cholesterol 0mg; Sodium 680mg; Carbohydrate 52g (Dietary Fiber 4g); Protein 9g

TiP **THE COOKING TIME** over low heat for the sauce allows the flavor to develop.

TiP **A TIGHTLY HELD BUNDLE** of spaghetti, about the diameter of a quarter, weighs about 4 ounces, which makes about 2 servings.

Simmering Tomato Sauce

Heat to boiling. Reduce heat just enough so mixture bubbles gently and does not spatter.

Italian Tomato Sauce with Pasta

PESTO WITH PASTA

MAKES 4 servings • COOK: 12 minutes

INGREDIENTS

DIRECTIONS

ESSENTIAL EQUIPMENT: *Dutch oven (about 4-quart size); blender or food processor*

3 cups uncooked rigatoni pasta (8 ounces)

1 cup fresh basil leaves

2 cloves garlic

1/3 cup grated Parmesan cheese

1/3 cup olive or vegetable oil

2 tablespoons pine nuts or walnut pieces

Grated Parmesan cheese, if desired

1 Fill the Dutch oven about half full of water. Add 1/2 teaspoon salt if desired. Cover and heat over high heat until the water is boiling rapidly. Add the pasta. Heat to boiling again. Boil uncovered 9 to 11 minutes, stirring frequently, until tender. While the water is heating and the pasta is cooking, continue with the recipe to make the pesto.

2 To measure basil, firmly pack basil leaves into a measuring cup. Use the style of cup designed for dry ingredients, usually made of metal instead of glass. Rinse the basil leaves with cool water, and pat dry thoroughly with a paper towel or clean, dry kitchen towel. Peel the garlic.

3 Place the basil leaves, garlic, 1/3 cup cheese, the oil and pine nuts in the blender. Cover and blend on medium speed about 3 minutes, stopping blender occasionally to scrape sides, until smooth.

4 Drain the pasta in a strainer or colander, and place in a large serving bowl or back in the Dutch oven. Immediately pour the pesto over the hot pasta, and toss until pasta is well coated. Serve with additional cheese.

CILANTRO PESTO: Substitute 3/4 cup firmly packed fresh cilantro leaves and 1/4 cup firmly packed fresh parsley leaves for the fresh basil.

SPINACH WINTER PESTO: Substitute 1 cup firmly packed fresh spinach leaves and 1/4 cup firmly packed fresh basil leaves, or 2 tablespoons dried basil leaves, for the 1 cup fresh basil.

1 SERVING: Calories 440 (Calories from Fat 215); Fat 24g (Saturated 4g); Cholesterol 5mg; Sodium 160mg; Carbohydrate 46g (Dietary Fiber 2g); Protein 12g

TiP **STORE PESTO AIRTIGHT** in the refrigerator up to 5 days or in the freezer up to 1 month. Cover and store immediately because its color will darken as it stands.

TiP **PESTO CAN BE USED** as a spread on sandwiches, mixed into salads or used as a topping for hot meats or vegetables.

Measuring Basil Leaves

Firmly pack basil leaves into a measuring cup.

Pesto with Pasta

FETTUCCINE ALFREDO

MAKES 6 servings • COOK: 15 minutes

INGREDIENTS

ESSENTIAL EQUIPMENT: *Dutch oven (about 4-quart size); medium saucepan (about 2-quart size)*

8 ounces uncooked fettuccine

1/2 cup (1 stick) margarine or butter

1/2 cup whipping (heavy) cream

3/4 cup grated Parmesan cheese

1/2 teaspoon salt

Dash of pepper

Chopped fresh parsley

DIRECTIONS

1 Fill the Dutch oven about half full of water. Add 1/2 teaspoon salt if desired. Cover and heat over high heat until the water is boiling rapidly. Add the fettuccine. Heat to boiling again. Boil uncovered 11 to 13 minutes, stirring frequently, until tender. To test fettuccine for doneness, cut a strand of fettuccine on the side of the Dutch oven. While fettuccine is cooking, continue with the recipe to make the Alfredo sauce.

2 Heat the margarine and whipping cream in the saucepan over low heat, stirring constantly, until margarine is melted. Stir in the cheese, salt and pepper until the mixture is smooth.

3 Drain the fettuccine in a strainer or colander, and place in a large serving bowl or back in the Dutch oven. Pour the sauce over the hot fettuccine, and stir until fettuccine is well coated. Sprinkle with parsley.

1 SERVING: Calories 370 (Calories from Fat 235); Fat 26g (Saturated 9g); Cholesterol 65mg; Sodium 570mg; Carbohydrate 26g (Dietary Fiber 1g); Protein 9g

 Lighter

FETTUCCINE ALFREDO: For 16 grams of fat and 290 calories per serving, decrease margarine to 1/3 cup, and substitute evaporated milk for the whipping cream.

TiP **FRESHLY GRATED PARMESAN** cheese will make a thinner sauce than will canned grated cheese.

TiP **OTHER PASTAS MAY BE** substituted for the fettuccine. The sauce will cling best to a flat, narrow shape, such as linguine or spaghetti.

Cooking Fettuccine

Boil until desired doneness. To test, cut a strand of fettuccine on the side of the Dutch oven.

Fettuccine Alfredo

PASTA PRIMAVERA

MAKES 4 servings • COOK: 15 minutes

INGREDIENTS

ESSENTIAL EQUIPMENT: *Dutch oven (about 4-quart size); 12-inch skillet*

8 ounces uncooked fettuccine or linguine

2 medium carrots

1 small onion

1 tablespoon olive or vegetable oil

1 cup broccoli flowerets

1 cup cauliflowerets

1 cup frozen green peas

1 container (10 ounces) refrigerated Alfredo sauce

Grated Parmesan cheese, if desired

DIRECTIONS

1 Fill the Dutch oven about half full of water. Add 1/2 teaspoon salt if desired. Cover and heat over high heat until the water is boiling rapidly. Add the fettuccine. Heat to boiling again. Boil uncovered 11 to 13 minutes, stirring frequently, until tender. While the water is heating and the fettuccine is cooking, continue with the recipe.

2 Peel the carrots, and cut crosswise into thin slices. Peel and chop the onion.

3 Heat the oil in the skillet over medium-high heat 1 to 2 minutes. Add the carrots, onion, broccoli flowerets, cauliflowerets and frozen peas. Stir-fry with a turner or large spoon 6 to 8 minutes, lifting and stirring constantly, until vegetables are crisp-tender when pierced with a fork.

4 Stir the Alfredo sauce into the vegetable mixture. Cook over medium heat, stirring constantly, until hot.

5 Drain the fettuccine in a strainer or colander. Stir the fettuccine into the vegetable mixture. Serve with cheese.

1 SERVING: Calories 520 (Calories from Fat 280); Fat 31g (Saturated 12g); Cholesterol 100mg; Sodium 690mg; Carbohydrate 51g (Dietary Fiber 6g); Protein 15g

TiP **TO SAVE TIME,** substitute a 16-ounce bag of fresh vegetables for stir-fry, available in the produce section of the supermarket, for the vegetables in this recipe.

TiP **MANY SUPERMARKETS** carry fresh broccoli flowerets and cauliflowerets already washed and ready to use. You'll find them in the produce department.

Stir-Frying Vegetables

Stir-fry with a turner or large spoon 6 to 8 minutes, lifting and stirring constantly, until vegetables are crisp-tender.

Pasta Primavera

STUFFED PASTA SHELLS

MAKES 6 servings • COOK: 12 minutes • BAKE: 30 minutes

INGREDIENTS

ESSENTIAL EQUIPMENT: *Dutch oven (about 4-quart size); large skillet (about 10-inch size); 8- or 9-inch square pan or baking dish*

12 uncooked jumbo pasta shells

1 medium onion

1 pound lean ground beef

1 1/2 teaspoons chili powder

1 package (3 ounces) cream cheese at room temperature

1/4 cup taco sauce

Cooking spray

1/2 cup taco sauce

1 cup shredded Colby-Monterey Jack cheese (4 ounces)

1/2 cup crushed corn chips

4 medium green onions with tops

1/2 cup sour cream

DIRECTIONS

1 Fill the Dutch oven about half full of water. Add 1/2 teaspoon salt if desired. Cover and heat over high heat until the water is boiling rapidly. Add the pasta shells. Heat to boiling again. Boil uncovered 11 to 13 minutes, stirring frequently, until tender. While the water is heating and the pasta shells are cooking, continue with the recipe.

2 Peel and chop the onion. Cook the ground beef and onion in the skillet over medium-high heat 5 to 6 minutes, stirring occasionally, until beef is brown; drain.

3 Stir the chili powder, cream cheese and 1/4 cup taco sauce into the beef in the skillet. Heat over medium-low heat 2 to 3 minutes, stirring occasionally, until cheese is melted. Remove the skillet from the heat.

4 Heat the oven to 350°. Spray the square pan with cooking spray.

5 Drain the pasta shells in a strainer or colander. Fill the shells with the beef mixture, using about 2 tablespoons for each shell. Place filled shells in the sprayed pan. Pour 1/2 cup taco sauce over the shells.

6 Cover with aluminum foil and bake 20 minutes. Remove the pan from the oven. Sprinkle the Colby-Monterey Jack cheese and corn chips over the shells. Bake uncovered about 10 minutes longer or until cheese is melted. Peel and slice the green onions. Garnish pasta shells with sour cream and green onions.

1 SERVING: Calories 585 (Calories from Fat 270); Fat 30g (Saturated 14g); Cholesterol 90mg; Sodium 340mg; Carbohydrate 53g (Dietary Fiber 3g); Protein 29g

STUFFED PASTA SHELLS: For 24 grams of fat and 540 calories per serving, use 1 pound lean ground turkey instead of the ground beef and use reduced-fat cream cheese (Neufchâtel), available in 8-ounce packages.

TiP **BE SURE TO PURCHASE** jumbo-size pasta shells, so they'll hold all the filling. Shells also come in small and medium sizes.

TiP **TO DO AHEAD,** cover and refrigerate pan of unbaked stuffed pasta shells up to 24 hours. Increase first bake time to 25 minutes.

Stuffing Jumbo Pasta Shells

Fill pasta shells with beef mixture, using about 2 tablespoons for each shell. Place in sprayed pan.

Stuffed Pasta Shells

DO-AHEAD VEGETABLE LASAGNA DINNER

Whether cooking for family or friends, using do-ahead recipes makes dinner on a busy night easy and delicious. Invite friends over after work or the ball game to enjoy this special dinner, complete with dessert. Purchase the snacks, a 10-ounce bag of ready-to-eat salad greens, bottled dressing and a loaf of crusty bread from the supermarket along with the other ingredients you need, and let our timetable and recipes take away the guesswork. Your friends may offer to help set the table or toss the salad, which will make the dinner even easier for you. Plan to serve buffet-style from your kitchen counter.

SERVES FOUR

Peanuts or a purchased snack mix

Vegetable Lasagna

Crispy Green Salad

Crusty Bread

Creamy Lemon Dessert (page 216)

READY, SET, GO!

The night before dinner or up to 24 hours ahead
- Make Vegetable Lasagna, cover and refrigerate.
- Make Creamy Lemon Dessert, cover and refrigerate.

1 hour and 10 minutes before dinner
- Turn the oven to 400°, and allow to heat about 10 minutes.
- Set out a bowl of peanuts or snacks.
- Set the table, and select serving dishes for the salad and bread.

65 minutes before dinner
- Place Vegetable Lasagna in oven.
- Visit with your friends!

20 minutes before dinner
- Uncover lasagna, and continue baking 10 minutes.

10 minutes before dinner
- Remove lasagna from oven when it is bubbly around the edges and let stand 10 minutes.
- Place salad greens in a serving bowl, and toss with dressing.
- Cut wedges or slices of bread, and place in basket or on serving plate.
- Relax and enjoy your dinner!

After dinner
- Clear the table (accept help, if offered).
- Cut Creamy Lemon Dessert, and serve on small plates.

VEGETABLE LASAGNA

MAKES 6 servings • BAKE: 55 minutes • LET STAND: 10 minutes

INGREDIENTS

ESSENTIAL EQUIPMENT: *8-inch or 9-inch square pan or baking dish*

1 medium zucchini

2 cups spaghetti sauce

1 package (10 ounces) frozen chopped spinach, thawed

1 1/2 cups reduced-fat cottage cheese or ricotta cheese (12 ounces)

1/3 cup grated Parmesan cheese

2 tablespoons chopped fresh or 1 1/2 teaspoons dried oregano leaves

1 can (4 ounces) mushroom stems and pieces

8 purchased precooked or oven-ready lasagna noodles (each about 7×3 inches)

2 cups shredded mozzarella cheese (8 ounces)

DIRECTIONS

1 Shred the zucchini by rubbing it across the largest holes of a shredder. You will need about 1 cup. Mix the spaghetti sauce and zucchini in a medium bowl.

2 Drain the thawed spinach in a strainer, then squeeze out the excess moisture from the spinach, using paper towels or a clean kitchen towel, until the spinach is dry.

3 Mix the spinach, cottage cheese, Parmesan cheese and oregano in a medium bowl. Drain the mushrooms in a strainer. Spread 1/2 cup of the sauce mixture in the ungreased square pan.

4 Top sauce mixture in pan with 2 noodles, placing them so they do not overlap or touch the sides of the pan because they will expand as they bake. Spread one fourth of the remaining sauce mixture (about 1/2 cup) over the noodles.

5 Drop one fourth of the spinach mixture by small spoonfuls over the sauce mixture; spread carefully, pulling with the tines of a fork if necessary. Sprinkle with one fourth of the mushrooms and 1/2 cup of the mozzarella cheese.

6 Repeat layering three more times, beginning with 2 more noodles and following directions in steps 4 and 5 Cover with plastic wrap and then with aluminum foil and refrigerate up to 24 hours. (The plastic wrap keeps the lasagna from touching the aluminum foil while being refrigerated.)

7 Heat the oven to 400°. Remove the plastic wrap from the lasagna, then cover the lasagna again with the aluminum foil. Bake 45 minutes. Carefully remove the foil, and continue baking about 10 minutes longer or until lasagna is bubbly around the edges. Remove from oven and let stand 10 minutes, so the lasagna will become easier to cut and serve.

1 SERVING: Calories 425 (Calories from Fat 115); Fat 13g (Saturated 6g); Cholesterol 30mg; Sodium 1030mg; Carbohydrate 53g (Dietary Fiber 4g); Protein 28g

TiP **TO COMPLETE THE LASAGNA** and serve just after assembling, heat oven to 400°. Cover with aluminum foil and bake as directed in step 7, decreasing the first bake time to 35 minutes.

TiP **PRECOOKED OR OVEN-READY** lasagna noodles are available with the other dried pastas in the supermarket.

Shredding Zucchini

Shred zucchini by rubbing it across the largest holes of a shredder.

Layering the Lasagna

Spread 1/2 cup sauce in the pan. Add 2 noodles, 1/2 cup sauce, one fourth of the spinach mixture, one fourth of the mushrooms and 1/2 cup mozzarella cheese.

Vegetable Lasagna

FRIED RICE

MAKES 4 servings • COOK: 30 minutes

INGREDIENTS

DIRECTIONS

ESSENTIAL EQUIPMENT: *2-quart saucepan; 10-inch skillet*

Hot Cooked Rice (below)

1 cup bean sprouts

3 ounces mushrooms

2 medium green onions with tops

1 tablespoon vegetable oil

2 eggs

1 tablespoon vegetable oil

3 tablespoons soy sauce

Dash of pepper

HOT COOKED RICE

1 cup uncooked regular long-grain white rice

2 cups water

1 Prepare Hot Cooked Rice. While the rice is cooking, continue with the recipe. If the rice is done before you need it, just remove the rice from the heat and let it stand a few minutes until you're ready.

2 Rinse the bean sprouts with cool water, and drain in a strainer. Cut off the ends of the mushroom stems, and slice the mushrooms. You should have about 1 cup. Peel and slice the green onions.

3 Heat 1 tablespoon oil in the skillet over medium heat 1 to 2 minutes. Cook the mushrooms in the oil about 1 minute, stirring frequently, until they are coated with oil.

4 Add the bean sprouts, onions and rice to the mushrooms. Stir-fry with a turner or large spoon, lifting and stirring constantly, until the mixture is hot. Remove the skillet from the heat.

5 Beat the eggs slightly in a small bowl with a fork. Push the rice mixture to one side of the skillet. Add 1 tablespoon oil to the cleared spot, then pour the eggs into this spot. Cook over medium heat, stirring constantly, until eggs are thickened and cooked but still moist.

6 Stir the eggs and rice mixture together. Stir in the soy sauce and pepper.

HOT COOKED RICE Heat the rice and water to boiling in the saucepan over high heat, stirring occasionally to prevent sticking. Once mixture is boiling, reduce heat just enough so mixture bubbles gently. Cover and cook about 15 minutes or until rice is fluffy and tender.

1 SERVING: Calories 320 (Calories from Fat 100); Fat 11g (Saturated 2g); Cholesterol 105mg; Sodium 810mg; Carbohydrate 45g (Dietary Fiber 1g); Protein 11g

TiP **COOK EXTRA RICE** the next time you are serving it with another meal. Refrigerate or freeze the leftover rice (you'll need about 3 cups) in an airtight container, and use it for Fried Rice.

TiP **SUBSTITUTE INGREDIENTS** in Fried Rice to suit your taste. Use chopped green bell pepper or sliced water chestnuts, or add leftover ham or chicken. Make it exactly as you like it.

Cooking Eggs in Fried Rice

Push the rice mixture to one side of the skillet. Add 1 tablespoon oil to the cleared spot, then pour eggs into this spot. Cook, stirring constantly, until eggs are thickened and cooked but still moist.

Fried Rice

SPANISH RICE

MAKES 4 servings • **COOK: 30 minutes**

INGREDIENTS

ESSENTIAL EQUIPMENT: *large skillet (about 10-inch size)*

1 medium onion

1 small green bell pepper

2 tablespoons vegetable oil

1 cup uncooked regular long-grain white rice

2 1/2 cups water

1 teaspoon salt

3/4 teaspoon chili powder

1/8 teaspoon garlic powder

1 can (8 ounces) tomato sauce

DIRECTIONS

1 Peel and chop the onion. Cut the bell pepper lengthwise in half, and cut out seeds and membrane. Chop the bell pepper.

2 Heat the oil in the skillet over medium heat 1 to 2 minutes. Cook the onion and uncooked rice in the oil about 5 minutes, stirring frequently, until rice is golden brown.

3 Remove the skillet from the heat. Stir in the bell pepper, water, salt, chili powder, garlic powder and tomato sauce. Heat to boiling over high heat, stirring occasionally.

4 Once mixture is boiling, reduce heat just enough so mixture bubbles gently. Cover and cook about 25 minutes, stirring occasionally, until rice is tender and tomato sauce is absorbed. You may have to lower the heat as the mixture becomes thicker.

1 SERVING: Calories 265 (Calories from Fat 65); Fat 7g (Saturated 1g); Cholesterol 0mg; Sodium 930mg; Carbohydrate 48g (Dietary Fiber 2g); Protein 5g

TiP **FOR EXTRA FLAVOR,** sprinkle 1/4 cup shredded Cheddar cheese over Spanish Rice just before serving.

TiP **SERVE WITH WARMED TORTILLAS** or toasted pita bread wedges and, for dessert, cool sherbet or sorbet.

Cooking Rice and Onion

Cook onion and rice in oil over medium heat about 5 minutes, stirring frequently, until rice is golden brown.

Cooking Spanish Rice

Reduce heat until rice mixture bubbles gently. Cover and cook about 25 minutes, stirring occasionally, until rice is tender and tomato sauce is absorbed. You may have to lower the heat as mixture becomes thicker.

Spanish Rice

QUESADILLAS

MAKES 6 servings • BAKE: 5 minutes

INGREDIENTS

DIRECTIONS

ESSENTIAL EQUIPMENT: *cookie sheet or large shallow baking pan (about 15×10 inches)*

1 small tomato

3 medium green onions with tops

6 flour tortillas (8 to 10 inches in diameter)

2 cups shredded Colby or Cheddar cheese (8 ounces)

2 tablespoons chopped green chilies (from a 4-ounce can)

Chopped fresh cilantro or parsley, if desired

1 Heat the oven to 350°.

2 Chop the tomato. Peel and chop the green onions.

3 Place the tortillas on a clean counter or on waxed paper. Sprinkle 1/3 cup of the cheese evenly over half of each tortilla. Top cheese with tomato, onions, chilies and cilantro, dividing ingredients so each tortilla has an equal amount.

4 Fold tortillas over filling, and place on the ungreased cookie sheet.

5 Bake about 5 minutes or just until cheese is melted. Cut each quesadillas into wedges or strips, beginning cuts from the center of the folded side.

1 SERVING: Calories 280 (Calories from Fat 145); Fat 16g (Saturated 0g); Cholesterol 40mg; Sodium 470mg; Carbohydrate 26g (Dietary Fiber 1g); Protein 13g

Lighter **QUESADILLAS:** For 10 grams of fat and 245 calories per serving, use reduced-fat cheese and reduced-fat tortillas.

TiP **QUESADILLAS CAN** be served as an appetizer or as a main dish. Add shredded cooked beef or chicken or refried beans to the filling for a heartier main dish.

TiP **IF NOT ALL** the tortillas will fit on your cookie sheet, bake just some of them at a time. Bake more as you need them, so they'll always be hot.

Chopping a Tomato

Cut tomato in half; place cut side down on cutting board, and chop into small pieces.

Quesadillas

CHEESE ENCHILADAS

MAKES 4 servings • **COOK: 5 minutes** • **BAKE: 25 minutes**

INGREDIENTS

ESSENTIAL EQUIPMENT: *rectangular baking dish or casserole (about 11×7 inches)*

1 small green bell pepper

1 clove garlic

1 medium onion

1 tablespoon chili powder

1 1/2 teaspoons chopped fresh or 1/2 teaspoon dried oregano leaves

1/4 teaspoon ground cumin

1 can (15 ounces) tomato sauce

2 cups shredded Monterey Jack cheese (8 ounces)

1 cup shredded Cheddar cheese (4 ounces)

1/2 cup sour cream

2 tablespoons chopped fresh parsley

1/4 teaspoon pepper

8 corn tortillas (5 or 6 inches in diameter)

Sour cream and chopped green onions, if desired

DIRECTIONS

1 Heat the oven to 350°. Cut the bell pepper lengthwise in half, and cut out seeds and membrane. Chop enough of the bell pepper to measure 1/3 cup. Wrap and refrigerate any remaining bell pepper. Peel and finely chop the garlic. Peel and chop the onion, and set aside.

2 Mix the bell pepper, garlic, chili powder, oregano, cumin and tomato sauce in a medium bowl, and set aside. Mix the onion, Monterey Jack cheese, Cheddar cheese, 1/2 cup sour cream, the parsley and pepper in a large bowl.

3 Place 2 tortillas between dampened microwavable paper towels or microwavable plastic wrap and microwave on High 15 to 20 seconds to soften them. Immediately spoon about 1/3 cup of the cheese mixture down one side of each softened tortilla to within 1 inch of edge. Roll tortilla around filling, and place seam side down in the ungreased baking dish. Repeat with the remaining tortillas and cheese mixture.

4 Pour the tomato sauce mixture over the tortillas.

5 Bake uncovered about 25 minutes or until hot and bubbly. Garnish with sour cream and chopped green onions.

1 SERVING: Calories 540 (Calories from Fat 305); Fat 34g (Saturated 20g); Cholesterol 105mg; Sodium 1290mg; Carbohydrate 38g (Dietary Fiber 5g); Protein 26g

QUICK CHEESE ENCHILADAS: Omit the bell pepper, garlic, chili powder, oregano, cumin and tomato sauce. Instead, use a 16-ounce jar of salsa, which is about 2 cups.

TiP **IF YOU LIKE ENCHILADAS** with a hotter flavor, seed and finely chop 2 green jalapeño chilies, and add to the tomato sauce mixture.

TiP **WHEN BUYING TORTILLAS,** check for freshness. They should not look dry or cracked around the edges.

Softening Tortillas

Place 2 tortillas between dampened paper towels or microwavable plastic wrap and microwave on High 15 to 20 seconds to soften them.

Filling Tortillas

Spoon about 1/3 cup of the cheese mixture down one side of each softened tortilla to within 1 inch of edge. Roll tortilla around filling, and place seam side down in baking dish.

Cheese Enchiladas

SOUTH-OF-THE-BORDER WRAPS

MAKES 4 servings • COOK: 3 minutes

INGREDIENTS

ESSENTIAL EQUIPMENT: *9-inch square microwavable dish or dinner plate*

1 can (8 ounces) kidney beans

1 can (8 ounces) whole kernel corn

1 small bell pepper

1/2 cup chunky-style salsa

1 tablespoon chopped fresh cilantro or parsley

4 flour tortillas (8 to 10 inches in diameter)

1/2 cup shredded Cheddar cheese (2 ounces)

TiP **IF YOU HAVE** leftover rice from another dinner, stir 1/2 cup of it into the filling for these wraps.

DIRECTIONS

1 Drain the kidney beans in a strainer, rinse with cool water and place in a bowl. Drain the corn in a strainer.

2 Cut the bell pepper lengthwise in half, and cut out seeds and membrane. Chop enough of the bell pepper to measure 1/4 cup. Wrap and refrigerate any remaining bell pepper.

3 Mix the beans, corn, bell pepper, salsa and cilantro.

4 Place the tortillas on a clean counter or on waxed paper. Spread about 1/2 cup of the bean mixture over each tortilla to within 1 inch of the edge. Sprinkle 2 tablespoons cheese over each tortilla.

5 Fold opposite sides of each tortilla up toward the center about 1 inch over the filling—the sides will not meet in the center. Roll up tortilla, beginning at one of the open ends. Place wraps, seam sides down, in the microwavable dish.

6 Microwave uncovered on High 1 minute. Rotate dish 1/4 turn. Microwave 1 minute to 1 minute 30 seconds longer.

1 SERVING: Calories 335 (Calories from Fat 90); Fat 10g (Saturated 4g); Cholesterol 15mg; Sodium 800mg; Carbohydrate 53g (Dietary Fiber 6g); Protein 14g

---

Filling Wraps

Fold opposite sides of each tortilla up toward the center about 1 inch over the filling—the sides will not meet in the center.

Rolling up Wraps and Placing in Dish

Roll up tortilla, beginning at one of the open ends. Place seam side down in microwavable dish.

South-of-the-Border Wraps

CHUNKY BROCCOLI SOUP

MAKES 4 servings • COOK: 10 minutes

INGREDIENTS

ESSENTIAL EQUIPMENT: *large saucepan (about 3-quart size)*

1 large or 2 small stalks broccoli (about 3/4 pound)

1 small carrot

1/4 teaspoon salt

1/8 teaspoon pepper

1 can (14 1/2 ounces) ready-to-serve chicken broth

2 tablespoons all-purpose flour

1/4 cup cold water

1 cup half-and-half

DIRECTIONS

1 Trim the large leaves from the broccoli, and cut off any tough ends of lower stems. Rinse broccoli with cool water. Cut flower end from stalk, and cut flowerets into bite-size pieces. Cut the stalk into small pieces, about 1/4- to 1/2-inch cubes. You should have about 3 cups of broccoli, including the flowerets, but having a little more or less is fine.

2 Peel and shred the carrot. Any size shreds is fine.

3 Heat the broccoli, shredded carrot, salt, pepper and chicken broth to boiling in the saucepan over high heat. Once mixture is boiling, reduce heat just enough so mixture bubbles gently. Cover and cook 6 to 8 minutes or until broccoli is tender when pierced with a fork.

4 Mix the flour and water in a small bowl or measuring cup with a fork or wire whisk until the flour is dissolved. Pour this mixture gradually into the broccoli mixture, stirring broccoli mixture constantly while pouring.

5 Heat to boiling over high heat, stirring constantly. Continue boiling 1 minute, stirring constantly.

6 Stir in the half-and-half. Cook, stirring occasionally, until hot. The soup should look hot and steamy, but do not let it boil.

1 SERVING: Calories 150 (Calories from Fat 70); Fat 8g (Saturated 5g); Cholesterol 20mg; Sodium 650mg; Carbohydrate 15g (Dietary Fiber 5g); Protein 9g

BROCCOLI-CHEESE SOUP: Make Chunky Broccoli Soup as directed. When soup is finished and very hot, gradually stir in 1 cup shredded Cheddar cheese until it is melted.

TiP **ONE 10-OUNCE PACKAGE** of frozen chopped broccoli may be substituted for the fresh broccoli. There's no need to thaw it before adding in step 3.

TiP **THE FLOUR MIXTURE** is used to thicken the broccoli soup. If it is not stirred constantly, it can form lumps instead of making the soup smooth and slightly thicker.

Thickening the Soup

Pour flour-and-water mixture gradually into broccoli mixture, stirring constantly.

Chunky Broccoli Soup

HOME-STYLE POTATO SOUP

MAKES 5 servings • COOK: 20 minutes

INGREDIENTS

ESSENTIAL EQUIPMENT: *large saucepan (about 3-quart size); potato masher or large fork*

3 medium potatoes (about 1 pound)

1 can (14 1/2 ounces) ready-to-serve chicken broth

2 medium green onions with tops

1 1/2 cups milk

1/4 teaspoon salt

1/8 teaspoon pepper

1/8 teaspoon dried thyme leaves

DIRECTIONS

1 Peel the potatoes, and cut into large pieces.

2 Heat the chicken broth and potatoes to boiling in the saucepan over high heat, stirring occasionally with a fork to make sure potatoes do not stick to the saucepan. Once mixture is boiling, reduce heat just enough so mixture bubbles gently. Cover and cook about 15 minutes or until potatoes are tender when pierced with a fork.

3 While the potatoes are cooking, peel and thinly slice the green onions. If you have extra onions, wrap them airtight and store in the refrigerator up to 5 days.

4 When the potatoes are done, remove the saucepan from the heat, but do not drain. Break the potatoes into smaller pieces with the potato masher or large fork. The mixture should still be lumpy.

5 Stir the milk, salt, pepper, thyme and onions into the potato mixture. Heat over medium heat, stirring occasionally, until hot and steaming, but do not let the soup boil.

1 SERVING: Calories 110 (Calories from Fat 20); Fat 2g (Saturated 1g); Cholesterol 5mg; Sodium 510mg; Carbohydrate 19g (Dietary Fiber 1g); Protein 5g

POTATO-CHEESE SOUP: Make Home-Style Potato Soup as directed. When soup is finished and very hot, gradually stir in 1 1/2 cups shredded Cheddar cheese until it is melted.

TiP **IF YOU REFRIGERATED** leftover soup and it seems too thick, just stir in some milk, a little at a time, while reheating it.

TiP **LOW-FAT OR NONFAT** milk can be used for this potato soup, but whole milk makes the soup a little richer and creamier.

Cutting Green Onions

Cut green onions into thin slices, using some of the green part. Throw away the tip with the stringy end.

Breaking up Potatoes

When potatoes are done, remove from heat, but do not drain. Break potatoes into smaller pieces using a potato masher or large fork.

Home-Style Potato Soup

BLACK BEAN SOUP

MAKES 4 servings • COOK: 30 minutes

INGREDIENTS

DIRECTIONS

ESSENTIAL EQUIPMENT: *medium or large saucepan (2- or 3-quart size)*

1 medium onion

1 large clove garlic

1 medium carrot

1 medium stalk celery

Parsley sprigs

1 slice bacon

1 can (14 1/2 ounces) ready-to-serve chicken broth

1/2 teaspoon dried oregano leaves

1/2 teaspoon crushed red pepper

1 can (15 ounces) black beans

4 lemon wedges

1 Peel and chop the onion. Peel and finely chop the garlic. Peel and coarsely chop the carrot. Coarsely chop the celery.

2 Rinse sprigs of parsley with cool water, and pat dry with a paper towel. Chop enough parsley leaves into small pieces on a cutting board using a chef's knife to measure about 2 tablespoons, or place the leafy portion of the parsley in a small bowl or cup and snip into very small pieces with kitchen scissors. Discard the stems.

3 Cut bacon slice crosswise into 1/2-inch strips. Cook the bacon strips in the saucepan over medium heat 1 minute, stirring constantly. Do not drain.

4 Add the onion and garlic to the bacon. Cook about 5 minutes, stirring frequently, until onion is tender when pierced with a fork and beginning to turn yellow. Bacon will still be soft. Remove the saucepan from the heat.

5 Stir in the chicken broth, carrot, celery, parsley, oregano and red pepper. Heat to boiling over high heat. Once mixture is boiling, reduce heat just enough so mixture bubbles gently. Cover and cook 10 minutes.

6 While broth mixture is cooking, drain the black beans in a strainer, and rinse with cool water. Measure out 1/2 cup of the beans. Place the 1/2 cup beans in a small bowl, and mash them with a fork.

7 Stir the whole beans and the mashed beans into the broth mixture. Cook about 1 minute or until beans are heated. Serve soup with lemon wedges.

1 SERVING: Calories 140 (Calories from Fat 20); Fat 2g (Saturated 1g); Cholesterol 0mg; Sodium 670mg; Carbohydrate 27g (Dietary Fiber 7g); Protein 10g

TiP **TO MAKE** this a meatless soup, substitute 1 tablespoon vegetable oil for the bacon, and use vegetable broth instead of chicken broth.

TiP **THE BACON** will be easier to cut up if you place it in the freezer for 5 minutes first.

✔ **BEFORE ADDING** the chicken broth, remove the saucepan containing the hot bacon fat and onion from the heat to prevent spattering and steam.

Rinsing Beans

Empty beans into a strainer, and rinse with cool water.

Mashing Beans

Place 1/2 cup of the beans in a bowl, and mash with a fork.

Black Bean Soup

VEGETARIAN CHILI

MAKES 4 servings • COOK: 17 minutes

INGREDIENTS

ESSENTIAL EQUIPMENT: *Dutch oven (about 4-quart size)*

2 medium potatoes (about 10 ounces)

1 medium onion

1 small yellow bell pepper

1 can (15 to 16 ounces) garbanzo beans

1 can (15 to 16 ounces) kidney beans

1 can (28 ounces) whole tomatoes, undrained

1 can (8 ounces) tomato sauce

1 tablespoon chili powder

1 teaspoon ground cumin

1 medium zucchini

DIRECTIONS

1 Scrub the potatoes thoroughly with a vegetable brush, but do not peel. Cut the potatoes into cubes that are 1/2 inch or slightly larger. Peel and chop the onion. Place the potatoes and onion in the Dutch oven.

2 Cut the bell pepper lengthwise in half, and cut out seeds and membrane. Chop the bell pepper into small pieces. Add to the Dutch oven.

3 Drain the garbanzo and kidney beans in a strainer, and rinse with cool water. Add to the Dutch oven.

4 Add the tomatoes with their liquid, the tomato sauce, chili powder and cumin to the Dutch oven. Heat to boiling over high heat, breaking up the tomatoes with a fork and stirring occasionally.

5 Once chili is boiling, reduce heat just enough so chili bubbles gently. Cover and cook 10 minutes.

6 While chili is cooking, cut the zucchini into 1/2 inch slices. Stir zucchini into chili. Cover and cook 5 to 7 minutes longer, stirring occasionally, until potatoes and zucchini are tender when pierced with a fork.

1 SERVING: Calories 315 (Calories from Fat 25); Fat 3g (Saturated 0g); Cholesterol 0mg; Sodium 1250mg; Carbohydrate 68g (Dietary Fiber 14g); Protein 18g

TiP **YOU MAY NOTICE** that zucchini comes in many sizes, with some homegrown ones reaching a foot or more in length. Choose a zucchini between 4 and 8 inches long because it will be younger and more tender than the bigger ones.

TiP **SUBSTITUTE** a green or red bell pepper if you can't find a yellow one. The flavor is similar.

Cubing Potatoes

Cut potatoes into cubes that are 1/2 inch or slightly larger.

Vegetarian Chili

EXCELLENT EGGS—FIVE WAYS

ALLOW 1 or 2 eggs per serving • **COOK: Will vary with the method used**

ESSENTIAL EQUIPMENT: *Saucepan or skillet large enough to hold desired number of eggs*

COOKED EGGS

HARD-COOKED EGGS: Place eggs in a saucepan. Add enough cold water until it is at least 1 inch above the eggs. Heat uncovered to boiling over high heat. Remove the saucepan from the heat. Cover and let stand 18 minutes. Immediately pour off the hot water from the eggs, then run cool water over them several seconds to prevent further cooking; drain. Tap egg lightly on kitchen counter to crackle the shell. Roll the egg between your hands to loosen the shell, then peel. If shell is hard to peel, hold egg under cold water while peeling.

SOFT-COOKED EGGS: Place eggs in a saucepan. Add enough cold water until it is at least 1 inch above the eggs. Heat uncovered to boiling over high heat. Remove the saucepan from the heat. Cover and let stand 3 minutes. Immediately pour off the hot water from the eggs, then run cool water over them several seconds to prevent further cooking; drain. Cut eggs lengthwise in half, and scoop eggs from shells.

FRIED EGGS

FRIED EGGS, SUNNY SIDE UP: Heat margarine or butter in a heavy skillet over medium heat until it begins to sizzle and look hot. Use enough margarine so when melted it is about 1/8 inch deep in the skillet. Break each egg into a custard cup or saucer. Slip the egg carefully into the skillet. Immediately reduce heat to low. You should still be able to see and hear the eggs sizzle as they cook. If they stop sizzling, turn the heat up a little. Cook uncovered 5 to 7 minutes, spooning margarine from the skillet over the eggs frequently, until the whites are set, a film forms over the yolks and the yolks are thickened.

FRIED EGGS, OVER EASY: Follow directions for Fried Eggs, Sunny Side Up (above), but after cooking 3 minutes, gently turn eggs over with a wide spatula and cook 1 to 2 minutes longer or until yolks are thickened.

SCRAMBLED EGGS

1 Using 1 tablespoon of milk, half-and-half or water for each egg, beat eggs and milk with a fork or wire whisk until well mixed. Add salt and pepper as desired. Heat margarine (about 1 tablespoon for 3 eggs) in a skillet over medium heat just until the margarine begins to sizzle.

2 Pour egg mixture into skillet. The egg mixture will become firm at the bottom and side very quickly. When this happens, gently lift the cooked portions around the edge with a spatula so that the thin, uncooked portion can flow to the bottom. Avoid constant stirring, but continue to lift the cooked portion and allow the thin uncooked portions to flow to the bottom.

3 Cook 3 to 4 minutes or until eggs are thickened throughout but still moist and creamy. Serve immediately.

TiP **STORE EGGS IN THEIR CARTON** in the refrigerator. Keeping them in the carton protects them from absorbing refrigerator odors.

TiP **WHETHER THE EGGSHELL** is white or brown depends on the breed and diet of the hen. Flavor, nutritive value and the way the egg cooks are the same for both kinds.

✔ **IF HARD-COOKED EGGS** are used for an egg hunt, avoid keeping them at room temperature for more than 2 hours. If you do, don't eat the eggs.

Peeling Hard-Cooked Eggs

Roll egg between hands to loosen shell, then peel. If shell is hard to peel, hold egg under cold water while peeling

Frying an Egg

Break each egg into a custard cup or saucer. Slip the egg carefully into the skillet.

Cooking Scrambled Eggs

Gently lift the cooked portions around the edge with a spatula so that the thin, uncooked portion can flow to the bottom.

OMELET

MAKES 1 serving • COOK: 5 minutes

INGREDIENTS

DIRECTIONS

ESSENTIAL EQUIPMENT: *8-inch skillet*

2 eggs

2 teaspoons margarine or butter

Salt and pepper, if desired

1 Beat the eggs in a small bowl with a fork or wire whisk until yolks and whites are well mixed.

2 Heat the margarine in the skillet over medium-high heat until margarine is hot and sizzling. As margarine melts, tilt skillet to coat bottom with margarine.

3 Quickly pour the eggs into the skillet. While sliding the skillet back and forth rapidly over the heat, quickly stir the eggs with a fork to spread them continuously over the bottom of the skillet as they thicken. When they are thickened, let stand over the heat a few seconds to lightly brown the bottom. Do not overcook—the omelet will continue to cook after being folded.

4 Tilt the skillet and run a spatula or fork under the edge of the omelet, then jerk the skillet sharply to loosen omelet from bottom of skillet. Fold the portion of the omelet nearest you just to the center. Allow for a portion of the omelet to slide up the side of the skillet. Turn the omelet onto a warm plate, flipping folded portion of omelet over so the far side is on the bottom. Tuck sides of omelet under if necessary. Sprinkle with salt and pepper.

1 SERVING: Calories 220 (Calories from Fat 160); Fat 18g (Saturated 5g); Cholesterol 425mg; Sodium 220mg; Carbohydrate 1g (Dietary Fiber 0g); Protein 13g

CHEESE OMELET: Before folding omelet, sprinkle with 1/4 cup shredded Cheddar, Monterey Jack or Swiss cheese or 1/4 cup crumbled blue cheese.

DENVER OMELET: Cook 2 tablespoons chopped fully cooked ham, 1 tablespoon finely chopped bell pepper and 1 tablespoon finely chopped onion in the margarine about 2 minutes, stirring frequently, before adding eggs.

TiP **TO WARM A PLATE** for serving the omelet, run hot water over the serving plate, then dry it thoroughly just before cooking the omelet.

TiP **USING A NONSTICK** skillet makes preparing an omelet easier.

Cooking an Omelet

Tilt skillet and run a spatula or fork under edge of omelet, then jerk skillet sharply to loosen omelet from bottom. Fold portion of omelet nearest you just to center.

Turning Omelet out of Skillet

Turn omelet onto warm plate, flipping folded portion of omelet over so the far side is on the bottom.

Omelet

ON THE SIDE

BLUEBERRY MUFFINS

MAKES 12 regular-size muffins • BAKE: 25 minutes

INGREDIENTS

ESSENTIAL EQUIPMENT: *muffin pan with 12 regular-size muffin cups*

Shortening to grease muffin cups

1 cup fresh or canned blueberries

1 cup milk

1/4 cup vegetable oil

1/2 teaspoon vanilla

1 egg

2 cups all-purpose or whole wheat flour

1/3 cup sugar

3 teaspoons baking powder

1/2 teaspoon salt

DIRECTIONS

1 Heat the oven to 400°. Grease just the bottoms of 12 regular-size muffin cups with the shortening, or line each cup with a paper baking cup.

2 If using canned blueberries, drain them in a strainer. Rinse fresh or canned blueberries with cool water, and discard any crushed ones. Break off any stems.

3 Beat the milk, oil, vanilla and egg in a large bowl with a fork or wire whisk until well mixed. Stir in the flour, sugar, baking powder and salt all at once just until the flour is moistened. The batter will be lumpy. If the batter is mixed too much, the muffins will have high peaks instead of being rounded.

4 Carefully stir in the blueberries. Spoon the batter into the greased muffin cups, dividing batter evenly among them. You can use an ice-cream scoop for this if you have one.

5 Bake 20 to 25 minutes or until golden brown. Immediately remove muffins from the pan to a wire cooling rack. Serve warm or cool.

1 MUFFIN: Calories 160 (Calories from Fat 55); Fat 6g (Saturated 1g); Cholesterol 20mg; Sodium 240mg; Carbohydrate 24g (Dietary Fiber 0g); Protein 3g

APPLE-CINNAMON MUFFINS: Omit blueberries. Stir in 1 cup chopped apple with the milk. Stir in 1/2 teaspoon ground cinnamon with the flour. Bake 25 to 30 minutes.

BLUEBERRY MUFFINS: For 3 grams of fat and 135 calories per serving, use skim milk, decrease the vegetable oil to 2 tablespoons and add 1/4 cup unsweetened applesauce.

TiP **SUBSTITUTE 3/4 CUP** frozen blueberries, thawed and well drained, for the fresh or canned blueberries if desired.

TiP **ALUMINUM FOIL** baking cups purchased at the supermarket can be used instead of a muffin pan. Place 12 foil cups on a cookie sheet or in a rectangular pan, and fill as directed.

Stirring Blueberries into Muffin Batter

Carefully stir blueberries into the muffin batter.

Filling Muffin Cups

Using an ice-cream scoop is an easy way to fill muffin cups.

Blueberry Muffins

CORN BREAD

MAKES 12 servings • BAKE: 25 minutes

INGREDIENTS

ESSENTIAL EQUIPMENT: *8-inch square pan or 9 × 1 1/2-inch round pan*

Shortening to grease pan

1 cup milk

1/4 cup (1/2 stick) stick margarine or butter, melted

1 egg

1 1/4 cups yellow, white or blue cornmeal

1 cup all-purpose flour

1/2 cup sugar

1 tablespoon baking powder

1/2 teaspoon salt

DIRECTIONS

1 Heat the oven to 400°. Grease the bottom and side of the pan with the shortening.

2 Beat the milk, margarine and egg in a large bowl with a fork or wire whisk until well mixed. Stir in the cornmeal, flour, sugar, baking powder and salt all at once just until the flour is moistened. The batter will be lumpy. Pour the batter into the greased pan.

3 Bake 20 to 25 minutes or until golden brown and when a toothpick inserted in the center comes out clean. Serve warm.

1 SERVING: Calories 175 (Calories from Fat 45); Fat 5g (Saturated 1g); Cholesterol 20mg; Sodium 280mg; Carbohydrate 29g (Dietary Fiber 1g); Protein 4g

CORN MUFFINS: Grease just the bottoms of 12 regular-size muffin cups with shortening, or line each cup with a paper baking cup. Fill each cup about 3/4 full with batter.

TiP IF USING MARGARINE, purchase regular margarine or a spread that contains at least 65 percent vegetable oil and is in a stick form. Spreads with less fat do not work well for cakes, cookies and other baked desserts.

TiP TO DO AHEAD, measure the cornmeal, flour, sugar, baking powder and salt into a plastic bag or a bowl ahead of time; seal or cover. Then finishing the cornbread at the last minute so it can be served warm will be as easy as using a mix.

Testing Corn Bread for Doneness

If corn bread is not fully baked, a toothpick inserted in the center will have uncooked batter clinging to it.

Corn Bread

GARLIC BREAD

MAKES 1 loaf (18 slices) • **BAKE: 20 minutes**

INGREDIENTS

ESSENTIAL EQUIPMENT: *heavy-duty aluminum foil*

1 clove garlic or 1/4 teaspoon garlic powder

1/3 cup margarine or butter at room temperature

1 loaf (1 pound) French bread

DIRECTIONS

1 Heat the oven to 400°.

2 Peel and finely chop the garlic. Mix the garlic and margarine.

3 Cut the bread crosswise into 1-inch slices. Spread margarine mixture over 1 side of each bread slice. Reassemble the loaf, and wrap securely in heavy-duty aluminum foil.

4 Bake 15 to 20 minutes or until hot.

1 SLICE: Calories 95 (Calories from Fat 35); Fat 4g (Saturated 1g); Cholesterol 0mg; Sodium 190mg; Carbohydrate 13g (Dietary Fiber 0g); Protein 2g

HERB-CHEESE BREAD: Omit the garlic. Mix 2 teaspoons chopped fresh parsley, 1/2 teaspoon dried oregano leaves, 2 tablespoons grated Parmesan cheese and 1/8 teaspoon garlic salt with the margarine.

ONION BREAD: Omit the garlic. Mix 2 tablespoons finely chopped onion or chives with the margarine.

SEEDED BREAD: Omit the garlic. Mix 1 teaspoon celery seed, poppy seed, dill seed or sesame seed with the margarine.

TiP **TO SAVE TIME, HEAT THE BREAD** in your microwave. Do not wrap loaf in foil. Instead, divide loaf in half, and place halves side by side in napkin-lined microwavable basket or on microwavable dinner plate. Cover with napkin and microwave on Medium (50%) 1 1/2 to 3 minutes, rotating basket 1/2 turn after 1 minute, until bread is hot.

TiP **IF USING MARGARINE,** purchase regular margarine or a spread that contains at least 65 percent vegetable oil and is in a stick form. Spreads with less fat have more water, and the bread may get slightly soggy.

Assembling Loaf of Bread

Spread margarine mixture over 1 side of each bread slice. Reassemble the loaf, and wrap securely in heavy-duty aluminum foil.

Garlic Bread

CAESAR SALAD

MAKES 6 servings

INGREDIENTS

ESSENTIAL EQUIPMENT: *large salad or mixing bowl*

1 large bunch or 2 small bunches romaine

1 clove garlic

8 flat anchovy fillets (from 2-ounce can), if desired

1/3 cup olive or vegetable oil

3 tablespoons lemon juice

1 teaspoon Worcestershire sauce

1/4 teaspoon salt

1/4 teaspoon ground mustard (dry)

Freshly ground pepper

1 cup garlic-flavored croutons

1/3 cup grated Parmesan cheese

DIRECTIONS

1 Remove any limp outer leaves from the romaine, and discard. Break remaining leaves off the core, and rinse with cool water. Shake off excess water, and blot to dry, or roll up the leaves in a clean, kitchen towel or paper towel to dry. Tear the leaves into bite-size pieces. You will need about 10 cups of romaine pieces.

2 Peel the garlic, and cut the clove in half. Rub the inside of the bowl—a wooden salad bowl works best—with the cut sides of the garlic. Allow a few small pieces of garlic to remain in the bowl if desired.

3 Cut up the anchovies, and place in the bowl. Add the oil, lemon juice, Worcestershire sauce, salt, mustard and pepper. Mix well with a fork or wire whisk.

4 Add the romaine, and toss with 2 large spoons or salad tongs until coated with the dressing. Sprinkle with the croutons and cheese. To keep salad crisp, serve immediately.

1 SERVING: Calories 165 (Calories from Fat 125); Fat 14g (Saturated 3g); Cholesterol 10mg; Sodium 430mg; Carbohydrate 7g (Dietary Fiber 2g); Protein 5g

Lighter **CAESAR SALAD:** For 9 grams of fat and 120 calories per serving, decrease oil to 3 tablespoons, increase lemon juice to 1/4 cup and add 2 tablespoons water to anchovy mixture. Decrease cheese to 3 tablespoons.

✔ **SOME TRADITIONAL** Caesar salad recipes may call for raw egg. Using uncooked eggs may cause certain types of food poisoning, so these recipes should be avoided.

TiP **TO SAVE TIME,** purchase romaine already washed, torn and ready to use. You will need 10 cups, which is about 14 ounces.

TiP **TO DO AHEAD,** wash and dry romaine and seal in a plastic bag or airtight container. It will keep up to a week in the refrigerator.

Drying Romaine

Shake off excess water, and blot to dry, or roll up the leaves in a clean, kitchen towel or paper towel to dry.

Caesar Salad

GREEK SALAD

MAKES 8 servings

INGREDIENTS

ESSENTIAL EQUIPMENT: *large salad or mixing bowl*

Lemon Dressing (below)

**1 bunch spinach
(1/2 pound)**

1 head Boston or Bibb lettuce

3 medium green onions with tops

1 medium cucumber

3 medium tomatoes

24 pitted whole ripe olives (from a 6-ounce can)

3/4 cup crumbled feta cheese (3 ounces)

LEMON DRESSING

1/4 cup vegetable oil

2 tablespoons lemon juice

1/2 teaspoon sugar

1 1/2 teaspoons Dijon mustard

1/4 teaspoon salt

1/8 teaspoon pepper

DIRECTIONS

1 Prepare Lemon Dressing (below).

2 Remove and discard the stems of the spinach. Rinse the leaves in cool water. Shake off excess water, and blot to dry, or roll up the leaves in a clean, dry kitchen towel or paper towel to dry. Tear the leaves into bite-size pieces, and place in the bowl. You will need about 5 cups of spinach pieces.

3 Separate the leaves from the head of lettuce. Rinse the leaves with cool water. Shake off excess water, and blot to dry. Tear the leaves into bite-size pieces, and add to the bowl.

4 Peel and slice the green onions. Slice the cucumber. Cut the tomatoes into wedges. Add these vegetables and the olives to the bowl.

5 Break up any large pieces of the cheese with a fork, and add to the bowl.

6 Pour the dressing over the salad ingredients, and toss with 2 large spoons or salad tongs. To keep salad crisp, serve immediately.

LEMON DRESSING Shake all ingredients in a tightly covered jar or container. Shake again before pouring over salad.

1 SERVING: Calories 135 (Calories from Fat 100); Fat 11g (Saturated 3g); Cholesterol 10mg; Sodium 350mg; Carbohydrate 7g (Dietary Fiber 2g); Protein 4g

Washing Spinach

Remove and discard spinach stems. Place leaves in a sink or bowl filled with cool water. Swish with your hands to rinse off the dirt. Lift the leaves up to drain off excess water. Repeat until no dirt remains.

Preparing Boston Lettuce

Separate the leaves from the head of lettuce. Rinse thoroughly, and blot to dry.

Greek Salad

SPINACH-STRAWBERRY SALAD

MAKES 4 servings

INGREDIENTS

ESSENTIAL EQUIPMENT: *large salad or mixing bowl*

Honey-Dijon Dressing (below)

1 small jicama

2 kiwifruit

1/2 pint (1 cup) strawberries

7 to 8 cups ready-to-eat spinach (from 10-ounce bag)

1 cup alfalfa sprouts

HONEY-DIJON DRESSING

2 tablespoons vegetable oil

2 tablespoons honey

2 tablespoons orange juice

1 tablespoon seasoned rice vinegar or white vinegar

1 teaspoon poppy seed, if desired

2 teaspoons Dijon mustard

DIRECTIONS

1 Prepare Honey-Dijon Dressing (below).

2 Peel the jicama, removing the brown skin and a thin layer of the flesh just under the skin. The skin can sometimes be slightly tough. Cut about half of the jicama into about 1 × 1/4-inch sticks to measure about 3/4 cup. Wrap remaining jicama, and refrigerate for another use.

3 Peel the kiwifruit. Cut lengthwise in half, then cut into slices.

4 Rinse the strawberries with cool water, and pat dry. Remove the leaves, and cut the berries lengthwise into slices.

5 Remove the stems from the spinach leaves, and tear any large leaves into bite-size pieces. Place the spinach, strawberries, alfalfa sprouts, jicama sticks and kiwifruit slices in the bowl. Pour the dressing over the salad ingredients, and toss with 2 large spoons or salad tongs. To keep salad crisp, serve immediately.

HONEY-DIJON DRESSING Shake all ingredients in a tightly covered jar or container. Shake again before pouring over salad.

1 SERVING: Calories 165 (Calories from Fat 90); Fat 8g (Saturated 1g); Cholesterol 0mg; Sodium 45mg; Carbohydrate 28g (Dietary Fiber 8g); Protein 3g

Shaking Dressing

Shake all ingredients for the Honey-Dijon Dressing in a tightly covered jar.

Cutting up Jicama

Peel jicama, and cut into 1/4-inch slices. Cut slices into sticks for a salad or raw vegetable platter.

Spinach-Strawberry Salad

CREAMY COLESLAW

MAKES 4 servings • REFRIGERATE: 1 hour

INGREDIENTS

DIRECTIONS

ESSENTIAL EQUIPMENT: *small and medium bowls*

1/4 cup sour cream

2 tablespoons mayonnaise or salad dressing

1 1/2 teaspoons sugar

1 teaspoon lemon juice

1 teaspoon Dijon mustard

1/4 teaspoon celery seed

1/8 teaspoon pepper

1/4 of a medium head of cabbage

1/2 of a small carrot

1/2 of a small onion

1 Mix the sour cream, mayonnaise, sugar, lemon juice, mustard, celery seed and pepper in the small bowl.

2 Place a flat side of the 1/4 head of cabbage on a cutting board, and cut off the core. Cut the cabbage into thin slices with a large sharp knife. Cut the slices several times to make smaller pieces. You should have about 2 cups.

3 Peel and shred the carrot. Peel and chop the onion.

4 Place the cabbage, carrot and onion in the medium bowl. Pour the sour cream mixture over the vegetables, and mix with a large spoon until the vegetables are evenly coated with the dressing.

5 Cover and refrigerate the coleslaw at least 1 hour to blend flavors. Cover and refrigerate any remaining coleslaw.

1 SERVING: Calories 115 (Calories from Fat 80); Fat 9g (Saturated 3g); Cholesterol 15mg; Sodium 75mg; Carbohydrate 7g (Dietary Fiber 1g); Protein 2g

CREAMY COLESLAW: For 1 gram of fat and 55 calories per serving, use reduced-fat sour cream and fat-free mayonnaise.

TiP **TO SAVE TIME,** purchase a prepackaged coleslaw mixture, washed and ready to use, from the produce section of the supermarket. Substitute it for the cabbage, carrots and onion. You will need about 3 cups of the mixture (6 to 7 ounces).

TiP **YOU CAN PURCHASE** lemon juice that's ready to use in bottles or lemon-shaped plastic containers.

Shredding Cabbage

Place a flat side of the 1/4 head of cabbage on a cutting board. Cut into thin slices with a large sharp knife. Cut slices several times to make smaller pieces.

Creamy Coleslaw

ITALIAN PASTA SALAD

MAKES 6 servings • REFRIGERATE: 30 minutes

INGREDIENTS

ESSENTIAL EQUIPMENT: *Dutch oven (about 4-quart size)*

Garlic Vinaigrette Dressing (below)

2 cups uncooked rotini or rotelle (spiral) pasta (6 ounces)

1 large tomato

1/2 of a medium cucumber

3 or 4 medium green onions with tops

1 small red or green bell pepper

1/4 cup chopped ripe olives, if desired

GARLIC VINAIGRETTE DRESSING

1 clove garlic

1/4 cup rice vinegar or white vinegar

2 tablespoons water

2 tablespoons olive or vegetable oil

1/2 teaspoon salt

1/2 teaspoon sesame or vegetable oil

DIRECTIONS

1 Prepare Garlic Vinaigrette Dressing (below).

2 Fill the Dutch oven about half full of water. Add 1/4 teaspoon salt if desired. Cover and heat over high heat until the water is boiling rapidly. Add the pasta. Heat to boiling again. Boil uncovered, stirring frequently, 8 to 10 minutes for rotini, 9 to 11 minutes for rotelle, until tender.

3 While the water is heating and pasta is cooking, chop the tomato and cucumber, and peel and chop the onions. Place the vegetables in a large bowl.

4 Cut the bell pepper lengthwise in half, and cut out seeds and membrane. Cut bell pepper into pieces, and add to vegetables in bowl.

5 Drain the pasta in a strainer or colander, and rinse thoroughly with cold water. Add pasta to vegetables in bowl. Add the olives.

6 Pour the dressing over the vegetables and pasta, and mix thoroughly. Cover and refrigerate about 30 minutes or until chilled.

GARLIC VINAIGRETTE DRESSING Peel and finely chop the garlic. Shake garlic and remaining ingredients in a tightly covered jar or container. Shake again before pouring over vegetables and pasta.

1 SERVING: Calories 170 (Calories from Fat 55); Fat 6g (Saturated 1g); Cholesterol 0mg; Sodium 200mg; Carbohydrate 26g (Dietary Fiber 1g); Protein 4g

RANCH PASTA SALAD: Use about 1/2 cup ranch dressing from the supermarket instead of the Garlic Vinaigrette Dressing.

TiP **THE WATER BEING HEATED** for cooking the pasta will boil sooner if it is covered with a lid.

TiP **WRAP ANY LEFTOVER** onions and cucumber in plastic wrap and store in the refrigerator.

Cutting up a Bell Pepper

Cut bell pepper lengthwise in half; cut out seeds and membrane.

Italian Pasta Salad

OLD-FASHIONED POTATO SALAD

MAKES 5 servings • **REFRIGERATE: 4 hours**

INGREDIENTS

DIRECTIONS

ESSENTIAL EQUIPMENT: *large saucepan (about 3-quart size); medium saucepan (about 2-quart size)*

3 medium boiling potatoes (about 1 pound)

2 eggs

1 medium stalk celery

1 medium onion

3/4 cup mayonnaise or salad dressing

1 1/2 teaspoons white vinegar

1 1/2 teaspoons mustard

1/2 teaspoon salt

1/8 teaspoon pepper

1 Peel the potatoes, and cut any large potatoes in half. Add 1 inch of water to the large saucepan. Cover and heat the water to boiling over high heat. Add potatoes. Cover and heat to boiling again. Once water is boiling, reduce heat just enough so water bubbles gently. Cook covered 20 to 25 minutes or until potatoes are tender when pierced with a fork. Drain potatoes in a strainer, and cool slightly. Cut potatoes into cubes.

2 While the potatoes are cooking, place the eggs in the medium saucepan. Cover with at least 1 inch of cold water, and heat to boiling over high heat. Remove the saucepan from the heat. Let stand covered 18 minutes. Immediately pour off the hot water from the eggs, then run cool water over them several seconds to prevent further cooking; drain.

3 Peel and chop the eggs. Chop the celery. Peel the onion, and chop enough of the onion to measure 1/4 cup. Wrap any remaining onion, and refrigerate for another use.

4 Mix the mayonnaise, vinegar, mustard, salt and pepper in a large bowl. Gently stir in the potatoes, celery and onion. Stir in the chopped eggs.

5 Cover and refrigerate at least 4 hours to blend flavors and to chill. Cover and refrigerate any remaining salad.

1 SERVING: Calories 330 (Calories from Fat 250); Fat 28g (Saturated 5g); Cholesterol 105mg; Sodium 470mg; Carbohydrate 17g (Dietary Fiber 1g); Protein 4g

Lighter **POTATO SALAD:** For 1 gram of fat and 100 calories per serving, substitute 1/4 cup fat-free mayonnaise and 1/2 cup plain fat-free yogurt for the 3/4 cup mayonnaise. Use 1 egg.

TiP CELERY IS GROWN AND SOLD as a bunch and can be stored in a plastic bag in the refrigerator for up to 2 weeks. A stalk, or rib, is one stem out of the bunch. Stalks should be left attached to the bunch until used. Be sure to rinse the stalks and cut off the base and the leaves.

TiP TO DO AHEAD, PEEL POTATOES 2 or 3 hours before you plan to cook them. Put them in a bowl of cold water to keep them from turning a dark color, then cover and refrigerate.

Choosing Potatoes for Boiling

Choose round red or round white potatoes to boil for potato salad because they will hold their shape when cooked. Russet potatoes do not work as well for potato salad.

Old-Fashioned Potato Salad

FRESH FRUIT WITH HONEY-POPPY SEED DRESSING

MAKES 6 servings

INGREDIENTS

DIRECTIONS

ESSENTIAL EQUIPMENT: *large salad or mixing bowl*

Honey-Poppy Seed Dressing (below)

1 large unpeeled apple or 2 medium apricots or nectarines

1 medium orange

1 medium pineapple

1 small bunch seedless green grapes

HONEY-POPPY SEED DRESSING

1/4 cup vegetable oil

3 tablespoons honey

2 tablespoons lemon juice

1 1/2 teaspoons poppy seed

1 Prepare Honey-Poppy Seed Dressing (below).

2 Cut the unpeeled apple into slices, or peel and slice the apricots or nectarines.

3 Peel the orange, then cut along the membrane of both sides of one orange section. Remove that section, and continue with the rest of the orange.

4 Cut the pineapple lengthwise into fourths. Cut off the rind and the core. Cut the pineapple into chunks, removing any "eyes" or spots left from the rind.

5 Wash the grapes, and cut in half.

6 Mix the fruits and the dressing in a large bowl. Cover and refrigerate until ready to serve. Cover and refrigerate any remaining salad.

HONEY-POPPY SEED DRESSING Shake all ingredients in a tightly covered jar or container. Shake again before pouring over fruit.

1 SERVING: Calories 215 (Calories from Fat 90); Fat 10g (Saturated 2g); Cholesterol 0mg; Sodium 5mg; Carbohydrate 32g (Dietary Fiber 2g); Protein 1g

TiP **IF YOU'RE IN A HURRY,** substitute 1/2 cup frozen whipped topping, thawed, and 1/2 teaspoon grated lemon peel for the Honey-Poppy Seed Dressing. Stir into fruit just before serving.

TiP **TWO CUPS STRAWBERRIES,** cut in half, can be substituted for half of the pineapple.

Cutting an Orange into Sections

Cut along the membrane of both sides of one orange section. Remove that section, and continue with the rest of the orange.

Peeling and Cutting up Pineapple

Cut pineapple lengthwise into fourths. Cut off the rind and the core. Cut pineapple into chunks, removing any "eyes" or spots left from the rind.

Fresh Fruit with Honey-Poppy Seed Dressing

ASPARAGUS

1 1/2 pounds is enough for 4 servings

When Shopping: Look for smooth, firm, medium-size spears with tightly closed tips. Cover stem ends with damp paper towel, wrap airtight and store in the refrigerator up to 3 days.

Preparing for Cooking: Break off and discard the tough ends of the asparagus stalks where they snap easily. Wash asparagus thoroughly, including the tips, to remove any sandy soil. Remove the scales if sandy or tough. If stalk ends are quite large, peel about 2 inches of the end with a vegetable peeler, so they will be more tender after cooking.

Boiling: Add 1 inch of water (and 1/4 teaspoon salt if desired) to a large skillet (about 10-inch size). Cover and heat to boiling over high heat. Add asparagus spears. Cover and heat to boiling again. Once water is boiling, reduce heat just enough so water bubbles gently. Cook covered 8 to 12 minutes or until crisp-tender when pierced with a fork. Thinner, young asparagus will cook more quickly than the more mature, thicker stalks. Lift asparagus from water with tongs, allowing extra water to drip off.

Steaming: Place a steamer basket in 1/2 inch of water in a skillet or saucepan. The water should not touch the bottom of the basket. Place asparagus spears in basket. Cover tightly and heat to boiling over high heat. Once water is boiling, reduce heat to low. Steam covered 6 to 8 minutes or until crisp-tender when pierced with a fork.

Microwaving: Place asparagus spears and 1/4 cup water in an 8-inch square microwavable dish. Cover with plastic wrap, folding back 2-inch edge to vent. Microwave on High 6 to 9 minutes, rotating dish 1/2 turn after 3 minutes, until crisp-tender when pierced with a fork. Let stand covered 1 minute; drain in a strainer.

1 SERVING: Calories 20 (Calories from Fat 0); Fat 0g (Saturated 0g); Cholesterol 0mg; Sodium 5mg; Carbohydrate 4g (Dietary Fiber 1g); Protein 2g

Storing Asparagus

Cover stem ends with damp paper towel, wrap airtight and store in refrigerator up to 4 days.

Preparing Asparagus for Cooking

Break off tough ends of asparagus stalks where they snap easily; discard.

GREEN AND YELLOW WAX BEANS

1 pound is enough for 4 servings

When Shopping: The wax bean is a pale yellow variety of green bean. For green or yellow beans, look for long, smooth, crisp pods with fresh-looking tips and bright green or waxy yellow color. Wrap airtight and store in the refrigerator up to 5 days.

Preparing for Cooking: Wash beans, and cut off ends. Leave whole, or cut crosswise into about 1-inch pieces. To save time when cutting, place 3 to 4 beans side by side on a cutting board, and cut off all the ends at one time.

Boiling: Add 1 inch of water (and 1/4 teaspoon salt if desired) to a medium saucepan (about 2-quart size). Add the beans. Cover and heat to boiling over high heat. Once water is boiling, reduce heat just enough so water bubbles gently. Cook uncovered 5 minutes. Cover and cook 5 to 10 minutes longer or until crisp-tender when pierced with a fork; drain in a strainer.

Steaming: Place a steamer basket in 1/2 inch of water in a skillet or saucepan. The water should not touch the bottom of the basket. Place beans in basket. Cover tightly and heat to boiling over high heat. Once water is boiling, reduce heat to low. Steam covered 10 to 12 minutes or until crisp-tender when pierced with a fork.

Microwaving Pieces: Place beans and 1/2 cup water in a 1 1/2-quart microwavable casserole. Cover with plastic wrap, folding back 2-inch edge to vent. Microwave on High 9 to 12 minutes, stirring every 5 minutes, until crisp-tender when pierced with a fork. Let stand covered 5 minutes; drain in a strainer.

1 SERVING: Calories 20 (Calories from Fat 0); Fat 0g (Saturated 0g); Cholesterol 0mg; Sodium 10mg; Carbohydrate 6g (Dietary Fiber 2g); Protein 1g

Purchasing Beans

Look for long, smooth, crisp pods with fresh-looking tips and bright green or waxy yellow color.

Cutting Beans

Lay 3 or 4 beans side by side on cutting board; cut off all the ends at one time. Cut crosswise into 1-inch pieces.

BROCCOLI

1 1/2 pounds is enough for 4 servings

When Shopping: Look for firm, compact dark green clusters, and avoid thick, tough stems. Wrap broccoli tightly and store in the refrigerator up to 5 days.

Preparing for Cooking: Trim the large leaves, and cut off any tough ends of lower stems. Rinse with cool water. For spears, cut lengthwise into 1/2-inch-wide stalks. For pieces, cut into 1/2-inch-wide stalks, then cut crosswise into 1-inch pieces.

Boiling: Add 1 inch of water (and 1/4 teaspoon salt if desired) to a medium saucepan (about 3-quart size). Add the broccoli spears or pieces. Cover and heat to boiling over high heat. Once water is boiling, reduce heat just enough so water bubbles gently. Cook uncovered 10 to 12 minutes or until crisp-tender when pierced with a fork; drain in a strainer.

Steaming: Place a steamer basket in 1/2 inch of water in a skillet or saucepan. The water should not touch the bottom of the basket. Place broccoli spears or pieces in basket. Cover tightly and heat to boiling over high heat. Once water is boiling, reduce heat to low. Steam covered 10 to 11 minutes or until stems are crisp-tender when pierced with a fork.

Microwaving Spears: Place broccoli in an 8-inch square microwavable dish, arranging in a spoke pattern with flowerets toward the center. Add 1 cup water. Cover with plastic wrap, folding back 2-inch edge to vent. Microwave on High 9 to 11 minutes, rotating dish 1/4 turn every 4 minutes, until crisp-tender when pierced with a fork. Let stand covered 5 minutes; drain in a strainer.

Microwaving Pieces: Place broccoli and 1 cup water in a 2-quart microwavable casserole. Cover with plastic wrap, folding back 2-inch edge to vent. Microwave on High 9 to 11 minutes, stirring every 4 minutes, until crisp-tender when pierced with a fork. Let stand covered 5 minutes; drain.

1 SERVING: Calories 20 (Calories from Fat 0); Fat 0g (Saturated 0g); Cholesterol 0mg; Sodium 30mg; Carbohydrate 5g (Dietary Fiber 3g); Protein 3g

Cutting Broccoli

To make spears, cut lengthwise into 1/2-inch stalks. For pieces, cut the 1/2-inch stalks crosswise into 1-inch pieces.

Arranging Broccoli Spears for Microwaving

Place broccoli in an 8-inch square microwavable dish, arranging in a spoke pattern with flowerets toward the center.

CARROTS

1 pound (6 or 7 medium) is enough for 4 servings

When Shopping: Look for firm, smooth carrots, and avoid carrots with cracks or any that have become soft or limp. Store airtight in the refrigerator up to 2 weeks.

Preparing for Cooking: Peel carrots with a vegetable peeler, and cut off ends. Cut carrots crosswise into 1/4-inch slices.

Boiling: Add 1 inch of water (and 1/4 teaspoon salt if desired) to a medium saucepan (about 2-quart size). Cover and heat to boiling over high heat. Add the carrot slices. Cover and heat to boiling again. Once water is boiling, reduce heat just enough so water bubbles gently. Cook covered 12 to 15 minutes or until tender when pierced with a fork; drain in a strainer.

Steaming: Place a steamer basket in 1/2 inch of water in a skillet or saucepan. The water should not touch the bottom of the basket. Place carrot slices in basket. Cover tightly and heat to boiling over high heat. Once water is boiling, reduce heat to low. Steam covered 9 to 11 minutes or until tender when pierced with a fork.

Microwaving: Place carrot slices and 1/4 cup water in a 1-quart microwavable casserole. Cover with plastic wrap, folding back 2-inch edge to vent. Microwave on High 6 to 8 minutes, stirring after 4 minutes, until tender when pierced with a fork. Let stand covered 1 minute; drain in a strainer.

1 SERVING: Calories 35 (Calories from Fat 0); Fat 0g (Saturated 0g); Cholesterol 0mg; Sodium 40mg; Carbohydrate 11g (Dietary Fiber 3g); Protein 1g

Purchasing Carrots

Look for firm, smooth carrots; avoid carrots with cracks or any that have become soft or limp.

Cutting up Carrots

Peel carrots with a vegetable peeler, and cut off ends. Cut carrots crosswise into 1/4-inch slices.

 CAULIFLOWER

1 medium head (2 pounds) is enough for 4 servings

When Shopping: Look for a clean, firm cauliflower with nonspreading flower clusters (the white portion) and green leaves. Some supermarkets sell just the flower clusters, which are already removed from the stalks. Wrap tightly and store in the refrigerator up to 1 week.

Preparing for Cooking: Remove outer leaves, and cut off the core, or stem, close to the head. Cut any discoloration off of the flower clusters. Wash cauliflower. Cut the flower clusters (flowerets) off the core, and discard the core.

Boiling: Add 1 inch of water (and 1/4 teaspoon salt if desired) to a medium saucepan (about 3-quart size). Cover and heat to boiling over high heat. Add the flowerets. Cover and heat to boiling again. Once water is boiling, reduce heat just enough so water bubbles gently. Cook covered 10 to 12 minutes or until tender when pierced with a fork; drain in a strainer.

Steaming: Place a steamer basket in 1/2 inch of water in a skillet or saucepan. The water should not touch the bottom of the basket. Place flowerets in basket. Cover tightly and heat to boiling over high heat. Once water is boiling, reduce heat to low. Steam covered 6 to 8 minutes or until tender when pierced with a fork.

Microwaving: Place flowerets and 1/4 cup water in a 2-quart microwavable casserole. Cover with plastic wrap, folding back 2-inch edge to vent. Microwave on High 12 to 14 minutes, stirring after 6 minutes, until tender when pierced with a fork. Let stand covered 1 minute; drain in a strainer.

1 SERVING: Calories 30 (Calories from Fat 0); Fat 0g (Saturated 0g); Cholesterol 0mg; Sodium 45mg; Carbohydrate 7g (Dietary Fiber 3g); Protein 3g

Cutting off Cauliflower Core

Cut off the core, or stem, close to the head.

Cutting Flower Clusters from Cauliflower Head

Cut flower clusters (flowerets) off the core; discard the core.

CORN

4 ears of corn is enough for 4 servings

When Shopping: Look for bright green, tight-fitting fresh-looking silk and kernels that are plump but not too large. Corn tastes best if it is purchased and cooked the same day that it was picked. If that's not possible, wrap unhusked ears in damp paper towels and refrigerate the corn up to 2 days.

Preparing for Cooking: Pull the green husks off the ears and remove the silk just before cooking. Do not put the corn husks or silk in your garbage disposal. If there are any bad spots on the ears, cut them out. Break off any long stems, so the corn will fit easily into the pan. If any ears are too long for your pan, cut or break them in half.

Boiling: Fill a Dutch oven about half full of water. Do not add any salt because that will make the corn tough. Place the corn in the water. Cover and heat to boiling over high heat. Once water is boiling, continue cooking uncovered 2 minutes. Remove from heat, and let stand uncovered about 10 minutes or until tender when pierced with a fork. Lift corn from water with tongs, allowing extra water to drip off. Serve immediately with margarine or butter, salt and pepper.

Microwaving: Place corn and 1/4 cup water in an 8-inch square microwavable dish. Cover with plastic wrap, folding back 2-inch edge to vent. Microwave on High 9 to 14 minutes, rearranging ears with tongs after 5 minutes, until tender when pierced with a fork. Let stand covered 5 minutes. Lift corn from water with tongs, allowing extra water to drip off.

1 SERVING: Calories 90 (Calories from Fat 10); Fat 1g (Saturated 0g); Cholesterol 0mg; Sodium 15mg; Carbohydrate 19g (Dietary Fiber 2g); Protein 3g

Husking Corn

Pull the green husks off the ears and remove silk just before cooking. Do not put the corn husks or silk in your garbage disposal.

MUSHROOMS

1 pound is enough for 4 servings

When Shopping: Look for creamy white to light brown caps that are tightly closed around the stems. If the caps have started to open and show the underside, or "gills," the mushrooms may not be fresh. To store, do not wash. Wrap in damp paper towels and refrigerate in a plastic bag up to 4 days.

Preparing for Cooking: Rinse mushrooms with cool water, but do not soak them because they will absorb water and become mushy. Dry thoroughly. Do not peel. Cut off and discard the end of each stem. Cut each mushroom lengthwise into 1/4-inch slices.

Sautéing: Heat 2 tablespoons margarine or butter in a large skillet (about 10-inch size) over medium-high heat 1 to 2 minutes or until margarine begins to bubble. Add 1/2 pound mushroom slices (about 3 cups). Cook 6 to 8 minutes, lifting and stirring constantly with a turner or large spoon, until tender when pierced with a fork. If using a nonstick pan, you can use just 1 tablespoon margarine.

Steaming: Place a steamer basket in 1/2 inch of water in a skillet or saucepan. The water should not touch the bottom of the basket. Place mushroom slices in basket. Cover tightly and heat to boiling over high heat. Once water is boiling, reduce heat to low. Steam covered 6 to 8 minutes or until tender when pierced with a fork.

Microwaving: Place mushroom slices and 1/4 cup water in a 1 1/2-quart microwavable casserole. Cover with plastic wrap, folding back 2-inch edge to vent. Microwave on High 5 to 7 minutes or until tender when pierced with a fork; drain in a strainer.

1 SERVING: Calories 130 (Calories from Fat 110); Fat 12g (Saturated 2g); Cholesterol 0mg; Sodium 140mg; Carbohydrate 5g (Dietary Fiber 1g); Protein 2g

Washing Mushrooms

Rinse mushrooms with cool water.

Slicing Mushrooms

Cut mushrooms lengthwise into 1/4-inch slices by placing them on a cutting board with the stems up.

ACORN SQUASH

1 1/2 to 2 pounds is enough for 4 servings

When Shopping: Look for hard, tough rinds with no soft spots. The squash should feel heavy for its size.

Preparing for Cooking: Wash squash. Cut lengthwise in half. You will need to do this on a cutting board and using your biggest knife because the shell is quite tough. Scrape out the seeds and fibers with a soup spoon.

Baking: Heat the oven to 400°. Place squash, cut sides up, in a baking dish. Sprinkle cut sides with salt and pepper. Place small dabs of margarine or butter over cut surface and in cavity, using about 1 tablespoon margarine for each squash. Pour water into baking dish until it is about 1/4 inch deep. Cover with aluminum foil. The squash will probably be taller than the baking dish, so the foil may touch the squash.

Bake 30 to 40 minutes or until tender when pierced with a fork. When removing the foil to test for doneness, open a side of the foil away from you to allow steam to escape. Lift the squash from the baking dish with a large spoon or spatula. Scrape the cooked squash out of the shell and into a serving dish.

Microwaving: Pierce whole squash with knife in several places to allow steam to escape. Place on paper towel. Microwave 4 to 6 minutes or until squash is hot and rind is firm but easy to cut; cool slightly. Carefully cut in half; remove seeds. Arrange halves, cut sides down, on 10-inch plate. Cover and microwave 5 to 8 minutes or until squash is tender when pierced by knife.

1 SERVING: Calories 115 (Calories from Fat 25); Fat 3g (Saturated 1g); Cholesterol 0mg; Sodium 190mg; Carbohydrate 25g (Dietary Fiber 5g); Protein 2g

TiP **USE A GLASS BAKING DISH** if possible. If you use a metal pan, the water may leave a dark mark on it.

TiP **FOR MORE FLAVOR,** mash the cooked squash with a fork, then stir in about 1 tablespoon margarine or butter and 1 tablespoon packed brown sugar.

Testing Squash for Doneness

Carefully open a side of the foil farthest away from you, so you will not get burned by the steam that escapes.

MASHED POTATOES

MAKES 4 to 6 servings • **COOK: 25 minutes**

INGREDIENTS

ESSENTIAL EQUIPMENT: *large saucepan (about 3-quart size); potato masher or electric mixer*

6 medium potatoes (about 2 pounds)

1/4 cup (1/2 stick) margarine or butter

1/4 teaspoon salt, if desired

1/2 cup milk

1/2 teaspoon salt

Dash of pepper

DIRECTIONS

1 Wash and peel the potatoes, and cut into large pieces. Remove the margarine from the refrigerator so it can soften while the potatoes cook.

2 Add 1 inch of water (and the 1/4 teaspoon salt if desired) to the saucepan. Cover and heat to boiling over high heat. Add potato pieces. Cover and heat to boiling again. Once water is boiling, reduce heat just enough so water bubbles gently.

3 Cook covered 20 to 25 minutes or until tender when pierced with a fork. The cooking time will vary, depending on the size of the potato pieces and the type of potato used. Drain potatoes in a strainer.

4 Return the drained potatoes to the saucepan, and cook over low heat about 1 minute to dry them. While cooking, shake the pan often to keep the potatoes from burning, which can happen very easily once the water has been drained off.

5 Place the potatoes in a medium bowl to be mashed. You can mash them in the same saucepan they were cooked in if the saucepan will not be damaged by the potato masher or electric mixer.

6 Mash the potatoes with a potato masher or electric mixer until no lumps remain. Add the milk in small amounts, beating after each addition. You may not use all the milk because the amount needed to make potatoes smooth and fluffy depends on the type of potato used. Add the margarine, 1/2 teaspoon salt and the pepper. Beat vigorously until potatoes are light and fluffy.

1 SERVING: Calories 265 (Calories from Fat 110); Fat 12g (Saturated 3g); Cholesterol 5mg; Sodium 450mg; Carbohydrate 38g (Dietary Fiber 3g); Protein 4g

Lighter MASHED POTATOES: For 6 grams of fat and 210 calories per serving, use skim milk and decrease the margarine to 2 tablespoons.

GARLIC MASHED POTATOES: Peel 6 cloves of garlic, and cook them with the potatoes. Mash the garlic cloves with the potatoes.

TiP MOST TYPES OF POTATOES can be used for mashed potatoes. Although russets are known as baking potatoes, they also can be boiled and mashed. Look for potatoes that are nicely shaped, smooth and firm with unblemished skin that is free from discoloration.

TiP PLACE THE MILK in a microwavable measuring cup and microwave uncovered on High 40 seconds before adding to the mashed potatoes. The potatoes will stay hotter.

Mashed Potatoes

Mashing Potatoes

Use a handheld potato masher for the fluffiest mashed potatoes. If using an electric mixer, do not mix too long; overmixing releases more potato starch, and the potatoes can become gummy.

BAKED POTATOES

MAKES 1 potato for each serving • **BAKE: 1 hour 15 minutes**

INGREDIENTS

DIRECTIONS

ESSENTIAL EQUIPMENT: *nothing special*

1 or more medium baking potatoes (russet or Idaho), all about the same size

Margarine or butter, if desired

Sour cream or plain yogurt, if desired

1 Heat the oven to 375°. Scrub the potatoes thoroughly with a vegetable brush, but do not peel.

2 Pierce the potatoes on all sides with a fork to allow steam to escape while the potatoes bake. Place potatoes directly on the oven rack.

3 Bake 1 hour to 1 hour 15 minutes or until potatoes feel tender when squeezed gently. Be sure to use a pot holder because potatoes will be very hot to the touch.

4 To serve, cut an X in the top of each potato. Gently squeeze potato from the bottom to force the potato open. Serve with margarine or sour cream.

1 SERVING: Calories 85 (Calories from Fat 0); Fat 0g (Saturated 0g); Cholesterol 0mg; Sodium 5mg; Carbohydrate 20g (Dietary Fiber 1g); Protein 2g

TO MICROWAVE 4 POTATOES: Scrub the potatoes thoroughly with a vegetable brush, but do not peel. Pierce potatoes on all sides with a fork to allow steam to escape while the potatoes cook. Arrange potatoes about 2 inches apart in a circle on a microwavable paper towel in microwave oven. Microwave uncovered on High 11 to 13 minutes, turning potatoes over after 6 minutes, until tender when squeezed gently. Be sure to use a pot holder because potatoes will be very hot to the touch. Let stand uncovered 5 minutes. Continue with step 4

TiP **THE BAKE TIME** and oven temperature for baking potatoes can be adjusted so that other foods can be baking in the oven at the same time. Bake potatoes in a 350° oven 1 hour 15 minutes to 1 hour 30 minutes, in a 325° oven about 1 hour 30 minutes.

TiP **IF POTATOES ARE WRAPPED** in aluminum foil before being baked, the steam cannot escape during baking, so the potatoes will be gummy instead of fluffy.

Cutting X in Baked Potato

Cut an X in the top of each potato, then gently squeeze from the bottom to force the potato open.

Baked Potato

TWICE-BAKED POTATOES

MAKES 4 servings • BAKE: 1 hour 15 minutes for first baking plus 20 minutes for second baking

INGREDIENTS

ESSENTIAL EQUIPMENT: *potato masher or electric mixer; cookie sheet*

2 large baking potatoes (russet or Idaho), 8 to 10 ounces each

2 tablespoons margarine or butter

2 to 4 tablespoons milk

1/8 teaspoon salt

Dash of pepper

1/2 cup shredded Cheddar cheese (2 ounces)

2 teaspoons chopped fresh chives, if desired

DIRECTIONS

1 Heat the oven to 375°. Scrub the potatoes thoroughly with a vegetable brush, but do not peel. Pierce the potatoes on all sides with a fork to allow steam to escape while the potatoes bake. Place potatoes directly on the oven rack. Measure margarine, and let it stand at room temperature to soften.

2 Bake potatoes 1 hour to 1 hour 15 minutes or until potatoes feel tender when squeezed gently. Be sure to use a pot holder because potatoes will be very hot to the touch.

3 When potatoes are cool enough to handle, cut them lengthwise in half. Scoop out the insides into a medium bowl, leaving about a 1/4-inch shell in the potato skin.

4 Increase the temperature of the oven to 400°.

5 Mash the potatoes with a potato masher or electric mixer until no lumps remain. Add the milk in small amounts, beating after each addition. The amount of milk needed to make potatoes smooth and fluffy depends on the type of potato used.

6 Add the margarine, salt and pepper. Beat vigorously until potatoes are light and fluffy. Stir in the cheese and chives. Fill the potato shells with the mashed potato mixture. Place on an ungreased cookie sheet. Bake potatoes uncovered about 20 minutes or until hot.

1 SERVING: Calories 180 (Calories from Fat 100); Fat 11g (Saturated 4g); Cholesterol 15mg; Sodium 230mg; Carbohydrate 16g (Dietary Fiber 1g); Protein 5g

TiP **TO SAVE TIME,** arrange filled potato shells in a circle on a 10-inch microwavable plate. Cover with waxed paper and microwave on High 6 to 8 minutes, rotating plate 1/2 turn after 3 minutes, until hot.

TiP **TO DO AHEAD,** wrap filled potato shells airtight and refrigerate no longer than 24 hours or freeze no longer than 2 months. Unwrap potatoes and place on cookie sheet. Heat in 400° oven about 30 minutes for refrigerated potatoes, about 40 minutes for frozen potatoes, until hot.

Scooping Potato from Shells

Using a soup spoon, carefully scoop out the inside of each potato half, leaving about a 1/4-inch shell.

Twice-Baked Potatoes

BAKED POTATO WEDGES

MAKES 4 servings • **BAKE: 30 minutes**

INGREDIENTS

ESSENTIAL EQUIPMENT: *rectangular pan (about 13×9 inches)*

3/4 teaspoon salt

1/2 teaspoon sugar

1/2 teaspoon paprika

1/4 teaspoon ground mustard (dry)

1/4 teaspoon garlic powder, if desired

3 medium baking potatoes (russet or Idaho), 8 to 10 ounces each

Cooking spray

DIRECTIONS

1 Heat the oven to 425°. Mix the salt, sugar, paprika, mustard and garlic powder in a small bowl or measuring cup.

2 Scrub the potatoes thoroughly with a vegetable brush, but do not peel. Cut each potato lengthwise in half. Turn potatoes cut sides down, and cut each half lengthwise into 4 wedges. Place potato wedges, skin sides down, in the pan.

3 Spray the potato wedges with cooking spray until lightly coated. Sprinkle with the salt mixture.

4 Bake uncovered 25 to 30 minutes or until potatoes are tender when pierced with fork. The baking time will vary, depending on the size and type of the potato used.

1 SERVING: Calories 90 (Calories from Fat 0); Fat 0g (Saturated 0g); Cholesterol 0mg; Sodium 115mg; Carbohydrate 23g (Dietary Fiber 2g); Protein 2g

TiP FOR RECIPE SUCCESS, cut up potatoes just before using, or the cut sides will turn brown.

TiP USE RUSSET OR IDAHO potatoes because they are best for baking.

Cutting Potato Wedges

Cut each potato lengthwise in half. Turn potatoes cut sides down, and cut each half lengthwise into 4 wedges.

Baked Potato Wedges

PARSLEY POTATOES

MAKES 4 servings • COOK: 25 minutes

INGREDIENTS

ESSENTIAL EQUIPMENT: *Dutch oven (about 4-quart size)*

10 to 12 new potatoes (about 1 1/2 pounds)

2 tablespoons margarine or butter

Parsley sprigs

1/4 teaspoon salt, if desired

1/8 teaspoon pepper, if desired

DIRECTIONS

1 Scrub the potatoes thoroughly with a vegetable brush to remove all the dirt. Peel a narrow strip around the center of each potato with a vegetable peeler. This will make the potatoes look prettier when they are served. If you're in a hurry, you don't need to peel this strip.

2 Add 1 inch of water to the Dutch oven. Cover and heat the water to boiling over high heat. Add potatoes. Cover and heat to boiling again. Once water is boiling, reduce heat just enough so water bubbles gently. Cook covered 20 to 25 minutes or until tender when pierced with a fork; drain in a strainer.

3 While the potatoes are cooking, place the margarine in a small microwavable bowl or measuring cup. Microwave uncovered on High 15 to 30 seconds or until melted.

4 Rinse a few sprigs of the parsley with cool water, and pat dry with a paper towel. Chop enough parsley leaves into small pieces on a cutting board using a chef's knife to measure 1 tablespoon, or place the leafy portion of the parsley in a small bowl or cup and snip into very small pieces with kitchen scissors. Discard the stems.

5 After draining the potatoes, return them to the Dutch oven. Drizzle the melted margarine over the potatoes, and sprinkle with the chopped parsley, salt and pepper. Stir gently to coat the potatoes.

TO MICROWAVE 4 POTATOES: Choose potatoes of similar size. Pierce potatoes with a fork to allow steam to escape. Place potatoes and 1/4 cup water in a 2-quart microwavable casserole, arranging larger potatoes to the outside edge. Cover with plastic wrap, folding back 2-inch edge to vent. Microwave on High 10 to 12 minutes, stirring after 5 minutes, until tender when pierced with a fork. Let stand covered 1 minute; drain in a strainer. Melt margarine as directed in step 3, and continue with the recipe.

1 SERVING: Calories 270 (Calories from Fat 55); Fat 6g (Saturated 1g); Cholesterol 0mg; Sodium 85mg; Carbohydrate 54g (Dietary Fiber 5g); Protein 5g

TiP **WHEN SHOPPING,** look for nicely shaped, smooth, firm potatoes with unblemished skins that are free from discoloration. Store in a cool, dark place, and use within 3 days.

TiP **FOR EASY PREPARATION,** purchase potatoes that are all about the same size so they will cook in the same length of time.

Scrubbing New Potatoes

Scrub potatoes thoroughly with a vegetable brush to remove all the dirt.

Chopping Fresh Parsley

Place parsley leaves in a small bowl or cup and snip into very small pieces with kitchen scissors. Discard the stems.

Parsley Potatoes

ROASTED RED POTATOES

MAKES 4 servings • BAKE: 1 hour 15 minutes

INGREDIENTS

ESSENTIAL EQUIPMENT: *baking pan, such as 8- or 9-inch square or 13×9-inch rectangle*

12 small red potatoes (about 1 1/2 pounds)

2 medium green onions with tops

2 tablespoons olive or vegetable oil

2 tablespoons chopped fresh or 2 teaspoons dried rosemary leaves, crumbled

DIRECTIONS

1 Heat the oven to 350°.

2 Scrub the potatoes thoroughly with a vegetable brush to remove all the dirt.

3 Peel and slice the green onions.

4 Place the potatoes in the ungreased pan. Drizzle the oil over the potatoes, and turn potatoes so all sides are coated.

5 Sprinkle the onions and rosemary over the potatoes, and stir the potatoes.

6 Bake uncovered about 1 hour 15 minutes, stirring occasionally, until potatoes are tender when pierced with a fork.

1 SERVING: Calories 325 (Calories from Fat 65); Fat 7g (Saturated 1g); Cholesterol 0mg; Sodium 20mg; Carbohydrate 66g (Dietary Fiber 6g); Protein 6g

TiP **MOST SMALL RED POTATOES** are about 2 inches in diameter. If they are much bigger, cut them in half so they will roast more quickly.

TiP **LEFTOVER ROASTED POTATOES** can be cut into pieces and panfried for quick fried potatoes. To panfry, cook potato pieces in a small amount of oil over medium heat, stirring occasionally, until hot.

Drizzling Oil over Potatoes

Place potatoes in pan. Drizzle the oil over the potatoes, and turn potatoes so all sides are coated.

Roasted Red Potatoes

AU GRATIN POTATOES

MAKES 6 servings • **BAKE: 1 hour 10 minutes** • **LET STAND: 5 minutes**

INGREDIENTS

ESSENTIAL EQUIPMENT: *shallow 2-quart casserole or 8-inch square baking dish; medium saucepan (about 2-quart size)*

Cooking spray

6 medium potatoes (about 2 pounds)

1 small onion

2 tablespoons margarine or butter

1 tablespoon all-purpose flour

1/2 teaspoon salt

1/4 teaspoon pepper

2 cups milk

2 cups shredded natural sharp Cheddar cheese (8 ounces)

1/4 cup dry bread crumbs

DIRECTIONS

1 Heat the oven to 375°. Spray the casserole with cooking spray. Scrub the potatoes thoroughly with a vegetable brush. Peel the onion, and chop into very small pieces.

2 Melt the margarine in the saucepan over medium heat. Cook the onion in the margarine about 2 minutes, stirring occasionally, until softened.

3 Stir in the flour, salt and pepper. Cook 1 to 2 minutes, stirring constantly, until smooth and bubbly. Remove the saucepan from the heat.

4 Stir in the milk. Heat to boiling over medium heat, stirring constantly. Continue boiling 1 minute, stirring constantly. Remove the saucepan from the heat. Stir in 1 1/2 cups of the cheese until it is melted.

5 Peel the potatoes if you like, but peeling is not necessary. Cut the potatoes into enough thin slices to measure about 6 cups. Spread half the slices in the sprayed casserole. Pour half the sauce over the potatoes. Repeat with the remaining potatoes and sauce.

6 Bake uncovered 1 hour. Remove the casserole from the oven. Sprinkle with the bread crumbs and remaining 1/2 cup cheese. Bake uncovered about 10 minutes longer or until cheese is melted and potatoes are tender when pierced with a fork. Let stand 5 minutes before serving.

1 SERVING. Calories 370 (Calories from Fat 160); Fat 18g (Saturated 10g); Cholesterol 45mg; Sodium 50mg; Carbohydrate 39g (Dietary Fiber 3g); Protein 16g

TiP **THE SAUCE MAY SEPARATE** a bit after the potatoes bake. Cool, and the flavor will be just as good.

TiP **TO MEASURE THE CAPACITY** of your casserole dish, fill it with water using a measuring cup. A 2-quart casserole will hold 8 cups of water.

Making Cheese Sauce

Stir the flour, salt and pepper into the cooked onions. Cook, stirring constantly, until the mixture is smooth and bubbly.

Au Gratin Potatoes

STIR-FRIED GREEN BEANS AND PEPPER

MAKES 4 servings • COOK: 8 minutes

INGREDIENTS

ESSENTIAL EQUIPMENT: *10-inch skillet*

1/2 pound green beans

1 medium yellow or red bell pepper

1/4 cup water

1 tablespoon vegetable oil

2 teaspoons chopped fresh or 1/2 teaspoon dried marjoram leaves

DIRECTIONS

1 Cut off ends of green beans and discard. Cut beans crosswise in half.

2 Cut the bell pepper lengthwise in half, and cut out seeds and membrane. Cut bell pepper into 1/2-inch pieces.

3 Heat the water and beans to boiling in the skillet over high heat. Reduce heat just enough so water bubbles gently. Cover and cook about 5 minutes or until beans are crisp-tender when pierced with a fork. Larger, more mature beans will need to cook longer than young, small beans. If necessary, drain off any excess water.

4 Add the bell pepper and oil to the beans in the skillet. Increase heat to medium-high. Stir-fry with a turner or large spoon about 2 minutes, lifting and stirring constantly, until bell pepper is crisp-tender when pierced with a fork. Stir in marjoram.

1 SERVING. Calories 50 (Calories from Fat 35); Fat 4g (Saturated 1g); Cholesterol 0mg; Sodium 5mg; Carbohydrate 4g (Dietary Fiber 1g); Protein 1g

TiP **TO DO AHEAD,** wash and cut up green beans and bell pepper. Store airtight in refrigerator until needed.

TiP **DRAIN ANY REMAINING** water from the beans by pouring them into a strainer or colander. Then return them to the skillet.

Cutting a Bell Pepper

Cut the bell pepper lengthwise in half, and cut out seeds and membrane. Cut bell pepper into 1/2-inch pieces.

Stir-Fried Green Beans and Pepper

DILLED CARROTS AND PEA PODS

MAKES 4 servings • COOK: 7 minutes

INGREDIENTS

ESSENTIAL EQUIPMENT: *medium saucepan (about 2-quart size)*

1 1/2 cups snow (Chinese) pea pods (about 5 ounces)

1 1/2 cups baby-cut carrots

1 tablespoon margarine or butter

2 teaspoons chopped fresh or 1/2 teaspoon dried dill weed

1/8 teaspoon salt

DIRECTIONS

1 Snap off the stem end of each pea pod, and pull the string across the pea pod to remove it.

2 Add 1 inch of water to the saucepan. Cover and heat the water to boiling over high heat. Add carrots. Cover and heat to boiling again. Once water is boiling, reduce heat just enough so water bubbles gently. Cook covered about 4 minutes or until carrots are crisp-tender when pierced with a fork. Do not drain water.

3 Add pea pods to carrots in saucepan. Heat uncovered until water is boiling again; continue boiling uncovered 2 to 3 minutes, stirring occasionally, until pea pods are crisp-tender. Pea pods cook very quickly, so be careful not to overcook them. Drain carrots and pea pods in a strainer, then return to saucepan.

4 Stir margarine, dill weed and salt into carrots and pea pods until margarine is melted.

1 SERVING. Calories 45 (Calories from Fat 25); Fat 3g (Saturated 1g); Cholesterol 0mg; Sodium 130mg; Carbohydrate 6g (Dietary Fiber 2g); Protein 1g

TIP **SNOW PEA PODS** are very similar to snap pea pods, and they can be used interchangeably. Both are edible pea pods with tender, sweet peas inside.

TIP **ONE 6-OUNCE PACKAGE** of frozen snow (Chinese) pea pods can be substituted for the fresh pea pods. Thaw them before cooking in step 3

Removing Tips and Strings from Pea Pods

Snap off the stem end of pea pod, and pull the string across the pea pod to remove it.

Dilled Carrots and Pea Pods

ROASTED VEGETABLES

MAKES 4 servings • **BAKE: 25 minutes**

INGREDIENTS	DIRECTIONS

INGREDIENTS

ESSENTIAL EQUIPMENT: *rectangular pan (about 13×9 inches)*

1 medium red or green bell pepper

1 medium onion

1 medium zucchini

1/4 pound mushrooms

Olive oil-flavored or regular cooking spray

1/4 teaspoon salt

1/8 teaspoon pepper

2 tablespoons chopped fresh or 2 teaspoons dried basil leaves, if desired

DIRECTIONS

1 Cut the bell pepper lengthwise in half, and cut out seeds and membrane. Cut each half lengthwise into 4 strips.

2 Peel the onion, and cut in half. Wrap one half of onion, and refrigerate for another use. Cut remaining half into 4 wedges, then separate into pieces.

3 Cut the zucchini crosswise into 1-inch pieces. Cut off and discard the end of each mushroom stem, and leave the mushrooms whole.

4 Heat the oven to 425°. Spray the bottom of the pan with cooking spray. Arrange the vegetables in a single layer in the sprayed pan. Spray the vegetables with cooking spray until lightly coated. Sprinkle with salt, pepper and basil.

5 Bake uncovered 15 minutes. Remove the pan from the oven. Turn vegetables over. Bake uncovered about 10 minutes longer or until vegetables are crisp-tender when pierced with a fork.

1 SERVING. Calories 30 (Calories from Fat 0); Fat 0g (Saturated 0g); Cholesterol 0mg; Sodium 150mg; Carbohydrate 6g (Dietary Fiber 1g); Protein 2g

TiP **IN MANY SUPERMARKETS,** you can buy mushrooms that have not been prepackaged. Just buy as many as you need.

TiP **REMOVE THE PAN** of vegetables from the oven when it's time to turn them over. Place pan on a heatproof surface such as the burners of your range, and close the oven door to retain the heat.

Cutting an Onion

Cut the onion half into 4 wedges, then separate into pieces.

Roasted Vegetables

CHAPTER 6

Snacks and Desserts

QUICK GUACAMOLE

MAKES about 2 cups dip

INGREDIENTS

ESSENTIAL EQUIPMENT: *large knife, such as a chef's knife*

2 large ripe avocados

1 tablespoon lime juice

1/3 cup chunky-style salsa

Tortilla chips, if desired

DIRECTIONS

1 Cut the avocado lengthwise in half around the pit, and pull apart the halves. The pit will stay in one of the halves. Firmly and carefully strike the exposed pit with the sharp edge of the large knife. While grasping the avocado, twist the knife to loosen and remove the pit.

2 Scoop out the avocado pulp into a medium bowl, using a spoon. Add the lime juice, and mash the avocado with a fork.

3 Stir in the salsa. Serve with tortilla chips. Cover and refrigerate any remaining dip.

1 TABLESPOON: Calories 20 (Calories from Fat 20); Fat 2g (Saturated 0g); Cholesterol 0mg; Sodium 10mg; Carbohydrate 1g (Dietary Fiber 0g); Protein 0g

TiP **FIRM, UNRIPE AVOCADOS** are usually what are available in the supermarket. Let the avocado ripen at room temperature until it yields to gentle pressure but is still firm.

TiP **THE LIME JUICE** keeps the color of the mashed avocado from darkening. Add it to the avocado pulp as soon as possible.

Removing Avocado Pit

Firmly and carefully strike the exposed pit with the sharp edge of a knife. While grasping the avocado, twist the knife to loosen and remove the pit.

Quick Guacamole

HOT ARTICHOKE DIP

MAKES about 1 1/2 cups dip • BAKE: 20 to 25 minutes

INGREDIENTS

ESSENTIAL EQUIPMENT: *1-quart casserole*

4 medium green onions with tops

1 can (16 ounces) artichoke hearts

1/2 cup mayonnaise or salad dressing

1/2 cup grated Parmesan cheese

Crackers or cocktail rye bread, if desired

DIRECTIONS

1 Heat the oven to 350°.

2 Peel and chop the green onions.

3 Drain the artichoke hearts in a strainer. Chop the artichoke hearts into small pieces.

4 Mix the green onions, artichoke hearts, mayonnaise and cheese in the ungreased casserole.

5 Cover with lid or aluminum foil and bake 20 to 25 minutes or until hot. Serve with crackers.

1 TABLESPOON: Calories 45 (Calories from Fat 35); Fat 4g (Saturated 1g); Cholesterol 5mg; Sodium 105mg; Carbohydrate 2g (Dietary Fiber 1g); Protein 1g

Lighter **ARTICHOKE DIP:** For 1 gram of fat and 20 calories per serving, use 1/3 cup plain fat-free yogurt and 3 tablespoons reduced-fat mayonnaise for the 1/2 cup mayonnaise.

TiP **TO SAVE TIME,** mix ingredients in a microwavable casserole. Cover with plastic wrap, folding back 2-inch edge to vent. Microwave on Medium-High (70%) 4 to 5 minutes, stirring after 2 minutes.

TiP **PREPARE THIS DIP** ahead of time, and refrigerate up to 24 hours. Heat when you are ready to serve it. Increase bake time about 5 minutes.

Chopping Artichoke Hearts

Chop the artichoke hearts into small pieces.

Hot Artichoke Dip

Spinach Dip in Bread Bowl

MAKES 4 1/2 cups • **REFRIGERATE: 1 hour**

INGREDIENTS

ESSENTIAL EQUIPMENT:
serving plate

2 packages (10 ounces each) frozen chopped spinach, thawed

1 can (8 ounces) sliced water chestnuts

9 medium green onions with tops

1 clove garlic

1 cup sour cream

1 cup plain yogurt

2 teaspoons chopped fresh or 1/2 teaspoon dried tarragon leaves

1/2 teaspoon salt

1/2 teaspoon ground mustard (dry)

1/4 teaspoon pepper

1-pound unsliced round bread loaf

DIRECTIONS

1 Drain the thawed spinach in a strainer, then squeeze out the excess moisture from the spinach, using paper towels or a clean kitchen towel, until the spinach is dry. Place in a large bowl.

2 Drain the water chestnuts in a strainer. Chop them into small pieces, and add to the bowl.

3 Peel and chop the green onions. You will need about 1 cup. Add the onions to the bowl. Peel and crush the garlic, and add to the bowl.

4 Add the sour cream, yogurt, tarragon, salt, mustard and pepper to the bowl. Mix all ingredients thoroughly. Cover and refrigerate at least 1 hour to blend flavors.

5 Just before serving, cut a 1- to 2-inch slice from the top of the loaf of bread. Hollow out the loaf by cutting along the edge with a serrated knife, leaving about a 1-inch shell, and pulling out large chunks of bread. Cut or tear the top slice and the hollowed-out bread into bite-size pieces.

6 Fill the bread loaf with the spinach dip, and place on the serving plate. Arrange the bread pieces around the loaf to use for dipping.

1 TABLESPOON: Calories 30 (Calories from Fat 10); Fat 1g (Saturated 1g); Cholesterol 5mg; Sodium 60mg; Carbohydrate 4g (Dietary Fiber 0g); Protein 1g

Lighter **SPINACH DIP:** For 0 grams of fat and 25 calories per serving, substitute 1/2 cup reduced-fat sour cream for the 1 cup sour cream and 1 1/2 cups plain fat-free yogurt for the 1 cup yogurt.

TiP **A LOAF OF RYE BREAD** looks nice filled with the Spinach Dip, but white, whole wheat and multigrain breads also taste delicious with this snack.

TiP **PLACE THE FROZEN SPINACH** in the refrigerator the day before you need it so it can thaw, or thaw it in the microwave.

Draining Frozen Spinach

Squeeze excess moisture from spinach, using paper towels or a clean kitchen towel, until the spinach is dry.

Making a Bread Bowl

Cut a 1- to 2-inch slice from top of loaf. Hollow out the loaf by cutting along the edge with a serrated knife, leaving about a 1-inch shell, and pulling out large chunks of bread. Cut or tear the top slice and the hollowed-out bread into bite-size pieces for dipping.

Spinach Dip in Bread Bowl

MEXICAN SNACK PLATTER

MAKES about 16 servings

INGREDIENTS

ESSENTIAL EQUIPMENT: *12- or 13-inch round serving plate or pizza pan*

1 can (15 ounces) refried beans

2 tablespoons salsa, chili sauce or ketchup

1 1/2 cups sour cream

1 cup purchased guacamole

1 cup shredded Cheddar cheese (4 ounces)

2 medium green onions with tops

Tortilla chips, if desired

DIRECTIONS

1 Mix the refried beans and salsa in a small bowl. Spread in a thin layer over the serving plate.

2 Spread the sour cream over the beans, leaving about a 1-inch border of beans around the edge. Spread the guacamole over the sour cream, leaving a border of sour cream showing.

3 Sprinkle the cheese over the guacamole. Peel and chop the green onions; sprinkle over the cheese. Cover with plastic wrap and refrigerate until serving time.

4 Serve the dip with tortilla chips for dipping.

1 SERVING. Calories 115 (Calories from Fat 80); Fat 9g (Saturated 5g); Cholesterol 25mg; Sodium 210mg; Carbohydrate 7g (Dietary Fiber 2g); Protein 4g

TiP **PURCHASE GUACAMOLE** in the dairy section of the supermarket. It may be called "avocado dip" instead of "guacamole."

TiP **FOR A HOTTER FLAVOR,** use a flavored shredded cheese, such as pizza or nacho, instead of plain Cheddar.

Spreading Guacamole over Sour Cream

Spread guacamole over sour cream, leaving a border of sour cream showing.

Mexican Snack Platter

VEGETABLE TRAY WITH TANGY YOGURT DIP

MAKES about 1 cup • REFRIGERATE: 1 hour

INGREDIENTS

ESSENTIAL EQUIPMENT:
serving plate

1 cup plain fat-free yogurt

2 tablespoons chili sauce

1 teaspoon prepared horseradish

Assorted Fresh Vegetables (below)

ASSORTED FRESH VEGETABLES

Bell pepper strips

Broccoli flowerets

Carrot slices or sticks or baby-cut carrots

Cauliflowerets

Celery sticks

Cherry tomatoes

Cucumber slices

Jicama sticks

Snow (Chinese) pea pods or snap pea pods

Zucchini sticks

DIRECTIONS

1 Mix the yogurt, chili sauce and horseradish in a medium bowl. Cover and refrigerate at least 1 hour to blend flavors.

2 Arrange at least 4 or 5 different raw Assorted Fresh Vegetables on the serving plate. Serve with the dip.

1 TABLESPOON: Calories 10 (Calories from Fat 0); Fat 0g (Saturated 0g); Cholesterol 0mg; Sodium 35mg; Carbohydrate 2g (Dietary Fiber 0g); Protein 1g

TiP **TASTE THE DIP** before serving it, and add another teaspoon of horseradish if you want a stronger flavor.

TiP **YOU CAN PURCHASE** whole baby-cut carrots, broccoli flowerets and cauliflowerets cleaned and ready to eat in the produce section of the supermarket.

Cutting Carrots into Diagonal Slices

Cut carrots diagonally to make large slices that are easy to dip.

Removing Strings from Pea Pods

Snap off the stem end of pea pod, and pull the string across the pea pod to remove it.

Vegetable Tray with Tangy Yogurt Dip

FRESH TOMATO SALSA

MAKES about 3 1/2 cups • **REFRIGERATE: 1 hour**

INGREDIENTS

ESSENTIAL EQUIPMENT:
large bowl

3 medium tomatoes

1 small green bell pepper

6 medium green onions
with tops

3 cloves garlic

1 medium jalapeño chili

2 tablespoons chopped
fresh cilantro

2 tablespoons lime juice

1/2 teaspoon salt

Flour tortillas or tortilla
chips, if desired

DIRECTIONS

1 Place the bowl near your cutting board. After cutting or chopping each ingredient, add each one to the bowl. Cut the tomato crosswise in half. Gently squeeze each half, cut side down, to remove the seeds. Chop the tomatoes.

2 Cut the bell pepper lengthwise in half, and cut out seeds and membrane. Chop the bell pepper.

3 Peel and slice the green onions. Peel and finely chop the garlic.

4 Cut the stem off the jalapeño chili, cut the chili lengthwise in half and scrape out the seeds. Cut the chili into strips, and then finely chop.

5 Add the cilantro, lime juice and salt. Mix all the ingredients. Cover and refrigerate at least 1 hour to blend flavors but no longer than 7 days.

6 Serve salsa with flour tortillas or tortilla chips or as an accompaniment to chicken, fish and other main dishes.

1 TABLESPOON: Calories 5 (Calories from Fat 0); Fat 0g (Saturated 0g); Cholesterol 0mg; Sodium 20mg; Carbohydrate 1g (Dietary Fiber 0g); Protein 0g

TiP **IF YOU DESIRE** a hotter salsa, leave some of the seeds in the jalapeño chili.

✔ **THE FLESH, RIBS AND SEEDS** of chilies contain irritating, burning oils. Wash hands and utensils in soapy water, and be especially careful not to rub your face or eyes until the oils have been washed away.

Seeding a Jalapeño Chili

Cut the stem off the jalapeño chili, cut the chili lengthwise in half and scrape out the seeds.

Fresh Tomato Salsa

CREAM CHEESE FIESTA SPREAD

MAKES 8 servings

INGREDIENTS

ESSENTIAL EQUIPMENT: *serving plate or dinner plate*

1 package (8 ounces) cream cheese

1/4 cup salsa

1/4 cup apricot preserves or orange marmalade

1 tablespoon chopped fresh cilantro or parsley

1 tablespoon finely shredded Cheddar or Monterey Jack cheese

1 tablespoon chopped ripe olives

Assorted crackers, if desired

DIRECTIONS

1 Place block of cream cheese on the plate, and let stand at room temperature about 30 minutes to soften it slightly before serving. Or to soften in the microwave, remove foil wrapper and place cream cheese on microwavable plate; microwave on medium (50%) 1/2 to 1 minute.

2 Mix the salsa and preserves, and spread over cream cheese. Sprinkle with the cilantro, cheese and olives. Serve with crackers.

1 SERVING. Calories 135 (Calories from Fat 90); Fat 10g (Saturated 6g); Cholesterol 30mg; Sodium 125mg; Carbohydrate 8g (Dietary Fiber 0g); Protein 3g

CRUNCHY CREAM CHEESE-RASPBERRY SPREAD: Omit salsa, preserves, cilantro, cheese and olives. Spread 1/3 cup raspberry spreadable fruit over the cream cheese. Sprinkle with 2 tablespoons each of finely chopped toasted almonds, miniature semisweet chocolate chips and flaked coconut.

CURRIED CREAM CHEESE-CHUTNEY SPREAD: Omit salsa, preserves, cilantro, cheese and olives. Spread 1/3 cup chopped chutney over the cream cheese. Sprinkle generously with curry powder. Sprinkle with 1 tablespoon each of chopped peanuts, chopped green onions, raisins and chopped cooked egg yolk.

CREAM CHEESE FIESTA SPREAD: For 1 gram of fat and 55 calories per serving, use fat-free cream cheese.

TiP **IF THE PRESERVES** or marmalade contain large pieces of fruit, snip them into smaller pieces with a kitchen scissors.

TiP **A WIDE SELECTION** of salsas is available in the supermarket, including fresh salsa in the refrigerated section. Some are mild, some quite spicy. Choose the one you prefer.

Spreading Salsa Mixture over Cream Cheese

Mix salsa and preserves; spread over cream cheese.

Cream Cheese Fiesta Spread

ROASTED GARLIC

MAKES 2 to 8 servings • BAKE: 50 minutes

INGREDIENTS

ESSENTIAL EQUIPMENT:
aluminum foil; baking pan or pie plate

1 to 4 garlic bulbs

2 teaspoons olive or vegetable oil for each garlic bulb

Salt and pepper to taste

Sliced French bread, if desired

TiP **GARLIC BECOMES** rich and mellow when roasted.

DIRECTIONS

1 Heat the oven to 350°.

2 Carefully peel the paperlike skin from around each bulb of garlic, leaving just enough to hold the cloves together. Cut a 1/4- to 1/2-inch slice from the top of each bulb to expose the cloves. Place bulb, cut side up, on a 12-inch square of aluminum foil.

3 Drizzle 2 teaspoons oil over each bulb. Sprinkle with salt and pepper. Wrap foil securely around the bulb. Place in the baking pan or pie plate.

4 Bake 45 to 50 minutes or until garlic is tender when pierced with a toothpick or fork. Cool slightly. To serve, gently squeeze one end of each clove to release the roasted garlic. Spread on slices of bread.

1 SERVING. Calories 75 (Calories from Fat 45); Fat 5g (Saturated 1g); Cholesterol 0mg; Sodium 75mg; Carbohydrate 6g (Dietary Fiber 0g); Protein 1g

TiP **GARLIC BULBS,** sometimes called "heads" of garlic, are made up of as many as fifteen sections called "cloves," each of which is covered with a thin skin. You can find garlic bulbs in the produce section of the supermarket.

Preparing Garlic for Roasting

Carefully peel paperlike skin from around each garlic bulb, leaving just enough to hold the cloves together. Cut a 1/4- to 1/2-inch slice from top of each bulb to expose cloves.

Wrapping Garlic for Roasting

Place bulb, cut side up, on 12-inch square of aluminum foil. Drizzle 2 teaspoons oil over each bulb. Sprinkle with salt and pepper. Wrap foil securely.

Roasted Garlic

STRAWBERRY SMOOTHIE

MAKES 4 servings (about 1 cup each)

INGREDIENTS

DIRECTIONS

ESSENTIAL EQUIPMENT: *blender*

2 cups (1 pint) strawberries

1 cup milk

2 containers (6 ounces each) strawberry yogurt (2/3 cup)

1 Reserve 4 strawberries for the garnish. Cut out the hull, or "cap," from the remaining strawberries with the point of a paring knife (see page 215).

2 Place strawberries, milk and yogurt in a blender. Cover and blend on high speed about 30 seconds or until smooth.

3 Pour mixture into 4 glasses. Garnish each with a strawberry.

1 SERVING. Calories 150 (Calories from Fat 35); Fat 4g (Saturated 3g); Cholesterol 15mg; Sodium 80mg; Carbohydrate 24g (Dietary Fiber 1g); Protein 6g

ORANGE SMOOTHIE

MAKES 4 servings (about 1 cup each)

INGREDIENTS

DIRECTIONS

ESSENTIAL EQUIPMENT: *blender*

1 quart vanilla frozen yogurt or ice cream, slightly softened

1/2 cup frozen (thawed) orange juice concentrate

1/4 cup milk

Fresh orange slices, if desired

1 Place the yogurt, orange juice concentrate and milk in a blender. Cover and blend on medium speed about 45 seconds, stopping blender occasionally to scrape sides, until thick and smooth.

2 Pour mixture into 4 glasses. Garnish with orange slices.

1 SERVING. Calories 280 (Calories from Fat 55); Fat 6g (Saturated 4g); Cholesterol 20mg; Sodium 110mg; Carbohydrate 47g (Dietary Fiber 0g); Protein 9g

TiP **SERVE THESE** special drinks in your prettiest clear glasses for a quick, freshly made dessert.

TiP **LEAVE THE GREEN LEAVES** on the strawberries that will be used to garnish the Strawberry Smoothie.

Smoothies

Making a Strawberry Smoothie

Place strawberries, milk and yogurt in a blender. Cover and blend on high speed about 30 seconds or until smooth.

Frozen Chocolate Mousse

MAKES 8 servings • FREEZE: 4 hours

INGREDIENTS

ESSENTIAL EQUIPMENT: *electric mixer or hand beater; 9-inch square pan*

2 cups whipping (heavy) cream

1/4 cup almond-, chocolate- or coffee-flavored liqueur

1/2 cup chocolate-flavored syrup

Crushed cookies or chopped nuts, if desired

DIRECTIONS

1 Beat the whipping cream in a chilled large bowl with the electric mixer on high speed until stiff peaks form.

2 Gently pour the liqueur and chocolate syrup over the whipped cream. To fold ingredients together, use a rubber spatula to cut down vertically through the whipped cream, then slide the spatula across the bottom of the bowl and up the side, turning the whipped cream over. Rotate the bowl one-fourth turn, and repeat this down-across-up motion. Continue mixing in this way just until ingredients are blended.

3 Spread whipped cream mixture into the ungreased pan.

4 Cover and freeze at least 4 hours but no longer than 2 months. Cut mousse into squares. Garnish with crushed cookies. Serve immediately. Cover and freeze any remaining mousse.

1 SERVING. Calories 245 (Calories from Fat 170); Fat 19g (Saturated 12g); Cholesterol 65mg; Sodium 40mg; Carbohydrate 17g (Dietary Fiber 0g); Protein 2g

TiP **THE WHIPPING CREAM** will beat up more easily if the bowl and mixer beaters are chilled in the refrigerator for about 20 minutes before beating.

TiP **THE LIQUEUR KEEPS** this dessert from freezing totally solid. That's why the mousse can be served immediately after taking it from the freezer.

Folding Liqueur and Chocolate Syrup into Whipped Cream

To fold ingredients together, use a rubber spatula to cut down vertically through the whipped cream, then slide the spatula  across the bottom of the bowl and up the side, turning the whipped cream over. Rotate the bowl one-fourth turn, and repeat this down-across-up motion. Continue mixing in this way just until ingredients are blended.

Frozen Chocolate Mousse

FUDGY BROWNIE CAKE WITH RASPBERRY SAUCE

MAKES 8 servings • **BAKE: 40 minutes**

INGREDIENTS

ESSENTIAL EQUIPMENT: *9-inch round pan or 8-inch square pan; small saucepan (about 1-quart size)*

Shortening to grease pan

1 1/2 cups sugar

3/4 cup all-purpose flour

3/4 cup (1 1/2 sticks) margarine or butter, melted

1/2 cup baking cocoa

1 1/2 teaspoons vanilla

1/4 teaspoon salt

3 eggs

Raspberry Sauce (below)

Fresh raspberries for garnish, if desired

RASPBERRY SAUCE

3 tablespoons sugar

2 teaspoons cornstarch

1/3 cup water

1 package (10 ounces) frozen raspberries in syrup, thawed and undrained

DIRECTIONS

1 Heat the oven to 350°. Grease the bottom and side of the pan with shortening. Sprinkle a small amount of flour over the greased surface, shake the pan to distribute the flour evenly, then turn the pan upside down and tap the bottom to remove excess flour.

2 Mix the sugar, flour, margarine, cocoa, vanilla, salt and eggs in a medium bowl with a spoon or wire whisk. Pour into the greased and floured pan.

3 Bake 40 to 45 minutes or until the top appears dry. While the cake is baking, prepare Raspberry Sauce (below).

4 Cool the cake 10 minutes, then remove it from the pan and place on a wire cooling rack. Or you can leave the cake in the pan. Cool cake, and serve with the sauce. Garnish with fresh raspberries.

RASPBERRY SAUCE Mix the sugar and cornstarch in the saucepan. Stir in water and raspberries. Cook over medium heat, stirring constantly, until the mixture thickens and boils. Continue boiling 1 minute, stirring constantly. Remove the saucepan from the heat. Strain the sauce through a strainer to the remove the raspberry seeds if desired. Serve sauce slightly warm or cool.

1 SERVING. Calories 420 (Calories from Fat 180); Fat 20g (Saturated 5g); Cholesterol 80mg; Sodium 300mg; Carbohydrate 59g (Dietary Fiber 4g); Protein 5g

TiP **IF USING A MARGARINE** or spread, make sure it contains at least 65 percent vegetable oil. Spreads with less fat are not recommended for baking.

TiP **FOR EASIER CLEANUP,** heat the margarine in a microwavable mixing bowl on High for 30 to 45 seconds until melted, then add the remaining ingredients for the cake.

Straining Raspberry Sauce

Strain sauce through a strainer to remove the raspberry seeds.

Fudgy Brownie Cake with Raspberry Sauce

TIRAMISU

MAKES 9 servings • **REFRIGERATE: 4 hours**

INGREDIENTS

ESSENTIAL EQUIPMENT: *electric mixer or hand beater; 8-inch square pan or 9-inch round pan*

1 cup whipping (heavy) cream

1 package (8 ounces) cream cheese at room temperature

1/2 cup powdered sugar

2 tablespoons light rum or 1/2 teaspoon rum extract

1 package (3 ounces) ladyfingers (12 ladyfingers)

1/2 cup cold prepared espresso or strong coffee

2 teaspoons baking cocoa

Maraschino cherries with stems for garnish, if desired

DIRECTIONS

1 Pour the whipping cream into a medium bowl, and place in the refrigerator to chill. The cream will whip better in a cold bowl.

2 Beat the cream cheese and powdered sugar in another medium bowl with the electric mixer on medium speed until smooth. Beat in the rum on low speed, and set aside.

3 Beat the whipping cream on high speed until stiff peaks form. Gently spoon the whipped cream onto the cream cheese mixture. To fold together, use a rubber spatula to cut down vertically through the mixtures, then slide the spatula across the bottom of the bowl and up the side, turning the mixtures over. Rotate the bowl one-fourth turn, and repeat this down-across-up motion. Continue mixing in this way just until ingredients are blended.

4 Split each ladyfinger horizontally in half. Arrange half of them, cut sides up, over the bottom of the ungreased pan. Drizzle 1/4 cup of the cold espresso over the ladyfingers. Spread half of the cream cheese mixture over ladyfingers.

5 Arrange the remaining ladyfingers, cut sides up, over the cream cheese mixture. Drizzle with the remaining 1/4 cup cold espresso, and spread with the remaining cream cheese mixture.

6 Sprinkle the cocoa over the top of the dessert. If you have a small strainer, place the cocoa in the strainer and shake it over the dessert. Otherwise, shake the cocoa from a spoon. Cover and refrigerate about 4 hours or until the filling is firm. Garnish each serving with a cherry.

1 SERVING. Calories 240 (Calories from Fat 160); Fat 18g (Saturated 11g); Cholesterol 60mg; Sodium 115mg; Carbohydrate 17g (Dietary Fiber 0g); Protein 3g

 Lighter **TIRAMISU:** For 8 grams of fat and 165 calories per serving, use reduced-fat cream cheese (Neufchâtel) instead of regular cream cheese. Use 2 cups frozen (thawed) reduced-fat whipped topping for the whipping cream.

TiP **LADYFINGERS** are small, oval-shaped cakes usually found in the bakery department or freezer section of the supermarket.

TiP **TIRAMISU MAY BE FROZEN;** be sure to cover tightly. Allow to thaw several hours in the refrigerator before serving.

Arranging Ladyfingers in Pan

Split ladyfingers horizontally in half. Arrange half of them, cut sides up, over bottom of pan. Drizzle with 1/4 cup of the cold espresso.

Sprinkling with Cocoa

Place cocoa in a small strainer, and shake it over the dessert.

Tiramisu

APPLE CRISP

MAKES 6 servings • **BAKE: 30 minutes**

INGREDIENTS

DIRECTIONS

ESSENTIAL EQUIPMENT: *8-inch square pan or 9-inch round pan*

Shortening to grease pan

4 medium tart cooking apples, such as Granny Smith, Wealthy or Rome Beauty

2/3 cup packed brown sugar

1/2 cup all-purpose flour

1/2 cup quick-cooking or old-fashioned oats

1/3 cup margarine or butter at room temperature

3/4 teaspoon ground cinnamon

3/4 teaspoon ground nutmeg

Half-and-half or ice cream, if desired

1 Heat the oven to 375°. Grease the bottom and sides of the pan with the shortening.

2 Peel the apples if desired. Cut the apple into fourths, and remove seeds. Cut each fourth into slices. You will need about 4 cups of apple slices. Spread the slices in the greased pan.

3 Mix the brown sugar, flour, oats, margarine, cinnamon and nutmeg with a fork. The mixture will be crumbly. Sprinkle this mixture evenly over the apples.

4 Bake about 30 minutes or until the topping is golden brown and the apples are tender when pierced with a fork. Serve warm with half-or-half or ice cream.

1 SERVING. Calories 300 (Calories from Fat 100); Fat 11g (Saturated 2g); Cholesterol 0mg; Sodium 130mg; Carbohydrate 51g (Dietary Fiber 3g); Protein 2g

BLUEBERRY CRISP: Substitute 4 cups fresh or frozen blueberries for the apples. If using frozen blueberries, thaw and drain them first.

CHERRY CRISP: Substitute a 21-ounce can cherry pie filling for the apples.

TiP **MANY VARIETIES** of apples are available. The ones used for cooking and baking remain flavorful and firm when baked.

TiP **USE A VEGETABLE** peeler to peel apples. Doing so is quick, and the peeler removes just a thin skin.

Slicing Apples

Peel apples if desired. Cut the apple into fourths and remove seeds. Cut each fourth into slices.

Sprinkling Brown Sugar Mixture over Apples

Mix brown sugar, flour, oats, margarine, cinnamon and nutmeg with a fork. The mixture will be crumbly. Sprinkle evenly over apples.

Apple Crisp

STRAWBERRY SHORTCAKES

MAKES 6 servings • **LET STAND: 1 hour** • **BAKE: 12 minutes**

INGREDIENTS

DIRECTIONS

ESSENTIAL EQUIPMENT: *cookie sheet; electric mixer or hand beater*

1 quart (4 cups) strawberries

1/2 cup sugar

2 cups all-purpose flour

2 tablespoons sugar

3 teaspoons baking powder

1 teaspoon salt

1/3 cup shortening

3/4 cup milk

Sweetened Whipped Cream (below) or
1 1/2 cups frozen (thawed) whipped topping, if desired

SWEETENED WHIPPED CREAM

3/4 cup whipping (heavy) cream

2 tablespoons granulated or powdered sugar

1 Wash strawberries, and dry on paper towels. Cut out the hull, or "cap," with the point of a paring knife. Cut the strawberries lengthwise into slices. Mix sliced strawberries and 1/2 cup sugar in a large bowl. Let stand 1 hour.

2 Heat the oven to 450°.

3 Mix the flour, 2 tablespoons sugar, the baking powder and salt in a medium bowl. Cut the shortening into the flour mixture, using a pastry blender or crisscrossing 2 knives, until the mixture looks like fine crumbs.

4 Stir the milk into the crumb mixture just until blended and a dough forms. If the crumb mixture is not completely moistened, stir in an additional 1 to 3 teaspoons milk. Drop the dough by 6 spoonfuls onto the ungreased cookie sheet.

5 Bake 10 to 12 minutes or until golden brown.

6 Just before serving, prepare Sweetened Whipped Cream (below). Split warm or cool shortcakes horizontally. Spoon whipped cream and strawberries over bottoms of shortcakes. Top with tops of shortcakes and additional whipped cream and strawberries.

SWEETENED WHIPPED CREAM Beat the whipping cream and sugar in a chilled medium bowl with the electric mixer on high speed until stiff peaks form. Serve immediately.

1 SERVING. Calories 375 (Calories from Fat 115); Fat 13g (Saturated 3g); Cholesterol 5mg; Sodium 650mg; Carbohydrate 62g (Dietary Fiber 3g); Protein 6g

TiP **WASH STRAWBERRIES** just before you plan to use them.

TiP **THE WHIPPING CREAM** will beat up more easily if the bowl and beaters for the mixer are chilled in the refrigerator for about 20 minutes before beating.

Removing Hull from Strawberry

Cut out the hull, or "cap," with the point of a paring knife.

Dropping Shortcake Dough onto Cookie Sheet

Drop dough by 6 spoonfuls onto ungreased cookie sheet.

Strawberry Shortcakes

CREAMY LEMON DESSERT

MAKES 9 servings • **REFRIGERATE: 2 hours**

INGREDIENTS

DIRECTIONS

ESSENTIAL EQUIPMENT: *9-inch square pan or 9-inch pie pan; electric mixer or hand beater*

2 cups whipping (heavy) cream

Graham Cracker Crust (below)

1 can (14 ounces) sweetened condensed milk

1/2 cup lemon juice

2 teaspoons grated lemon peel, if desired

Few drops of yellow food color, if desired

Whole strawberries for garnish, if desired

GRAHAM CRACKER CRUST

16 graham cracker squares

2 tablespoons sugar

1/4 cup (1/2 stick) margarine or butter, melted

1 Pour the whipping cream into a large bowl, and place in the refrigerator to chill. The whipping cream will whip better in a cold bowl.

2 Prepare Graham Cracker Crust (below). While crust is cooling, continue with recipe.

3 Mix milk, lemon juice and lemon peel in a small bowl, and set aside.

4 Add the food color to the whipping cream. Beat the whipping cream with the electric mixer on high speed until stiff peaks form.

5 Gently pour the lemon mixture over the whipped cream. To fold together, use a rubber spatula to cut down vertically through the whipped cream, then slide the spatula across the bottom of the bowl and up the side, turning the whipped cream over. Rotate the bowl one-fourth turn, and repeat this down-across-up motion. Continue mixing in this way just until ingredients are blended.

6 Pour the folded mixture over the crust. Cover and refrigerate at least 2 hours but no longer than 48 hours.

7 Cut dessert into 3-inch squares. Garnish each serving with a strawberry. Cover and refrigerate any remaining dessert.

GRAHAM CRACKER CRUST Heat the oven to 350°. Place a few crackers at a time in a plastic bag. Seal the bag, and crush crackers into fine crumbs with a rolling pin or bottle. Mix the crumbs, sugar and margarine in a medium bowl. Press firmly and evenly on the bottom of the square pan. If using a pie pan, press crumb mixture against bottom and side of pan. Bake 10 minutes; cool.

1 SERVING. Calories 420 (Calories from Fat 245); Fat 27g (Saturated 14g); Cholesterol 75mg; Sodium 210mg; Carbohydrate 39g (Dietary Fiber 0g); Protein 5g

TiP **BE SURE TO PURCHASE** sweetened condensed milk, not evaporated milk. They are used very differently in recipes.

TiP **INSTEAD OF USING** graham crackers, purchase packaged graham cracker crumbs at the supermarket, and use 1 1/4 cups of them in the crust.

Crushing Graham Crackers

Place a few crackers at a time in a plastic bag. Seal bag, and crush crackers into fine crumbs with a rolling pin or bottle.

Creamy Lemon Dessert

PUMPKIN PIE

MAKES 8 servings • BAKE: 1 hour

INGREDIENTS

ESSENTIAL EQUIPMENT: *9-inch pie pan; electric mixer or hand beater*

Pat-in-the-Pan Pastry (below)

2 eggs

1/2 cup sugar

1 teaspoon ground cinnamon

1/2 teaspoon salt

1/2 teaspoon ground ginger

1/8 teaspoon ground cloves

1 can (16 ounces) pumpkin

1 can (12 ounces) evaporated milk

Sweetened Whipped Cream (below) or 1 cup frozen (thawed) whipped topping

PAT-IN-THE-PAN PASTRY

1 1/3 cups all-purpose flour

1/3 cup vegetable oil

1/2 teaspoon salt

2 tablespoons cold water

SWEETENED WHIPPED CREAM

1/2 cup whipping (heavy) cream

1 tablespoon granulated or powdered sugar

DIRECTIONS

1 Heat the oven to 425°. Prepare Pat-in-the-Pan Pastry (below).

2 Beat the eggs slightly in a large bowl with a wire whisk or hand beater. Beat in the sugar, cinnamon, salt, ginger, cloves, pumpkin and milk.

3 To prevent spilling, place pastry-lined pie plate on oven rack before adding filling. Carefully pour the pumpkin filling into the pie plate. Bake 15 minutes.

4 Reduce the oven temperature to 350°. Bake about 45 minutes longer or until a knife inserted in the center comes out clean. Place pie on a wire cooling rack after baking. If after 4 to 6 hours the pie has not been served, cover and refrigerate it.

5 Serve pie with Sweetened Whipped Cream (below). Cover and refrigerate any remaining pie up to 3 days.

PAT-IN-THE-PAN PASTRY Mix the flour, oil and salt with a fork in a medium bowl until all flour is moistened. Sprinkle with cold water, 1 tablespoon at a time, tossing with fork until all water is absorbed. Shape pastry into a ball, using your hands. Press pastry in bottom and up side of pie pan.

SWEETENED WHIPPED CREAM Beat the whipping cream and sugar in a chilled medium bowl with the electric mixer on high speed until stiff peaks form. Serve immediately, or continue with recipe to freeze and use later. Place waxed paper on cookie sheet. Drop whipped cream by 8 spoonfuls onto waxed paper. Freeze uncovered at least 2 hours. Place frozen mounds of whipped cream in a freezer container. Cover tightly and freeze no longer than 2 months.

1 SERVING. Calories 345 (Calories from Fat 160); Fat 18g (Saturated 7g); Cholesterol 85mg; Sodium 360mg; Carbohydrate 40g (Dietary Fiber 2g); Protein 8g

PUMPKIN PIE: For 2 grams of fat and 120 calories per serving, omit Pat-in-the-Pan Pastry. Heat the oven to 350°. Spray 9-inch pie pan with cooking spray. Use evaporated skimmed milk. Prepare filling as directed; pour into sprayed pie pan. Bake about 45 minutes or until knife inserted in center comes out clean.

TiP **BE SURE TO PURCHASE** canned pumpkin, not pumpkin pie mix, for this recipe. The pumpkin pie mix would require a different recipe.

TiP **THE WHIPPING CREAM** will beat up more easily if the bowl and beaters for the mixer are chilled in the refrigerator for about 20 minutes before beating.

Patting Pastry into pan

Press pastry in bottom and up side of pie pan.

Freezing Mounds of Whipped Cream

Drop whipped cream by 8 spoonfuls onto waxed paper. Freeze uncovered at least 2 hours.

Pumpkin Pie

BEYOND THE BASICS

COMMON PREPARATION TECHNIQUES

CHOP: Cut into pieces of irregular sizes.

GRATE: Cut into tiny particles by rubbing food across the small rough holes of a grater.

CRUSH: Press with side of knife, mallet or rolling pin to break into small pieces.

JULIENNE: Stack thin slices; cut into matchlike sticks.

CUBE: Cut into 1/2-inch or wider strips; cut across strips into cubes.

PEEL: Cut off outer covering with a knife or vegetable peeler, or strip off outer covering with fingers.

CUT UP: Cut into small irregular pieces with kitchen scissors or knife.

SHRED: Cut into long thin pieces by rubbing food across the large holes of a shredder or by using a knife to slice very thinly.

DICE: Cut into 1/2-inch or narrower strips; cut across strips into cubes.

SLICE: Cut into pieces of the same width.

SLICE DIAGONALLY: Cut with knife at 45-degree angle into pieces of the same width.

ROASTING BELL PEPPERS OR CHILIES: Broil whole peppers with tops 5 inches from heat, turning occasionally, until skin is blistered and evenly browned but not burned. Place peppers in a plastic bag and let stand 20 minutes. Peel skin from peppers.

SNIP: Cut into very small pieces with kitchen scissors.

SLICING AN APPLE: Cut apple into fourths, and remove seeds. Cut each fourth into wedges.

MAKING BREAD CRUMBS (DRY): Place bread on cookie sheet and heat in 200° oven about 20 minutes or until dry; cool. Place in heavy plastic bag; crush with rolling pin into very small pieces. Or blend in blender or food processor to make fine bread crumbs.

MAKING BREAD CRUMBS (SOFT): Tear soft bread with fingers into small pieces.

SEEDING AN AVOCADO: Cut avocado lengthwise in half. Hit the seed of the avocado with the sharp edge of a knife. Grasp the avocado half, then twist the knife to loosen and remove the seed.

SHREDDING CABBAGE: Place a flat side of one fourth of a head of cabbage on a cutting board; cut off core. Cut cabbage into thin slices with a large knife. Cut slices several times to make smaller pieces.

CUTTING A BELL PEPPER: Cut bell pepper lengthwise in half. Cut out seeds and membrane.

COATING CHICKEN OR FISH: Place seasonings and bread crumbs or flour in a paper or plastic bag. Add a few pieces of chicken or fish at a time; seal bag and shake until each piece is evenly coated. If chicken or fish is dipped into milk or egg mixture before coating with crumbs, use one hand for handling the wet food and the other for handling the dry food.

SOAKING SUN-DRIED TOMATOES: Soak tomatoes in enough hot water to cover about 20 minutes or until tender; drain. Chop or cut up tomatoes.

MELTING CHOCOLATE: Heat chocolate in small saucepan over low heat, stirring frequently, until melted. Or place 1 to 2 ounces chocolate in microwavable bowl. Microwave uncovered on Medium 3 to 4 minutes, stirring after 2 minutes.

TOASTING COCONUT OR NUTS: Bake coconut or nuts in shallow pan in 350° oven about 10 minutes, stirring occasionally, until golden brown. Or sprinkle 1/2 cup coconut or nuts in ungreased heavy skillet. Cook over medium-low heat 6 to 14 minutes for coconut or 5 to 7 minutes for nuts, stirring frequently until browning begins, then stirring constantly until golden brown. (Watch carefully; time varies greatly between gas and electric ranges.)

MAKING CROUTONS: Cut bread into 1/2-inch slices; spread one side with softened margarine or butter. Cut into 1/2-inch cubes. Sprinkle with chopped herbs, grated Parmesan cheese or spices if desired. Cook in ungreased heavy skillet over medium heat 4 to 7 minutes, stirring frequently, until golden brown.

SEPARATING EGGS: Eggs are easiest to separate when cold. Purchase an inexpensive egg separator. Place separator over a small bowl. Crack egg; open shell, allowing egg yolk to fall into center of separator.

The egg white will slip through the slots of the separator into the bowl. Do not pass the egg yolk back and forth from shell half to shell half; bacteria may be present in the pores of the shell, which could contaminate the yolk or white.

SKIMMING FAT: Remove fat floating on top of broth or soup by dipping large spoon or fat skimmer into broth. Remove fat, leaving as much of the broth as possible.

CHOPPING GARLIC: Hit garlic clove with flat side of heavy knife to crack the skin, which will then slip off easily. Finely chop garlic with knife.

PREPARING AND CHOPPING GINGERROOT: Peel gingerroot with a paring knife. Cut into thin slices, then chop finely or grate finely.

CRUSHING GRAHAM CRACKERS: Place a few crackers at a time in a plastic bag. Seal bag, and crush crackers into fine crumbs with a rolling pin. Use the same technique for crushing cookies and chips. Or blend in blender or food processor to make fine crumbs.

CUTTING GREEN ONIONS: Cut green onions into thin slices, using some of the green part. Discard the tip with the stringy end.

PREPARING MUSHROOMS: Rinse mushrooms, and cut off stem ends. Leave mushrooms whole, or cut into slices.

SEEDING A JALAPEÑO CHILI: Cut the stem off the jalapeño chili, cut the chili lengthwise in half and scrape out the seeds.

SOAKING DRIED MUSHROOMS: Soak mushrooms in enough warm water to cover about 30 minutes. Rinse well and squeeze out moisture. Cut off and discard the tough stems.

PEELING A KIWIFRUIT: Cut the fuzzy brown skin from the fruit with a paring knife. Cut fruit into slices or wedges.

CUTTING PINEAPPLE: Twist top from pineapple. Cut pineapple into fourths. Holding pineapple securely, cut fruit from rind. Cut off pineapple core and remove "eyes." Cut pineapple crosswise or lengthwise into chunks or spears.

MELTING MARGARINE OR BUTTER: To microwave 3 to 4 tablespoons margarine, remove foil wrapper and place margarine in microwavable bowl. Microwave uncovered on High 30 to 45 seconds. Or melt margarine in small saucepan over very low heat about 1 minute.

HULLING STRAWBERRIES (REMOVING THE CAPS): Use the tip of a paring knife to remove the hull, or use an inexpensive strawberry huller (very short, fat tweezers). Or push one end of a plastic drinking straw into the point of the berry and push it through to pop off the cap.

CUTTING GRAIN OF MEAT: The "grain" of the meat refers to the muscle fibers that run the length of a cut of meat. Cut with the grain into strips, then cut across the grain into slices.

SOFTENING TORTILLAS: Place 2 tortillas between dampened microwavable paper towels or microwavable plastic wrap. Microwave on High 15 to 20 seconds to soften.

TWELVE TERRIFIC HERBS TO ADD AROMA AND FLAVOR

Herbs can add great flavor and variety to your favorite dishes. Most herbs are available fresh, dried or ground. If you have the space, you can even grow your own.

Too much of any herb can overwhelm a food or become bitter, so use small amounts of herbs, then taste the dish before adding more. Dried herbs are more concentrated than fresh; if a recipe calls for 1 tablespoon chopped fresh herbs, substitute 1 teaspoon dried herbs. For the best flavor when using dried herbs, crumble the herbs in the palm of your hand after measuring them to release more flavor. To chop fresh herbs, see page 71.

To store fresh herbs such as basil, chives, cilantro, parsley and rosemary, snip off the stem ends, and place the herbs in a glass or jar with the stems in about 1 inch of water. Seal the glass or jar in a plastic bag, and refrigerate for up to a week. For other herbs, such as oregano, tarragon and thyme, store dry in a dry plastic bag in the refrigerator; they should last four to six days.

Dried and ground herbs begin to lose their flavor after six months on the shelf and should be replaced after one year. When you buy dried herbs, write the date on the box or jar, so you will know when to replace them. Because herbs are perishable, buy them in the smallest quantity; this is one time when buying the large economy size is not a good idea.

BASIL: Fresh and dried leaves; ground
Flavor: Sweet with pungent tang
Uses: Eggs, pesto, spaghetti sauce, tomatoes

BAY LEAF: Fresh and dried leaves
Flavor: Pungent and aromatic
Uses: Meats, sauces, soups, stews

CHIVES: Fresh and freeze-dried
Flavor: Onion-like
Uses: Appetizers, cream soups, eggs, salads

CILANTRO: Fresh and dried leaves
Flavor: Aromatic and parsleylike
Uses: Chinese, Italian and Mexican dishes, pesto

DILL WEED: Fresh and dried
Flavor: Pungent and tangy
Uses: Dips, fish, soups, stews

MARJORAM: Fresh and dried leaves; ground
Flavor: Aromatic with bitter overtone
Uses: Fish, poultry, soups, stews

OREGANO: Fresh and dried leaves; ground
Flavor: Aromatic with pleasant bitter overtone
Uses: Eggs, Italian dishes, meats, sauces

PARSLEY: Fresh and dried leaves
Flavor: Slightly peppery
Uses: Garnishes, herb mixtures, sauces, soups

ROSEMARY: Fresh and dried leaves
Flavor: Fresh, sweet flavor
Uses: Breads, casseroles, pork, vegetables

SAGE: Fresh and dried leaves; rubbed; ground
Flavor: Aromatic, slightly bitter
Uses: Fish, meats, poultry, stuffing

TARRAGON: Fresh and dried leaves
Flavor: Piquant, aniselike
Uses: Eggs, meats, salads, sauces

THYME: Fresh and dried leaves; ground
Flavor: Aromatic, pungent
Uses: Fish, meats, poultry, stews

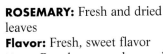

Top Five Spices for Flavor

The seeds, buds, fruit, bark or roots of plants, spices have added zest and a flavor boost to foods for hundreds of years. Store spices in a cool, dry place. Ground spices loose some of their flavor after six months and whole spices after one year. When you purchase spices, write the date on the box or jar, so you will know when to replace them.

CHILI POWDER: Ground
Flavor: Blend of chili peppers and spices; hot and spicy
Uses: Casseroles, Mexican dishes, soups, stews

CINNAMON: Stick and ground
Flavor: Aromatic, sweet and pungent
Uses: Cakes, cookies, desserts, pies

GINGER: Fresh and ground
Flavor: Pungent and spicy
Uses: Cookies, cakes, desserts, pies

NUTMEG: Whole and ground
Flavor: Fragrant, sweet and spicy
Uses: Beverages, cakes, cookies, desserts

PAPRIKA: Ground
Flavor: Slightly bitter; ranges from sweet to hot
Uses: Casseroles, eggs, garnishes, meats

ABOUT PASTA

The versatility of pasta makes it popular and convenient for today's meals. Pasta is available in three forms—dried, fresh and frozen—and in many shapes and sizes. Here are some of the most popular dried varieties; many are shown in the photo to the right.

ACINI DE PEPE (OR DOT SHAPE): Peppercorn-size pieces of cut spaghetti.

CAPELLINI (OR ANGEL HAIR): The thinnest of the long spaghettis.

CONCHIGLE: Medium to small shapes with or without grooves.

COUSCOUS: The tiniest form of pasta made from granular semolina.

EGG NOODLES: Flat or curly, short pasta strips usually made with eggs or egg yolks.

ELBOW MACARONI: Short, curved, tubular-shaped pasta.

FARFALLE (OR BOW-TIES): Shaped like bow-ties. Miniature bow-ties are known as tripolini.

FETTUCCINE: Long, flat noodles, usually 1/4 inch wide.

FUSILLI: Long or short spring-shaped pasta.

JAPANESE CURLY NOODLES: Wavy, thin, long noodles in thin "bricks."

LASAGNA: Flat noodle about 2 inches wide with either ruffled or straight edges.

LINGUINE: Long, flat, thin noodle usually 1/8 inch wide.

MANICOTTI (OR CANNELLONI): Large 4-inch hollow pasta tubes that are usually stuffed and baked.

NOVELTY SHAPES: Seasonal or other pasta shapes, such as trees, rabbits, hearts, etc., sometimes flavored.

PENNE: Narrow, short, diagonal-cut pasta about 1 1/4 inches long, smooth or with grooves.

RAMEN: Quick-cooking, deep-fried noodles used dry or cooked.

RAVIOLI: Filled pillow-shaped pasta usually stuffed with cheese or spinach.

RICE NOODLES: Translucent, thin strands made from rice flour and water.

RIGATONI: Short-cut, wide tubular pasta about 1 inch long with grooves.

ROSAMARINA (OR ORZO): Resembles rice but is slightly larger and longer.

ROTINI: Short-cut corkscrew-shaped pasta. Wider version is called rotelle.

SPAGHETTI: Long, thin, solid strands.

TORTELLINI: Filled, slightly irregularly shaped little rings.

WAGON WHEEL: Small, round pasta resembling a wheel with spokes.

ZITI: Short-cut, 2-inch tubular noodle with smooth surface.

STORING AND REHEATING COOKED PASTA

You can refrigerate or freeze leftover pasta for a future meal. Store in tightly sealed containers or plastic bags in the refrigerator up to five days, or freeze up to two months. To reheat pasta, choose one of these three quick and easy methods:

- Place pasta in rapidly boiling water for up to 2 minutes. Drain and serve immediately.

- Place pasta in colander and pour boiling water over it until heated through. Drain and serve immediately.

- Place pasta in microwavable dish or container. Cover and microwave on High for 1 to 3 minutes per 2 cups or until heated through. Serve immediately.

Japanese Curly Noodles

Rotini

Lasagna Noodles

Linguine

Fettuccine

Capellini

Spaghetti

Fusilli

Rice Noodles

Rigatoni

Rosamarina (orzo)

Manicotti

Farfelle (bow ties)

Tortellini

Egg Noodles

Wagon Wheels

Acini de Pepe

Couscous

Penne

Macaroni

Conchigle

Novelty Pasta Shapes

ABOUT SALAD GREENS

Once you know the different types of greens available, your salads can have more variety. Some greens tend to be bitter, and others are mild. You can have fun experimenting to find those you like best. Be sure to purchase fresh, crisp greens. Avoid limp or bruised greens and those with rust spots. Here are some of the more popular varieties, shown in the photo to the right.

ARUGULA (OR ROCKET) has small, slender, dark green leaves similar to radish leaves with a slightly bitter peppery mustard flavor. Choose smaller leaves for a less distinctive flavor.

BELGIAN (OR FRENCH) ENDIVE has closed, narrow, pale leaves with a distinct bitter flavor.

BIBB LETTUCE (OR LIMESTONE) has tender, pliable leaves similar to Boston lettuce leaves but smaller; it has a delicate, mild flavor.

BOSTON LETTUCE (OR BUTTERHEAD) has small rounded heads of soft, buttery leaves with the same delicate flavor of Bibb lettuce.

CABBAGE comes in a variety of types; the most familiar are green and red. Look for compact heads. Green cabbage also is available already shredded. Savoy cabbage has crinkled leaves, and Chinese (or napa) cabbage has long, crisp leaves. The flavor of cabbage can range from strong to slightly sweet.

CURLY ENDIVE has frilly narrow leaves with a slightly bitter taste.

ESCAROLE, also part of the endive family, has broad dark green leaves and a mild flavor.

GREENS (BEET, DANDELION, MUSTARD) all have a strong, biting flavor. When young, they are tender and milder in flavor and make a nice addition to tossed salads.

ICEBERG LETTUCE (OR CRISPHEAD) has a bland, mild flavor, making it the most popular and versatile green. Look for solid, compact heads with tight leaves that range from medium green on the outside to pale green inside.

LEAF LETTUCE, either red or green, has tender leaves that do not form heads. These leafy bunches have a mild, bland flavor.

MIXED SALAD GREENS, which you can find in bags in the produce section of most supermarkets, are already cleaned and ready to use. The package can include one type of green or a mixture of several varieties, which can add color, flavor and texture to your salads.

RADICCHIO, another member of the endive family, resembles a small, loose-leaf cabbage with smooth, tender leaves. The most familiar variety is usually rose-colored and may have a slightly bitter taste.

ROMAINE (OR COS) has narrow, elongated dark leaves with a crisp texture. This mild-flavored green is used in the traditional Caesar salad.

SPINACH has smooth, tapered, dark green leaves, sometimes with crumpling at the edges. Larger leaves may be tougher and stronger in flavor.

WATERCRESS has large, dark green leaves with a strong peppery flavor.

STORING AND HANDLING SALAD GREENS

Store greens in the crisper section of your refrigerator. You can keep them in the original wrap or place them in a plastic bag. Romaine and iceberg lettuce will keep up to one week. Most other greens will wilt within a few days.

Before using, be sure to wash greens thoroughly in several changes of cold water and then shake off excess moisture. For greens that may be sandy, such as spinach, after washing separate the leaves with your fingers to remove all grit. Toss them in a cloth towel and gently blot dry, or use a salad spinner to remove excess moisture. You can refrigerate unused washed greens in a sealed plastic bag or bowl with an airtight lid for three to four days.

BEYOND THE BASICS—EQUIPMENT

Special utensils and equipment will broaden the range of recipes you can prepare and will make some common tasks easier. If you enjoy cooking, plan to add some of these special things to your kitchen.

CASEROLE DISHES: Serving from beautiful casserole dishes adds color and interest to your table setting.

CUSTARD CUPS: Small glass cups that can be used in many ways, including combining ingredients or snipping fresh herbs.

EGG SEPARATOR: A tool for separating the egg white from the yolk.

FUNNEL: Helps when transferring liquids to a smaller container.

GARLIC PRESS: Pressing cloves of garlic is faster than chopping them and imparts more garlic flavor.

ICE-CREAM SCOOP: Choose a sturdy scoop that will work well in solidly frozen ice cream and yogurt.

KNIVES: Once you have the basic 3 knives—paring, chef's and all-purpose serrated, you may find that adding a utility knife, boning knife, carving knife and slicing knife would be helpful. Or simply add more sizes of the types of knives you use most often.

PANS

Having the pans shown below adds variety to your baking.

BUNDT CAKE PAN

ANGEL FOOD CAKE PAN

JELLY ROLL PAN

LOAF PAN

OMELET PAN

MUFFIN PAN

PASTRY BRUSH: Perfect for greasing baking pans, brushing meats and poultry with oil or a marinade and for use in making special pastries.

PEPPER MILL: Makes freshly ground pepper from peppercorns.

ROASTING PAN WITH A RACK: A large shallow pan for roasting meat and poultry. The rack suspends the meat so it doesn't cook in its own juices or fat.

ROLLING PIN: The best piece of equipment for rolling out cookie dough or pastry.

SALAD SPINNER: After rinsing greens, this is a quick and easy way to dry them.

SPAGHETTI SERVER: Separates long pasta strands for easy serving.

STOCKPOT: A large pot, usually 5-quart size or larger, used to simmer soups and stews and for cooking pasta.

WIRE COOLING RACKS: These allow air to circulate around freshly baked breads, cookies and desserts as they cool.

ZESTER: A special tool for removing the thin, flavorful colored layer, called the zest, from the peel of lemons, limes and oranges.

SMALL ELECTRICAL APPLIANCES

GRIDDLE

FOOD PROCESSOR

WAFFLE IRON

WOK

BASICS FOR GREAT GRILLING

Grilled food tastes delicious! Plus it's so easy to prepare and convenient, with little cleanup required. Outdoor grilling not only puts great-tasting food on the table, but also turns a meal into a special event.

SELECTING A GRILL

The variety of styles and sizes of grills can seem endless. To decide what model best fits your needs, consider how often you grill, where you grill, which technique you prefer, how many people you feed and how much money you're planning to spend.

Here are some features to look at: cooking grill racks that resist corrosion (such as those made of stainless steel), nonstick racks for easier cleanup, handles designed to be gripped easily and comfortably that are not too close to the heat source. On gas grills, look for an easy-to-replace gas tank with a fuel gauge, so you won't be caught on empty.

STYLES OF OUTDOOR GRILLS

Open

OPEN GRILLS OR BRAZIERS

This simplest form of a grill consists of a shallow firebox to hold the charcoal and a metal cooking grill rack for the food. The grill rack is usually just a few inches from the coals, so these grills are best for direct-heat grilling (grilling foods directly over charcoal) of burgers, chops, steaks and chicken. Braziers have a crank-type handle so you can raise and lower the cooking grill rack. They may be partially hooded for protection from the wind and for heat retention.

Covered

KETTLES AND COVERED COOKERS

"Kettle" describes the round version, whereas "covered cooker" describes the square and rectangular models. Because of their deep, rounded bottoms and generous lids, these grills are great for a wide range of cooking methods—grilling, roasting, steaming and smoking. Without their covers, they are used for direct-heat grilling. Covered, foods can be grilled and lightly smoked at the same time. Draft vents in the bottom and the cover help control the temperature.

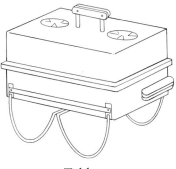

Tabletop

PORTABLE OR TABLETOP GRILLS

These grills are lightweight for transporting, are easy to clean and take up little storage space. They range from uncovered simple cast-metal hibachis of Japanese origin to miniature versions of kettles and covered cookers. They're great for direct-heat cooking for two, beach cookouts, tailgating parties and picnics. Because the cooking surface is much smaller than that of standard grills, portable grills are not designed for indirect-heat cooking of roasts or whole poultry, feeding crowds or long cooking times. Use them outdoors only.

Types of Grills by Fuel Source

CHARCOAL GRILLS

If there is a tradition in grilling, charcoal is it. Available in all types and sizes, the simplest charcoal grill consists of a firebox with a grate to hold the charcoal, a grill rack for the food and sometimes a cover or lid.

ELECTRIC GRILLS

If you live in an apartment or condominium building where charcoal or gas grills are prohibited, an electric outdoor grill may be your obvious choice. Mobility can be limited because these grills require a separate 110/120-volt grounded outlet with 1,600 to 1,800 watts of cooking power. Most electric grills include a smoking element, such as lava rock, which will give food a grilled flavor similar to that produced by charcoal and gas grills.

GAS GRILLS

Convenience is the key to the popularity of gas grills. They're quick and easy to start with no charcoal required. Heat controls let you cook food more evenly and accurately. Gas is used to heat semipermanent ceramic briquettes, or lava rock, made from natural volcanic stone. Most models are fueled by refillable liquid propane (LP) gas tanks; others are directly hooked up to a natural gas line.

Starting the Fire

CHARCOAL GRILLS

For greatest success, follow manufacturer's directions for lighting coals well before cooking. Most coals take between 30 and 45 minutes to reach proper temperature.

Arrange the desired number of charcoal briquettes in a pyramid shape in the firebox. This shape allows air to circulate, heating the briquettes faster. An electric coil starter or liquid fire starter will make starting the fire easier; follow manufacturer's directions.

In daylight, you can tell the coals are ready for grilling when they are about 80 percent ashy gray. If it's dark outside, coals should have an even red glow. Bright red coals are too hot, black coals are too cool and a mix of red and black coals gives off uneven heat.

Check the temperature of the coals by placing your hand, palm side down, near but not touching the cooking grill rack. If you can keep your hand there for two seconds (count: one thousand one, one thousand two), the temperature is high; three seconds is medium-high, four seconds is medium and five seconds is low.

GAS GRILLS

Follow manufacturer's directions, or heat 5 to 10 minutes before cooking.

The recipes in this book call for direct-heat cooking, where you cook the food directly over the heat. If you're using indirect heat for longer-cooking foods such as whole poultry and whole turkey breasts, arrange the coals around the edge of the firebox and place a drip pan under the grilling area.

SUCCESS TIPS FOR GRILLING

- Before lighting coals or turning on gas, grease or oil the rack or spray it with cooking spray.

- Place the grill rack 4 to 6 inches above the coals or gas burners.

- For even cooking, place thicker foods in the center of the grill rack and smaller pieces on the edges; turn pieces frequently.

- Keep the heat as even as possible throughout the grilling period.

- If you're not getting a sizzle, the fire may be too cool. Regulate the heat by spreading the coals or raking them together, opening or closing the vents or adjusting the control on a gas or electric grill. Raising or lowering the cooking grill or covering it will also help control the heat.

- Use long-handled barbecue tools to allow for a safe distance between you and the intense heat of the grill.

SETTING THE TABLE AND SERVING THE MEAL

How the dinner table looks and how you present the food are part of the overall dining experience. But setting the table with multiple pieces of flatware and glassware can be baffling. You can do it easily with the suggestions that follow.

● Place the flatware 1 inch from the edge of the table, arranging the pieces used first the farthest from the plate, so you can use the flatware from the outside toward the plate. The forks are typically to the left, and the knife (with the blade toward the plate), then the spoons, to the right.

● If a butter plate is used, place it above the forks.

● If salad is to be served with the main course, place the salad plate to the left of the forks. The salad fork may be placed at either side of the dinner fork.

● Arrange glasses above the knife. The water glass is usually at the tip of the knife, with beverage and wine glasses to the right of the water glass.

● If coffee or tea is served at the table, place the cup slightly above and to the right of the spoons.

● Place the napkin either in the center of the dinner plate or to the left of the forks at each place setting. There are many creative ways of folding napkins to make any meal festive.

● Before offering dessert, clear the table of all serving dishes, plates, salt and pepper shakers and any flatware that won't be used for the dessert course.

SERVING BUFFET STYLE

Buffet service is a convenient way for you to serve small or large groups. It works well for both casual and formal occasions. If you have limited seated or serving space, a buffet makes entertaining much easier. When the meal is served from a buffet, guests select food, beverage and flatware from the buffet table, then move to sit wherever they're comfortable. It's important to serve foods that do not need to be cut with a knife, because your guests will usually have to balance plates on their laps. Serve rolls or bread already buttered, and provide small tables on which your guests can place their beverages. You can go around to guests with any accompaniments such as sauce, gravy or salsa.

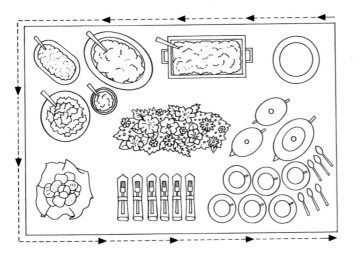

You can set up the buffet wherever it's most convenient—on the dining-room table, a picnic table, two card tables placed together, a kitchen counter or a desk.

The key to success is to create a buffet table setting so the traffic flows smoothly and easily. Place the buffet table in the center of the room, so guests can help themselves from all sides of the table. Or push it against a wall to save space.

Place the food in order so guests can serve themselves without backtracking. Plates first, main course and vegetables next, then salad, condiments, bread and flatware and napkins last. Placing flatware and napkins at the end of the line allows guests to have a hand free to serve themselves.

While guests finish the main course, you can clear the buffet table and arrange the dessert, dessert plates and flatware on the buffet table or on a side table.

CLASSY CENTERPIECES IN MINUTES

Centerpieces needn't be expensive or time-consuming to make. One of these easy ideas is sure to be a hit at your next dinner.

• Pile an assortment of lemons and limes in a rustic wooden bowl or basket. Accent with feathery greens from the florist, or tuck a trailing ivy plant among the fruit.

• Wrap the pot of your healthiest houseplant with a bright and colorful paper napkin or scarf, and hold the napkin in place with a raffia bow.

• Fill a favorite basket with a collection of fresh and aromatic garden herbs. The herbs can be potted or cut fresh and placed in small bottles or juice glasses filled with water.

• Fill a glass bowl with bright red apples and green pears. Tie yarn or a narrow ribbon around the stem of each piece of fruit.

• Arrange an assortment of fruits and vegetables in a large basket. Be creative with grapes, broccoli, savoy cabbage, radicchio, carrots with the green tops left on, oranges, miniature pumpkins, squash and leaf lettuce.

STOCKING THE PANTRY

You can prepare quick meals or make an easy snack or dessert without planning ahead if you keep the essential ingredients on hand in your kitchen. Check the lists below for the foods you like to serve, and add them to your cupboard, refrigerator or freezer. Then keep a running shopping list, and add items as your supply runs low. See our food-storage guide (pages 243–245) for information on how long you can plan to store some of these items.

Cupboard

Breads (buns, loaves, pitas, tortillas)
Canned
    Beans (black, kidney, navy)
    Broth (beef, chicken, vegetable)
    Meats (chicken, salmon, tuna)
    Tomatoes (diced or peeled whole)
Cereals
Coffee and tea
Cookies and crackers
Herbs and spices (see page 226)
Jams and jellies
Ketchup
Main-dish mixes
Mayonnaise
Mustard
Olives
Pasta (fettuccine, macaroni, spaghetti)
Pasta sauces (Alfredo, pesto, spaghetti)
Peanut butter
Pickles
Rice and rice mixtures
Salsa
Salt and pepper
Soft drinks
Soups (canned or dried)
Soy sauce and marinating sauces
Syrups (butterscotch, chocolate, maple)
Tomato sauce and tomato paste
Vegetable oil
Vinegar

Refrigerator

Cheeses (Cheddar, cottage, Parmesan)
Eggs
Fruit juice
Margarine or butter
Milk
Packaged salad greens
Sour cream
Yogurt

Freezer

Chicken (skinless, boneless breasts)
Fruit juice concentrate
Ground beef or turkey
Ice cream or frozen yogurt
Vegetables (packaged)

Baking

Baking cocoa
Baking mix (Bisquick®)
Baking powder and baking soda
Brownie mix
Cake mix and canned frosting
Flour
Sugars (brown, granulated, powdered)
Vanilla and almond extract

Nonfood Supplies

All-purpose spray cleanser
Aluminum foil
Dishwasher detergent
Food-storage bags
Liquid detergent
Napkins
Nonabrasive scrubbing pads
Paper towels
Plastic wrap
Sponges
Storage containers
Toothpicks
Waxed paper

THREE WAYS TO KEEP FOODS SAFE

Keeping the food you buy safe to eat is very easy and involves just three things: keep everything in the kitchen clean, keep hot foods hot and keep cold foods cold. Occasionally, a food will look or smell bad and should obviously be thrown away. Some foods, though, may look, smell and taste good but actually be harmful. If in doubt, don't taste it; just throw it out.

1 Keep everything in the kitchen clean

- Use hard plastic cutting boards for raw meat, poultry and fish. They are less porous than wooden cutting boards and can be cleaned easily with hot soapy water or washed in the dishwasher. Wash the board, as well as your knives, before using it for cutting any other foods.

- After using a plate for raw meat, poultry or fish, do not serve the cooked meat on the same unwashed plate. Either wash it in hot soapy water or use a clean plate for serving the cooked food.

- After working with raw foods, especially meat, poultry and fish, use disposable paper towels to wipe any spills from the counter. Then, wipe again with hot, soapy water.

- Always keep countertops, appliances, utensils and dishes clean. Remember to occasionally wipe all the special drawers or bins in the refrigerator for clean, safe food storage.

- Wash hands thoroughly before preparing food, and cover any cuts or infection with a bandage or wear rubber gloves.

- Keep kitchen towels and sponges clean.

2 Keep hot foods hot

- Hot foods can remain lukewarm or at room temperature for only two hours or less before they become unsafe to eat. Foods spoil easily and rapidly at lukewarm temperatures. If they need to stand out longer, be sure they are kept hot in an electric skillet or a chafing dish or on a hot tray. Warming units heated with a candle will not keep them hot enough to be safe.

- Lower temperatures can cause the meat to spoil before cooking is complete.

- Once food has been cooked, keep it hot until serving, or refrigerate it as soon as possible.

3 Keep cold foods cold

- Cold foods can remain lukewarm or at room temperature for only two hours or less before they become unsafe to eat. Foods spoil easily and rapidly at lukewarm temperatures.

- When shopping, purchase cold foods such as meats and dairy products last so they will stay cold until you can refrigerate them when you get home. Try to refrigerate them within 30 minutes after purchasing. Even short stops during hot weather can cause perishable groceries in a hot car to reach unsafe temperatures.

- When shopping, wrap foods from the meat department in plastic bags to prevent meat juices from dripping onto other foods in your shopping cart. These bags usually are available near the meat counter.

- Frozen foods should not be thawed at room temperature. Thaw them in the refrigerator or the microwave. If foods are thawed in the microwave, finish cooking them immediately because some cooking may have started during the thawing process.

FOOD SAFETY TIPS

1 CANNED FOODS: Do not buy or use food in a can that is leaking, bulging or dented. Jars of food should not have cracks or loose or bulging lids.

2 UNCOOKED EGGS:

• Store in refrigerator in the carton for as long as the date on the carton indicates.

• "Do-ahead" recipes that contain raw eggs should be refrigerated only 24 hours or less before they are baked.

• Do not eat cookie dough or cake batter containing raw eggs.

• Do not use uncooked eggs in recipes that will not be baked, such as Caesar salad, frostings or desserts unless you purchase eggs marked pasteurized or use egg substitutes.

3 FRUITS AND VEGETABLES: Wash with cool water, using a vegetable brush if necessary.

4 GROUND BEEF: Ground meats should be cooked at least until they are brownish pink in the center. Cooking them until well done is even safer. Any contamination that may have been on the outside of a piece of meat becomes mixed into the meat as it is ground up.

5 HAM: Most hams are already fully cooked and need only to be reheated. But check the label to be sure it does not need to be cooked. If you are uncertain, cook it until a meat thermometer reaches 165°.

6 MARINADES: Place foods to be marinated in a heavy plastic food-storage bag or non-metal utensil. Always refrigerate when marinating; do not leave at room temperature.

Discard leftover marinade or sauces that touched raw meat, fish or poultry, or heat the marinade or sauce to a full boil and boil for 1 minute before serving.

7 POULTRY: Cook all poultry until the juices are no longer pink when you cut into the centers of thickest pieces.

STORING FOODS

Many foods are labeled with a "sell by," "use by" or expiration date that will tell you how long they can be stored either in your cupboard at room temperature or in the refrigerator. This is helpful information you should check before purchasing to make sure all foods are fresh. Foods stored at room temperature should be kept in a cool, dry place to prolong their freshness. Avoid cupboards in areas over the stove or microwave, near the dishwasher or above the refrigerator because they tend to be warm.

The temperature in your refrigerator should be between 34° and 40°, and your freezer should be at 0° or below. Having a refrigerator thermometer and a freezer thermometer is helpful, so you know that your foods are being properly chilled or frozen. Allow space between foods when you place them in the refrigerator and freezer, so air can circulate and chill or freeze the food more quickly.

Refrigerated foods stay colder near the back of the refrigerator rather than in the door. Wrap foods that will be frozen tightly in aluminum foil or plastic food-storage bags. The storage times shown here are just a guide because the conditions under which foods are stored will affect the quality.

ROOM TEMPERATURE STORAGE

Foods		Length of Time	Storage Tips
Bread crumbs, dry		6 months	After opening, close tightly.
Breads and rolls		5 to 7 days	Store in tightly closed original package; refrigerate in hot humid weather.
Canned foods		1 year	Date the cans; use oldest first.
Cereals	Ready-to-cook	4 to 6 months	
	Ready-to-eat	Check package label	Refold inner lining after opening to keep crisp.
Chocolate syrup		Use within 2 years*	Refrigerate after opening.
Cookies, packaged and unopened		2 months	After opening, close tightly.
Crackers		8 months	After opening, close tightly.
Dressings, bottled		Check date on bottle.	Refrigerate after opening.
Flour	All-purpose	15 months	Store in airtight container; may be refrigerated or frozen. Bring to room temperature before using.
	Whole wheat	6 to 8 months	Same as for all-purpose flour.
Honey		1 year	
Jams and Jellies		1 year*	Refrigerate after opening.
Main-dish mixes		1 year	
Olives		Use within 1 year*	Refrigerate after opening.
Pasta, dried		1 year	Store in original packaging or in airtight glass or plastic containers.
Peanut butter	Unopened	Use within 9 months*	
	Opened	2 to 3 months	
Pickles		Use within 1 year*	Refrigerate after opening.
Rice	Brown or wild	6 months	Use seasoned mixes within 6 months.
	White	1 year	
Sugar	Brown or powdered	4 months	Store airtight.
	White (granulated)	2 years	
Syrups		1 year	Store in cool, dark place.
Vegetable oil	Unopened	Use within 6 months*	Store in cool, dark place.
	Opened	1 to 3 months	

This is total storage time, including the time after it has been opened.

Refrigerator and Freezer Storage

Foods	Refrigerator (34° to 40°)	Freezer (0° or below)
Breads, coffee cakes, muffins	5 to 7 days	2 to 3 months
Butter	Up to 2 weeks, if opened	Up to 2 months
Cakes	3 to 5 days	3 to 4 months unfrosted, 2 to 3 months, frosted
Cheesecakes, baked	3 to 5 days	4 to 5 months
Chocolate syrup	3 months, after opening	
Dairy foods (milk, yogurt, cheese)	Check package labels	
Eggs Raw and in the shell Cooked	3 weeks 1 week	Not recommended Not recommended
Ice cream, sorbet and frozen yogurt	Freeze only	2 to 4 months
Jams and jellies	1 year	
Margarine or spread	Up to 1 month, if opened	Up to 2 months
Meats, cooked, including meats purchased at the deli	3 to 5 days	2 to 3 months
Meats, processed Cold cuts	Check date on package, 3 to 5 days after opening	Not recommended
Cured bacon Hot dogs	5 to 7 days after opening Check date on package, 2 weeks after opening	Up to 1 month 1 to 2 months
Ham, canned, unopened	Check date on can	Not recommended
Ham, whole or half, cooked	5 to 7 days	1 to 2 months
Ham, slices fully cooked,	3 to 4 days	1 to 2 months

Foods		Refrigerator (34° to 40°)	Freezer (0° or below)
Meats, uncooked	Chops	3 to 5 days	4 to 6 months
	Ground	·1 to 2 days	3 to 4 months
	Roasts and steaks	3 to 5 days	6 to 12 months
Olives		2 months after opening	
Pasta, fresh		Check date on package	9 months, unopened; 3 months if opened
Pickles		2 months after opening	
Poultry	Cooked, including poultry purchased at the deli	3 to 4 days	4 months
	Uncooked, cut up	1 to 2 days	Up to 9 months
	Uncooked, whole (including game birds, ducks and geese)	1 to 2 days	Up to 12 months
Seafood	Fish, uncooked	1 to 2 days	2 to 3 months
	Shellfish, cooked	3 to 4 days	1 to 2 months
	Shellfish, uncooked	1 to 2 days	3 to 4 months

YIELDS AND EQUIVALENTS

Knowing how many apples or carrots you may need for a recipe can be difficult, so here's a guide of common ingredients to help you when shopping for groceries and preparing recipes.

Food		If Your Recipe States	You Will Need Approximately
Apples		1 cup chopped	1 medium
		1 medium apple, thinly sliced	1 1/3 cups
Asparagus		16 to 20 stalks	1 pound
Bacon		1/2 cup crumbled	8 slices, crisply cooked
Beans, dried	Black, kidney, lima, pinto, red	5 to 6 cups cooked	1 pound dried (2 1/4 cups)
	Green or wax	3 cups 1-inch pieces	1 pound
Bread, white		12 slices (1/2 inch)	1-pound loaf
		1 cup soft crumbs	1 1/2 slices
		1 cup dry crumbs	4 to 5 slices, oven-dried
Broccoli		1 bunch	1 1/2 pounds
		2 cups flowerets, 1-inch pieces or chopped	6 ounces
Cabbage	Green	1 medium head	1 1/2 pounds
		4 cups shredded	1 pound
	Slaw (bag)	7 cups	16 ounces
Carrots		1 medium	7 inches
		1 cup shredded	1 1/2 medium
		1 cup 1/4-inch slices	2 medium
Cauliflower		1 medium head	2 pounds (with leaves)
		3 cups flowerets	1 pound
Celery		1 medium bunch	2 pounds (11 inches)
		1 cup thinly sliced or chopped	2 medium stalks

Food		If Your Recipe States	You Will Need Approximately
Cheese	Hard (blue, Cheddar, feta, mozzarella, Swiss), shredded or crumbled	1 cup	4 ounces
	Cottage	2 cups	16 ounces
	Cream	1 cup	8 ounces
Chocolate	Chips	1 cup	6 ounces
	Unsweetened or semisweet baking	1 square or bar	1 ounce
Corn, sweet		1 medium ear	8 ounces
		1 cup kernels	2 medium ears
Cream	Sour	1 cup	8 ounces
	Whipping (heavy)	1 cup (2 cups whipped)	1/2 pint
Crumbs, finely crushed			
	Chocolate wafer cookie	1 1/2 cups	27 cookies
	Graham cracker	1 1/2 cups	21 squares
	Saltine cracker	1 cup	29 squares
	Vanilla wafer cookie	1 1/2 cups	38 cookies
Eggs, large	Whole	1 cup	4 large eggs
		1 egg	1/4 cup fat-free cholesterol-free egg product
Flour		3 1/2 cups	1 pound
Garlic		1/2 teaspoon finely chopped	1 medium clove
Jalapeño chili		1 tablespoon	1 medium, seeded and chopped
Lemon or lime		1 1/2 to 3 teaspoons grated peel	1 medium
		2 to 3 tablespoons juice	1 medium
Lettuce	Iceberg or romaine	1 medium head	1 1/2 pounds
		2 cups shredded	5 ounces
		6 cups bite-size pieces	1 pound

(CONTINUED)

Food	If Your Recipe States	You Will Need Approximately
Margarine, butter or spread	2 cups 1/2 cup	1 pound 1 stick
Marshmallows	1 large	10 miniature
Meat, cooked Beef, pork and poultry	bite-size pieces	1 cup chopped or 6 ounces
Mushrooms Fresh Canned	6 cups sliced 2 1/2 cups chopped 4-ounce can sliced, drained	1 pound 8 ounces 2/3 cup fresh, sliced and cooked (5 ounces uncooked)

Nuts (without shells)
  Chopped, sliced or
    slivered
  Whole or halves
	
	1 cup
	3 to 4 cups
		
		4 ounces
		1 pound

Olives Pimiento-stuffed Ripe, pitted	1 cup sliced 1 cup sliced	24 large or 36 small 32 medium
Onions Green, with tops Yellow or white	1 medium 2 tablespoons chopped 1/4 cup sliced 1 medium 1/2 cup chopped	1/2 ounce 2 medium 3 or 4 medium 3 ounces 1 medium
Orange	1 to 2 tablespoons grated peel 1/3 to 1/2 cup juice	1 medium 1 medium

Pasta   Macaroni
    Noodles, egg
    Spaghetti
	4 cups cooked
	4 cups cooked
	4 cups cooked
		6 to 7 ounces uncooked (2 cups)
		7 ounces uncooked (4 to 5 cups)
		7 to 8 ounces uncooked

Peppers, bell	1/2 cup chopped 1 cup chopped 1 1/2 cups chopped	1 small 1 medium 1 large

Food		If Your Recipe States	You Will Need Approximately
Potatoes	New Red, white, sweet or yams Red or white	10 to 12 small 1 medium 1 cup 1/2-inch pieces	1 1/2 pounds 5 to 6 ounces 1 medium
Rice	Brown Parboiled(converted) Precooked (white) instant Regular long grain Wild	4 cups cooked 3 to 4 cups cooked 2 cups cooked 3 cups cooked 3 cups cooked	1 cup uncooked 1 cup uncooked 1 cup uncooked 1 cup uncooked 1 cup uncooked
Shrimp, uncooked, with shells	Jumbo Large Medium Small	1 pound 1 pound 1 pound 1 pound	10 to 12 count 15 to 20 count 26 to 30 count 40 to 50 count
Shrimp, cooked without shells		1 pound	1 1/3 pounds uncooked (with shells)
Sugar	Brown Granulated Powdered	2 1/4 cups packed 2 1/4 cups 4 cups	1 pound 1 pound 1 pound
Tomatoes		3/4 cup chopped (1 medium) 1 cup chopped 1/2 cup chopped	5 ounces 1 large 1 small

SUBSTITUTIONS

Using the ingredients recommended in a recipe is best. Sometimes, no practical alternatives or substitutions exist. If you must substitute, try the following:

Food		Instead of: Amount	Use
Arborio rice		1 cup uncooked	1 cup uncooked short grain white rice, regular long-grain rice or brown rice
Balsamic vinegar		1 tablespoon	1 tablespoon sherry or cider vinegar
Bread crumbs, dry		1/4 cup	1/4 cup finely crushed cracker crumbs, cornflakes or quick-cooking or old-fashioned oats
Broth, chicken, beef or vegetable		1 cup	1 teaspoon chicken, beef or vegetable bouillon granules (or 1 cube) dissolved in 1 cup boiling water
Buttermilk or sour milk		1 cup	1 tablespoon lemon juice or white vinegar plus enough milk to measure 1 cup. Let stand a few minutes. Or use 1 cup plain yogurt.
Chocolate	Semisweet baking	1 ounce	1 ounce unsweetened baking Chocolate plus 1 tablespoon sugar
	Semisweet chips	1 cup	6 ounces semisweet baking chocolate, chopped
	Unsweetened baking	1 ounce	3 tablespoons baking cocoa plus 1 tablespoon shortening or margarine
Cornstarch		1 tablespoon	2 tablespoons all-purpose flour
Eggs		1 large	2 egg whites or 1/4 cup fat-free cholesterol-free egg product
Flour	All-purpose	1 cup	1 cup plus 2 tablespoons cake flour
	Cake	1 cup	1 cup minus 2 tablespoons all-purpose flour
Garlic, finely chopped		1 medium clove	1/8 teaspoon garlic powder or 1/4 teaspoon instant minced garlic
Gingerroot, grated or finely chopped		1 teaspoon	3/4 teaspoon ground ginger

Food	Instead of: Amount	Use
Herbs, chopped fresh	1 tablespoon	3/4 to 1 teaspoon dried herbs
Honey	1 cup	1 1/4 cups sugar plus 1/4 cup water or apple juice
Lemon juice, fresh	1 tablespoon	1 tablespoon bottled lemon juice or white vinegar
Lemon peel, grated	1 teaspoon	1 teaspoon dried lemon peel
Mushrooms, fresh	2/3 cup sliced and cooked	1 can (4 ounces) mushroom stems and pieces, drained
Mustard	1 tablespoon	1 teaspoon ground mustard (dry)
Orange peel, grated	1 teaspoon	1 teaspoon dried orange peel
Raisins	1/2 cup	1/2 cup currants, dried cherries, dried cranberries or chopped dates
Red pepper sauce	3 or 4 drops	1/8 teaspoon ground red pepper (cayenne)
Sugar Brown, packed	1 cup	1 cup granulated sugar plus 2 tablespoons molasses or dark corn syrup
White, granulated	1 cup	1 cup light brown sugar (packed) or 2 cups powdered sugar
Tomato paste	1/2 cup	1 cup tomato sauce cooked uncovered until reduced to 1/2 cup
Tomato sauce	2 cups	3/4 cup tomato paste plus 1 cup water
Tomatoes, canned	1 cup	About 1 1/3 cups cut-up fresh tomatoes, simmered 10 minutes
Whipping cream, whipped	1 cup	1 cup frozen (thawed) whipped topping or prepared whipped topping mix
Wine Red	1 cup	1 cup apple cider or beef broth
White	1 cup	1 cup apple juice, apple cider or chicken broth
Yogurt, plain	1 cup	1 cup sour cream

GLOSSARY OF INGREDIENTS

Using the right ingredient helps you to be successful when you cook. This glossary lists the ingredients used in this cookbook, as well as other ingredients you might find in your supermarket.

BAKING POWDER: Leavening mixture made from baking soda, an acid and a moisture absorber. Double-acting baking powder forms carbon dioxide twice: once when mixed with moist ingredients and once during baking. Do not substitute baking powder for baking soda because acid proportions in the recipe may be unbalanced.

BAKING SODA: Leavening known as bicarbonate of soda. Must be mixed with an acid ingredient (such as lemon juice, buttermilk or molasses) to release carbon dioxide gas bubbles.

BALSAMIC VINEGAR: Italian vinegar that has been aged in barrels, resulting in darker color and sweeter flavor. May contain sulfites, which can cause allergic reactions.

BISQUICK® ORIGINAL BAKING MIX: A convenience baking mix made from flour, shortening, baking powder and salt. Used for biscuits, muffins, other quick breads, cakes, cookies and some main dishes.

BOUILLON/BROTH/STOCK: Strained liquid made from cooking vegetables, meat, poultry or fish. Used for making soups and sauces. Beef, chicken and vegetable broths are available canned; dehydrated bouillon is available in granules or cubes.

CAPERS: Unopened flower buds of a Mediterranean plant that are usually pickled in vinegar brine. Used to flavor salad dressings, sauces and condiments.

CHILIES: A family of more than 200 varieties, chilies are used in cooking around the world. Available fresh and dried in red, green, yellow and purple. Length ranges from 1/4 inch to 12 inches. The seeds of chilies are hotter than the flesh. Chilies contain oils that can irritate. To avoid transferring these oils to your eyes or skin, wash hands thoroughly after seeding or wear rubber gloves when handling.

- **Anaheim chilies:** Slim and various shades of green, between 5 and 8 inches long, mildly hot. They are occasionally stuffed and can be purchased in cans as "mild green chilies."

- **Ancho chilies:** Are dried ripened poblano chilies.

- **Cascabel chilies:** Hot, with a distinctive flavor. Round, 1 1/2 inches in diameter.

- **Chipotle chilies:** Smoked, dried jalapeño chilies. Can be purchased loose (dry) or canned in adobo sauce. Often used in sauces.

- **Jalapeño chilies:** Very hot, jade green or red chilies, 2 to 3 inches long. Smallest ones are the hottest. Favorite for nachos, salsas and other sauces. Available fresh and pickled.

- **Poblano chilies:** Chilies most frequently used for *chiles rellenos*. Dark green; range from mild to hot.

- **Serrano chilies:** Short, thin chilies that start out green then develop to brilliant red when ripe. Among the hottest of chilies.

CHEESE: There are four categories of identification for all cheeses: natural cheese, pasteurized process cheese, cheese food and pasteurized cheese spread.

- **Natural cheese:** Made from the milk or cream of cows, sheep or goats that has been solidified by the process of curdling and the liquid (whey) removed. These cheeses range from soft to hard and from mild to sharp flavor. They may or may not be aged or ripened. Examples of soft cheeses are Boursin, Brie, cottage cheese, cream cheese and ricotta. Semisoft varieties are Colby, feta, Monterey Jack and mozzarella. Examples of hard cheeses are Cheddar, Edam, Swiss and Gruyère. Very hard cheeses, such as Parmesan and Romano, tend to be sharp in flavor; hard and semisoft cheeses range from sharp to mild. Many soft cheeses, such as Brie and Camembert vary from mild to pungent.

- **Cheese food:** Cheese made from one or more varieties of natural cheese that are blended, then combined with cream, milk, skim milk or whey. This results in a higher moisture content than in other cheeses. Cheese food usually is sold in tubs or jars and is sometimes flavored.

- **Pasteurized cheese spread:** This cheese is similar to pasteurized process cheese except it is easily spreadable at room temperature. Cheeses in aerosol cans are examples of pasteurized cheese spread.

- **Pasteurized process cheese:** Usually a blend of one or more varieties of natural cheese that are ground, blended and heated. This process stops the aging, or ripening, of the cheese. The very popular American cheese is a good example of this type of cheese.

CHOCOLATE: Made from cocoa beans that are shelled, roasted, ground and liquefied. Chocolate liquor is the product of cocoa beans that have been shelled, roasted and ground; hardened chocolate liquor becomes unsweetened baking chocolate. Cocoa butter is the fat or oil of the cocoa bean. Chocolate is processed in various ways:

- **Baking cocoa:** Dried chocolate liquor (cocoa butter removed) is ground into unsweetened cocoa. Does not substitute directly for cocoa drink mixes, which contain added milk powder and sugar.

- **Semisweet, bittersweet, sweet and milk chocolates:** Contain from 10 to 35 percent chocolate liquor, varying amounts of cocoa butter, sugar and, for some, milk and flavorings. Available in bars and chips; use for baking or eating. Quality varies, so follow package directions when melting.

- **"White" chocolate:** Not a true chocolate. Contains some cocoa butter but no cocoa or chocolate liquor. Often called vanilla milk chips or vanilla baking bar.

COCONUT: From the meat of the coconut fruit. Available shredded or flaked, either sweetened or unsweetened, in cans or plastic bags.

CONDIMENT: Term for an accompaniment to food. Examples are ketchup, mustard, salsa and relish.

CORN SYRUP: Clear, thick liquid (dark and light are interchangeable in recipes) made from corn sugar mixed with acid. It's one sweetener that doesn't crystallize and is especially good for pecan pie, frostings, fruit sauces and jams.

CORNSTARCH: A thickener for soups, sauces and desserts that comes from a portion of the corn kernel. This finely ground flour keeps sauces clear, not opaque as are sauces thickened with wheat flour. To substitute for all-purpose flour, use half as much cornstarch.

CREAM: Smooth, rich product made by separating butterfat from the liquid in whole milk. Pasteurized and processed into several forms:

- **Half-and-half:** Milk and cream are mixed; contains 10 to 12 percent butterfat. It won't whip, but it can be used in place of whipping (heavy) cream in many recipes.

- **Sour cream:** Commercially cultured with lactic acid to give a tangy flavor. Regular sour cream is 18 to 20 percent butterfat. Reduced-fat sour cream is made from half-and-half and can be substituted for regular sour cream in most recipes. Fat-free sour cream has all the fat removed and may not be successful in all recipes that call for regular sour cream.

- **Whipping (heavy) cream:** The richest cream available in the United States, it has 36 to 40 percent butterfat. It doubles in volume when whipped.

CREAM OF TARTAR: After wine is made, the acid left in wine barrels is processed into cream of tartar. When cream of tartar is added to egg whites in beginning beating stages, the egg whites are more stable and have more volume. Also contributes to creamier frostings and candy.

CRÈME FRAÎCHE: Very thick cream often served with soup, fresh fruit and cobblers. Unlike sour cream, it does not curdle when heated.

CRUDITÉS: Fresh, raw vegetables, usually served with a dip.

EGGS: For preparation, see page 132; for food safety, see page 242.

FATS AND OILS: In cooking, fats and oils add richness and flavor to food, aid in browning, help bind ingredients together, tenderize baked goods and are used for frying. But not all fats are created equal in texture and flavor. In our recipes, ingredient listings for fats vary because of their cooking and baking characteristics. See specific examples that follow.

● **Butter:** A saturated fat made from cream that must be at least 80 percent butterfat by USDA standards. It is high in flavor and has a melt-in-your-mouth texture. Butter is sold in sticks, whipped in tubs and as butter-flavored granules. For baking, use only the sticks; whipped butter will give a different texture because of the air beaten into it.

● **Margarine:** An unsaturated butter substitute made with no less than 80 percent fat (most use vegetable oils made from soybeans, cottonseed and corn) by weight and flavoring from dairy products. Textures and flavors vary. Use as a table spread and for cooking and baking. Sold in sticks and as soft spreads in tubs.

● **Oils for cooking:** Low in saturated fats and containing no cholesterol, these liquid fats are delicate to blend in flavor and are treated to withstand high-temperature cooking and long storage. In our recipes, they are listed as follows:

● **Cooking spray:** Used to spray cookware and bakeware before using to prevent food from sticking during cooking and baking. Sometimes used directly on foods in low-fat cooking.

● **Olive oil:** Pressed from pitted ripe (black) olives. Olive oil is graded based on its acidity. The lower the acidity, the stronger the olive flavor. Cold-pressed (processed without heat) oil is called extra virgin and is the result of the first pressing of the olives. For the second olive pressing, solvents are used, and this yields "virgin olive oil." Successive pressings yield less-delicate oils. Use olive oil for marinades, salad dressings and cooking.

● **Vegetable oil:** An economical blend of oils from various vegetables, such as corn, cottonseed, peanut, safflower and soybean. Use for all cooking and baking.

● **Reduced-calorie or low-fat butter or margarine:** These products have water and air added and contain at least 20 percent less fat than regular butter or margarine. Do not use for baking.

● **Shortening:** Vegetable oils that are hydrogenated to change them from liquid to solid at room temperature. Shortening is used especially for flaky, tender pastry and to grease baking pans. Sold in cans and in stick form.

● **Vegetable-Oil Spreads:** Margarine products with less than 80 percent fat (vegetable oil) by weight usually are labeled as vegetable-oil spreads. These products, like margarine, can be used for a variety of purposes, from spreading to cooking to baking. Vegetable-oil spreads are sold in sticks (for all-purpose use, including some baking if more than 65 percent fat), in tubs (to use as a table spread—do not use for baking) and as liquid squeeze spreads (to use for topping vegetables and popcorn or for basting—do not use for baking).

FLOUR: The primary ingredient in breads, cakes, cookies and quick breads.

● **All-purpose flour:** Selected wheats blended to be used for all kinds of baking. Available both bleached and unbleached.

● **Bread flour:** Wheats higher in gluten-forming protein, which gives more structure to bread, than all-purpose flour. For other bakings, bread flour can make some recipes too tough.

● **Cake flour:** Milled from soft wheats. Cake flour results in tender, fine-textured cakes.

● **Self-rising flour:** A convenience flour made from a blend of hard and soft wheats that includes leavening and salt. For best results, don't substitute self-rising flour for other kinds of flour, unless directed in a recipe, because leavening and salt proportions won't be accurate.

● **Whole wheat flour:** Ground from the complete wheat kernel, whole wheat flour gives a nutty flavor and dense texture to breads and other baked goods. Baked goods made with whole wheat flour rise less than those made with all-purpose flour.

GELATIN: An odorless and colorless powder; its thickening power is released when it is mixed with hot liquid. Gelatin is pure protein, processed from beef and veal bones and cartilage or pig skin. Available flavored and sweetened.

GINGERROOT: Plump tubers with knobby branches. Side branches have a milder tangy ginger flavor than the main root. Grate unpeeled gingerroot, or peel and chop or slice it, to add flavor to foods such as stir-fries, sauces and baked goods.

HERBS: Available fresh and dried. Before using fresh herbs, chop them finely. Crumble dried herb leaves between fingers before using. (See also "Twelve Terrific Herbs" and "Top Five Spices," pages 226–227.)

LEGUMES: A term for beans, peas and lentils, which are the nutritious seeds of leguminous plants. They can be purchased dried, canned or frozen. Legumes are rich with soluble fiber and are virtually fat-free. Legumes are a staple part of the diet all around the world.

Top: great northern beans, kidney beans, black beans, baby lima beans

Middle: navy beans, pinto beans, lima beans

Bottom: yellow split peas, green split beans, garbanzo beans

LEAVENING: Ingredients that cause baked goods to rise and develop lighter textures. (*See also* Baking Powder, Baking Soda, Yeast.)

MAYONNAISE: Smooth, rich mixture made from egg yolks, vinegar and seasonings. Beaten to make a permanent emulsion that retains its creamy texture through storage. Available in jars. The product "salad dressing" is similarly prepared but is lower in fat because it's made with a starch thickener, vinegar, eggs and sweetener.

MERINGUE: A soft topping for desserts such as pies or a hardened baked shell for fruit.

- A mixture of stiffly beaten egg whites and sugar spread over pie or other desserts and baked at high temperature until lightly browned.

- Egg white and sugar mixture spooned onto cookie sheet and baked several hours at low temperature until dry and set. Can be used as individual shells or as single large shell to hold fruit, ice cream or pudding.

MILK: Refers to cow's milk throughout this cookbook.

- **Buttermilk:** Thick, smooth liquid that results when skim or part-skim milk is cultured with lactic acid bacteria. Used in baking for tangy flavor.

- **Evaporated milk:** Whole milk with more than half the water removed before mixture is homogenized. Mixture is slightly thicker than whole milk. Use in recipes calling for evaporated milk, or mix with equal amount of water to substitute for whole milk in recipes.

- **Low-fat milk:** Milk with 0.5 to 2 percent of milk fat removed.

- **Skim milk:** Contains less than 0.5 percent fat.

- **Sweetened condensed milk:** Made when about half of the water is removed from whole milk and sweetener is added. Use for such desserts as Creamy Lemon Dessert (page 216).

- **Whole milk:** Contains at least 3.25 percent butterfat.

MOCHA: A hot drink combining coffee and chocolate. Also used to describe coffee/chocolate combination in food.

MUSHROOMS: Available fresh, canned or dried. To prepare fresh mushrooms, cut thin slice from bottom end of stem if necessary. Rinse carefully in cool water just before using. Blot dry with towel.

MUSTARD: From plants grown for sharp-tasting seeds and calcium-rich leaves (mustard greens). Use to add pungent flavor to foods.

- **Ground mustard:** Dried mustard seed that has been finely ground.

- **Mustard:** Yellow mustard (also called American mustard) is prepared from mild white mustard seeds and mixed with sugar, vinegar and seasonings. Dijon mustard, originating in Dijon, France, is prepared from brown mustard seeds mixed with wine, unfermented grape juice and seasonings. Many other flavors of mustards are available.

● **Mustard seed:** Whole seeds used for pickling and to season savory dishes.

ORGANIC: Term used for food or drink that has been produced or grown without chemicals such as fertilizers, additives or pesticides and that has been grown according to federal organic standards.

PASTA: See page 228.

PEPPERCORNS: The spice berry that is ground to produce black and white peppers. Available as whole berries to use in soups and main dishes. Green peppercorns are underripe berries that are packed in brine; they are available in bottles and cans.

PESTO: A sauce traditionally made from fresh basil, pine nuts, Parmesan cheese and garlic. The mixture can be ground or blended until smooth. Most often served with pasta.

PHYLLO (FILO): Paper-thin pastry sheets whose name comes from the Greek word for "leaf"; is the basis of many Greek and Middle Eastern main dishes and sweets. Available frozen or refrigerated. Sheets dry out quickly, so when working with phyllo, cover unused sheets with waxed paper and a damp kitchen towel.

PILAF: Near Eastern dish made by browning rice or bulgur in butter or oil, then cooking in broth or water. Chopped vegetables, meat or poultry can be stirred into cooked mixture.

PINE NUTS: Small white nuts from several varieties of pine trees. Often used in Mediterranean and Mexican dishes. These nuts turn rancid quickly, so refrigerate or freeze to slow the rancidity process.

PUFF PASTRY: Dozens of layers of chilled butter rolled between sheets of pastry dough. Is the basis of croissants, puff pastry shells for creamed poultry or seafood and such desserts as Napoleons and fruit pastries.

RED PEPPER SAUCE: Condiment made from hot chili peppers and cured in either salt or vinegar brine. Many varieties and levels of hotness are available.

RICE: Grain that is a staple in cuisines around the world.

Top: Short grain rice, medium grain rice, long grain rice
Middle: Instant (precooked), parboiled (converted)
Bottom: Brown rice, wild rice

ROASTED BELL PEPPERS: Sweet red or other color bell peppers that have been roasted and packed in jars. Use for appetizers, soups and main dishes.

ROUX: Mixture of flour and fat used to thicken soups, sauces and gravy.

SALAD DRESSING: *See* Mayonnaise.

SALSA: Mexican sauce of tomatoes, onions, green chilies and cilantro. Available fresh, canned and bottled. Green salsa, or "salsa verde," is made with tomatillos.

SCALLION: A vegetable with a white base and green top that's a member of the onion family. Green onions and scallions are used interchangeably in cooking.

SHALLOT: An onion with multiple cloves that looks like garlic. The papery skin that covers the bulbs ranges in color from beige to purple and should be removed before using the shallot. Shallots and onions are used interchangeably.

SOUFFLÉ: A mixture of beaten egg whites and flavored sauce that expands during baking to produce a puffy, light dish. Soufflés can be savory with cheese, seafood or vegetables or sweet with chocolate or lemon flavor. There are also chilled or frozen dessert soufflés.

SOY SAUCE: Chinese and Japanese specialty. A brown sauce made from soybeans, wheat, yeast and salt used for main dishes and vegetables and as a condiment.

SUGAR: Sweetener that may come from sugar beets or cane sugar. Available in several forms:

● **Artificial sweeteners:** A variety of products are available. Best if used in nonbaked items because flavor of some sweeteners may break down during baking.

● **Brown (packed):** Either is produced after refined white sugar is removed from beets or cane or is the result of mixing refined molasses syrup with white sugar crystals. Dark brown sugar has a more intense flavor. If brown sugar hardens, store in a closed container with a slice of apple or a moist slice of bread.

● **Granulated:** Standard white sugar available in sizes from 1-pound boxes to 100-pound bags, as well as in cubes and 1-teaspoon packets.

● **Powdered:** Crushed granulated sugar used for frostings and for dusting pastries and cakes.

SUN-DRIED TOMATOES: Tomatoes dried for use in appetizers, sauces, main dishes and other foods. Available packed in oil or dry; rehydrate the dry form by soaking in hot water until plump, then draining before using.

TOMATILLO: A fruit that resembles a small green tomato. It is covered with a paperlike husk, which is removed before use. Tomatillos have a citrus flavor and are used in salsas and Mexican sauces.

TRUFFLE: A European fungus that is one of the world's most expensive foods. It grows near roots of trees and is hand-harvested, resulting in the high cost. Used in sauces, omelets and as an accompaniment. Available fresh, frozen, canned and in paste form. *Truffle* is also the term for a rich confection of cream, sugar and various flavorings such as chocolate, liqueur, nuts and spices; usually dipped in chocolate.

VINAIGRETTE: A dressing of oil, vinegar, salt and pepper that can be flavored with mustard and a little Worcestershire sauce.

WORCESTERSHIRE SAUCE: Common condiment made from exotic blend of ingredients: garlic, soy sauce, tamarind, onions, molasses, lime, anchovies, vinegar and other seasonings. Named for Worcester, England, where it was first bottled, but it was developed in India by the English.

YEAST: Leavening whose fermentation is the essence of yeast bread. The combination of warmth, food (sugar) and liquid causes yeast to release carbon dioxide bubbles that cause dough to rise. Always use yeast before its expiration date.

● **Bread machine yeast:** A strain of yeast that is finely granulated and works exceptionally well in bread machines.

● **Quick active dry yeast:** Dehydrated yeast that allows bread to rise in less time than regular yeast. Quick active dry yeast can be substituted directly for bread machine yeast.

● **Regular active dry yeast:** Dehydrated yeast that can be substituted directly for quick active dry yeast. When using in bread machines, you may need to increase regular yeast by 1/4 to 1/2 teaspoon, depending on the recipe.

Glossary of Cooking Terms and Techniques

Cooking has its own vocabulary, just as does any other activity. Although not all-inclusive, this glossary is a handy reference as you select recipes and begin to cook. We've included examples of foods, in some cases, to help familiarize you with the terms. For other food or cooking definitions, see "Glossary of Ingredients" (page 252), "Basics for Great Grilling" (page 234) and "Common Preparation Techniques" (page 222).

AL DENTE: Doneness description for pasta cooked until tender but firm to the bite.

BAKE: Cook in oven surrounded by dry heat. Bake uncovered for dry, crisp surfaces (breads, cakes, cookies, chicken) or covered for moistness (casseroles, chicken, vegetables).

BASTE: Spoon liquid over food (pan drippings over turkey) during cooking to keep it moist.

BATTER: An uncooked mixture of flour, eggs and liquid in combination with other ingredients; thin enough to be spooned or poured (muffins, pancakes).

BEAT: Combine ingredients vigorously with spoon, fork, wire whisk, hand beater or electric mixer until mixture is smooth and uniform.

BLANCH: Plunge food into boiling water for a brief time to preserve color, texture and nutritional value or to remove skin (vegetables, fruits, nuts).

BLEND: Combine ingredients with spoon, wire whisk or rubber scraper until mixture is very smooth and uniform. A blender or food processor also may be used.

BOIL: Heat liquid until bubbles rise continuously and break on the surface and steam is given off. For rolling boil, the bubbles form rapidly.

BREAD: Coat a food (fish, meat, vegetables) by usually first dipping into a liquid (beaten egg or milk) then into bread or cracker crumbs or cornmeal before frying or baking. *See also* Coat.

BROIL: Cook directly under or above a red-hot heating unit.

BROWN: Cook quickly over high heat, causing food surface to turn brown.

CARAMELIZE: Melt sugar slowly over low heat until it becomes a golden brown, caramel-flavored syrup. Or sprinkle granulated, powdered or brown sugar on top of a food, then place under a broiler until the sugar is melted and caramelized. Also a technique for cooking vegetables, especially onions, until golden brown.

CASSEROLE: A deep, usually round, ovenproof baking dish made of glass or ceramic with handles and a cover that's also suitable for serving. Also a mixture that usually contains meat, vegetables, a starch such as pasta or rice and a sauce; in some parts of the country is called a *hot dish*.

CHILL: Place food in the refrigerator until it becomes thoroughly cold.

CHOP: Cut into coarse or fine irregular pieces, using knife, food chopper, blender or food processor.

COAT: Cover food evenly with crumbs or sauce. *See also* Bread.

COOL: Allow hot food to stand at room temperature for a specified amount of time. Placing hot food on a wire rack will help it cool more quickly. Stirring mixture occasionally also will help it cool more quickly and evenly.

CORE: Remove the center of a fruit (apple, pear, pineapple). Cores contain small seeds (apple, pear) or have a woody texture (pineapple).

COVER: Place lid, plastic wrap or aluminum foil over a container of food.

CUT IN: Distribute solid fat in dry ingredients until particles are desired size by crisscrossing two knives, using the side of a table fork, using a wire whisk or cutting with a pastry blender in a rolling motion.

CRISP-TENDER: Doneness description of vegetables cooked until they retain some of the crisp texture of the raw food.

CRUSH: Press into very fine particles (crushing a clove of garlic, using side of chef's knife or a garlic press).

CUBE: Cut food into squares 1/2 inch or larger, using knife.

CUT UP: Cut into small irregular pieces with kitchen scissors or knife. Or cut into smaller pieces (broiler-fryer chicken).

DASH: Less than 1/8 teaspoon of an ingredient.

DEEP-FRY OR FRENCH-FRY: Cook in hot fat that's deep enough to float the food. *See also* Fry, Panfry, Sauté.

DEGLAZE: Remove excess fat from skillet after food has been panfried, add small amount of liquid (broth, water, wine) and stir to loosen browned bits of food in skillet. This mixture is used as base for sauce.

DICE: Cut food into squares smaller than 1/2 inch, using knife.

DISSOLVE: Stir a dry ingredient (flavored gelatin) into a liquid ingredient (boiling water) until the dry ingredient disappears.

DIP: Moisten or coat by plunging below the surface of a liquid, covering all sides (dipping onion ring into batter, dipping bread into egg mixture for French toast).

DOT: Drop small pieces of an ingredient (margarine, butter) randomly over food (sliced apples in an apple pie).

DOUGH: Mixture of flour and liquid in combination with other ingredients (often including a leavening) that is stiff but pliable. Dough can be dropped from a spoon (for cookies), rolled (for pie crust) or kneaded (for bread).

DRAIN: Pour off liquid by putting a food into a strainer or colander that has been set in the sink or over another container. When draining fat from meat, place strainer in disposable container to discard. When liquid is to be saved, place the strainer in a bowl or other container.

DRIZZLE: Pour topping in thin lines from a spoon or liquid measuring cup in an uneven pattern over food (glaze over cake or cookies).

DUST: Sprinkle lightly with flour, granulated sugar, powdered sugar or baking cocoa (dusting coffee cake with powdered sugar).

FLAKE: Break lightly into small pieces, using fork (cooked fish).

FLUTE: Squeeze pastry edge with fingers to make a finished, ornamental edge.

FOLD: Combine mixtures lightly while preventing loss of air. Gently spoon or pour one mixture over another mixture in a bowl. Using a rubber spatula, first cut down vertically through mixtures. Next, slide spatula across bottom of bowl and up the side, turning the bottom mixture over the top mixture. Rotate bowl one-fourth turn, and repeat this down-across-up motion. Continue mixing in this way *just* until mixtures are blended (folding beaten egg yolks into beaten egg whites for soufflé, folding liqueur into whipped cream).

FRY: Cook in hot fat over moderate or high heat. *See also* Deep-fry, Panfry, Sauté.

GARNISH: Decorate food with small amounts of other foods that have distinctive color or texture (parsley, fresh berries, carrot curls) to enhance appearance.

GLAZE: Brush, spread or drizzle an ingredient or mixture of ingredients (meat stock, heated jam, melted chocolate) on hot or cold foods to give a glossy appearance or hard finish.

GRATE: Rub a hard-textured food (chocolate, citrus peel, Parmesan cheese) against the small, rough, sharp-edged holes of a grater to reduce it to tiny particles. For citrus peel, grate only the skin, not the bitter white membrane.

GREASE: Rub the bottom and sides of a pan with shortening, using pastry brush, waxed paper or paper towel, to prevent food from sticking during baking (muffins, some casseroles). Also may use cooking spray. Margarine and butter usually contain salt and may cause hot foods to stick, so they should not be used for greasing unless specified in recipe.

GREASE AND FLOUR: After greasing a pan with shortening, sprinkle a small amount of flour over greased surface and shake the pan to distribute the flour evenly, then turn the pan upside down and tap the bottom to remove excess flour. Is done to prevent food from sticking during baking.

GRILL: See Basics for Great Grilling (page 234).

HEAT OVEN: Turn the oven control(s) to the desired temperature, allowing the oven to heat thoroughly before adding food. Heating takes about ten minutes for most ovens. Also called *preheat.*

HULL: Remove the stem and leaves, using knife or huller (strawberries).

HUSK: Remove the leaves and outer shell (corn on the cob).

JULIENNE: Cut into thin, match-like strips, using knife or food processor (fruits, vegetables, meats).

KNEAD: Work dough on a floured surface, using hands or an electric mixer with dough hooks, into a smooth, elastic mass. Kneading develops the gluten in flour and results in breads, biscuits and other baked goods with an even texture and a smooth, rounded top. Kneading by hand can take up to about 15 minutes.

MARINATE: Let food stand usually in refrigerator in a savory, usually acidic, liquid in a glass or plastic container to add flavor or to tenderize. *Marinade* is the savory liquid in which the food is marinated.

MELT: Turn a solid (chocolate, margarine) into liquid by heating.

MICROWAVE: Cook, reheat or thaw food in a microwave oven.

MINCE: Cut food into very fine pieces; smaller than chopped food.

MIX: Combine ingredients in any way that distributes them evenly.

PANFRY: Fry meat or other food starting with a cold skillet, using little or no fat and usually pouring off fat from meat as it accumulates during cooking. *See also* Deep-fry, Fry, Sauté.

PEEL: Cut off outer covering, using knife or vegetable peeler (apples, potatoes). Also, strip off outer covering, using fingers (bananas, oranges).

POACH: Cook in simmering liquid just below the boiling point (eggs, fish).

POUND: Flatten boneless cuts of chicken and meat to uniform thickness, using mallet or flat side of meat pounder.

PUREE: Mash or blend food until smooth and uniform consistency, using a blender or food processor or by forcing food through a sieve.

REDUCE: Boil liquid uncovered to evaporate some of the liquid and intensify flavor of remaining liquid.

REDUCE HEAT: Lower heat on range top to allow mixture to continue cooking slowly and evenly without scorching pan.

REFRIGERATE: Place food in refrigerator until it becomes thoroughly cold or to store it.

ROAST: Cook meat uncovered on rack in shallow pan in oven without adding liquid.

ROLL: Flatten dough into a thin, even layer, using a rolling pin (cookies, pie crust).

ROLL UP: Roll a flat food covered with a filling (or with filling placed at one end) from one end until it is tube shaped (enchilada, jelly roll).

SAUTÉ: Cook in hot fat over medium-high heat with frequent tossing or turning motion. *See also* Deep-fry, Fry, Panfry.

SCALD: Heat liquid to just below the boiling point. Tiny bubbles form at the edge. A thin skin will form on the top of scalded milk.

SCORE: Cut surface of food about 1/4 inch deep, using knife, to aid in cooking, flavoring or tenderizing or for appearance (meat, yeast bread).

SEAR: Brown meat quickly over high heat to seal in juices.

SEASON: Add flavor, usually with salt, pepper, herbs or spices.

SHRED: Cut into long, thin pieces, using round, smooth holes of shredder, a knife or a food processor (cabbage, carrots, cheese).

SIMMER: Cook in liquid on range top at just below the boiling point. Usually done after reducing heat from a boil. Bubbles will rise slowly and break just below the surface.

SKIM: Remove fat or foam from a soup, broth, stock or stew, using a skimmer (a flat utensil with holes in it), spoon or ladle.

SLICE: Cut into uniform-size flat pieces (bread, meat).

SNIP: Cut into very small pieces, using kitchen scissors.

SOFT PEAKS: Egg whites beaten until peaks are rounded or curl when beaters are lifted from bowl, while still moist and glossy. *See also* Stiff peaks.

SOFTEN: Let cold food stand at room temperature, or microwave at low power setting, until no longer hard (margarine, butter, cream cheese).

STEAM: Cook food by placing on a rack or special steamer basket over a small amount of boiling or simmering water in a covered pan. Also see Vegetables (pages 158–165). Steaming helps retain flavor, shape, color, texture and nutritional value.

STEW: Cook slowly in a small amount of liquid for a long time (stewed fruit, beef stew).

STIFF PEAKS: Egg whites beaten until peaks stand up straight when beaters are lifted from bowl, while still moist and glossy. *See also* Soft Peaks.

STIR: Combine ingredients with circular or figure-eight motion until uniform consistency. Stir once in a while for "stirring occasionally," stir often for "stirring frequently" and stir continuously for "stirring constantly."

STIR-FRY: A Chinese method of cooking uniform pieces of food in small amount of hot oil over high heat, lifting and stirring constantly with a turner or large spoon.

STRAIN: To pour mixture or liquid through a fine sieve or strainer to remove larger particles.

TEAR: Break into pieces, using fingers (lettuce for a salad, bread slices for soft bread crumbs).

TOAST: Brown lightly, using toaster, oven, broiler or skillet (bread, coconut, nuts).

TOSS: Tumble ingredients lightly with a lifting motion (salads).

WHIP: Beat ingredients to add air and increase volume until ingredients are light and fluffy (whipping cream, egg whites).

ZEST: Outside colored layer of citrus fruit (oranges, lemons) that contains aromatic oils and flavor. Also, to remove outside colored layer of citrus fruit in fine strips, using knife, citrus zester or vegetable peeler.

UNDERSTANDING RESTAURANT MENUS

If you've ever been too embarrassed or intimidated to ask what an item on a menu is or have refrained from trying unfamiliar food at a restaurant because you don't know how to pronounce it, this section can help you. Terms used on restaurant menus can be confusing. Many are foreign words that describe a specific cuisine or dish; others describe ingredients or techniques. Here's a list of the most commonly used terms to guide you when you're eating out.

AIOLI (ay-OH-le): Garlic mayonnaise, often served with fish, meat or vegetables; from southern France.

ALFREDO (al-FRAY-doh): Rich Parmesan cheese sauce with butter and cream, usually served over fettuccine with fresh ground pepper; from Italy.

AU GRATIN (oh-GRAH-tihn): Any dish topped with bread crumbs or cheese then baked or broiled.

AU LAIT (oh-LAY): Food or beverages served or prepared with milk.

BEEF TARTARE (tar-TAR): Finely chopped raw lean beef, sometimes served with capers, chopped parsley and onions.

BORDELAISE (bor-dl-AYZ): Sauce made with red or white wine, beef stock or broth, shallots, parsley and herbs; usually served with beef.

BRIOCHE (BREE-osh): A rich yeast bread made with butter and eggs; from France. It can be baked in a large round loaf or individual rolls; each usually has a "top-knot."

BRUSHCETTA (brew-SHEH-tah): An appetizer of bread rubbed with garlic, drizzled with olive oil, heated and served warm.

CALAMARI (kal-a-MAHR-ee): Squid, known for chewy texture and mild flavor, often served as an appetizer.

CAPPUCCINO (kap-poo-CHEE-no): Italian coffee topped with foam from steamed milk. Sometimes sprinkled with sweetened cocoa powder or cinnamon.

CARBONNARA (kar-bo-NAH-rah): Dish of spaghetti, cream, eggs, Parmesan cheese and bacon.

CHILES RELLENOS (CHEE-lehs reh-YEH-nohs): Mexican dish of cheese-stuffed chilies that have been dipped in batter and deep-fried.

CROSTINI (kro-STEE-nee): An appetizer of thin slices of toasted bread, brushed with olive oil. Can also be topped with cheese, tomatoes and herbs.

FLAMBÉ (flahm-BAY): Food presentation created by sprinkling dish with liquor and igniting just before serving.

FRITTATA (frih-TAH-ta): Egg dish with ingredients such as cheese and vegetables, cooked over low heat on top of the stove.

GAZPACHO (gahz-PAH-cho): Spanish cold soup usually made from pureed tomatoes, peppers, onions, celery, cucumbers, olive oil, garlic, bread crumbs and vinegar.

HOLLANDAISE (HOL-un-dayz): Creamy, buttery sauce with a touch of lemon, usually served with fish and eggs.

LATTE (LAH-tay): Espresso with lots of foamy steamed milk, usually served in a tall glass mug.

MARINARA (Mah-ree-NAHR-a): Italian sauce for pasta and meat, made from tomatoes, onion, garlic and oregano.

NIÇOISE (nee-SWAHS): Dish that usually includes tomatoes, garlic, anchovies and black olives. A salad niçoise is made with green beans, onions, tuna, eggs and herbs.

PAELLA (pi-AY-yuh): Spanish dish of rice, saffron, seafood, meat, garlic, onion, peas, tomatoes and artichoke hearts, usually served in a wide, shallow pan.

POLENTA (poh-LEN-ta): A cornmeal porridge from northern Italy. Made from cornmeal that is heated with water, then cooled and cut into squares, and fried or baked. It is often mixed with Parmesan cheese and butter and served with a sauce.

PRAWN: Large shrimp; also the name of a seafood species that is more slender than shrimp and has longer legs.

PRIMAVERA (pree-ma-VEHR-ah): Dish that includes fresh vegetables; most well known is pasta primavera.

RAGOUT (ra-GOO): French stew of meat, poultry or fish.

RISOTTO (rih-SAW-to): Italian dish prepared with arborio rice and hot stock or broth. Unlike other rice recipes, stock is added to rice gradually and cooked and stirred constantly to produce a creamy mixture.

SATAY (say-TAY): Marinated cubes of meat, fish or poultry grilled on skewers and served with spicy peanut sauce, from Indonesia.

SCAMPI: Description of shrimp that have been split, brushed with butter and garlic, then broiled.

STRATA: Dish layered with bread and mixtures of cheese, poultry or seafood topped with an egg-milk mixture, which puffs when baked.

SUSHI (sue-SHEE): Japanese finger food consisting of slices of raw fish, rice, chopped vegetables, pickles and tofu all wrapped in sheets of seaweed.

TETRAZZINI (the-trah-ZEE-nee): Italian dish of cooked spaghetti, Parmesan cheese, cream sauce and chicken. Turkey or tuna is sometimes substituted for chicken.

HELPFUL NUTRITION INFORMATION

NUTRITION GUIDELINES:

We provide nutrition information for each recipe that includes calories, fat, cholesterol, sodium, carbohydrate, fiber and protein. Individual food choices can be based on this information

Recommended intake for a daily diet of 2,000 calories as set by the Food and Drug Administration

Total Fat	Less than 65g
Saturated Fat	Less than 20g
Cholesterol	Less than 300mg
Sodium	Less than 2,400mg
Total Carbohydrate	300g
Dietary Fiber	25g

CRITERIA USED FOR CALCULATING NUTRITION INFORMATION:

- The first ingredient is used wherever a choice is given (such as 1/3 cup sour cream or plain yogurt).

- The first ingredient amount is used wherever a range is given (such as 2 to 3 teaspoons milk).

- The first serving number is used wherever a range is given (such as 4 to 6 servings).

- "If desired" ingredients (such as "sprinkle with brown sugar if desired") and recipe variations are *not* included.

- Only the amount of a marinade or frying oil that is estimated to be absorbed by the food during preparation or cooking is calculated.

METRIC CONVERSION GUIDE

VOLUME

U.S. Units	Canadian Metric	Australian Metric
1/4 teaspoon	1 mL	1 ml
1/2 teaspoon	2 mL	2 ml
1 teaspoon	5 mL	5 ml
1 tablespoon	15 mL	20 ml
1/4 cup	50 mL	60 ml
1/3 cup	75 mL	80 ml
1/2 cup	125 mL	125 ml
2/3 cup	150 mL	170 ml
3/4 cup	175 mL	190 ml
1 cup	250 mL	250 ml
1 quart	1 liter	1 liter
1 1/2 quarts	1.5 liters	1.5 liters
2 quarts	2 liters	2 liters
2 1/2 quarts	2.5 liters	2.5 liters
3 quarts	3 liters	3 liters
4 quarts	4 liters	4 liters

WEIGHT

U.S. Units	Canadian Metric	Australian Metric
1 ounce	30 grams	30 grams
2 ounces	55 grams	60 grams
3 ounces	85 grams	90 grams
4 ounces (1/4 pound)	115 grams	125 grams
8 ounces (1/2 pound)	225 grams	225 grams
16 ounces (1 pound)	455 grams	500 grams
1 pound	455 grams	1/2 kilogram

Note: The recipes in this cookbook have not been developed or tested using metric measures. When converting recipes to metric, some variations in quality may be noted.

MEASUREMENTS

Inches	Centimeters
1	2.5
2	5.0
3	7.5
4	10.0
5	12.5
6	15.0
7	17.5
8	20.5
9	23.0
10	25.5
11	28.0
12	30.5
13	33.0
14	35.5
15	38.0

TEMPERATURES

Fahrenheit	Celsius
32°	0°
212°	100°
250°	120°
275°	140°
300°	150°
325°	160°
350°	180°
375°	190°
400°	200°
425°	220°
450°	230°
475°	240°
500°	260°

INDEX

Numbers in *italics* refer to photographs.

How-Tos

LIGHTER RECIPES